Happy birth[...]
Love Dave, Shelley, Livy.
5/21/85

ETHICAL
INVESTING

ETHICAL INVESTING

Amy L. Domini *with* Peter D. Kinder

♠ ADDISON-WESLEY PUBLISHING COMPANY

Reading, Massachusetts   Menlo Park, California
Wokingham, Berkshire   Amsterdam
Don Mills, Ontario   Sydney

Library of Congress Cataloging in Publication Data

Domini, Amy L.
  Ethical investing.

  Bibliography: p.
  Includes index.
  1. Investments — Moral and ethical aspects.

I. Kinder, Peter D.   II. Title.
HG4528.D65   1984   174'.4   84–2783
ISBN 0–201–10803–8

Cover design by Marshall Henrichs
Text design by Anna Post
Set in 11 point Goudy Old Style by DEKR Corporation

ISBN 0-201-10803-8

ABCDEFGHIJ-DO-8987654

First printing, October 1984

– To –

Enzo and Maggie Domini

Without whose encouragement, support, under-
standing and babysitting on short notice, we could
never have written this book.

CONTENTS

Acknowledgments

Writing a book like this requires what seems like endless hours of research and organization. We have been luckier than most in having had the help of many able people. What strengths this book has it owes to them. Its weaknesses are ours.

Over a period of more than a year Joan Bavaria of the Franklin Research and Development Corporation contributed information, research, criticism, and encouragement. Steve Moody and Robert Zevin of the U.S. Trust Company of Boston; Joan Shapiro of South Shore Bank, Chicago; Harry Tower of the Dreyfus Third Century Fund; Luther Tyson of Pax World Fund; Oliver Rodgers of the American Friends Service Committee; Walter Burrage of the Manchester Fund; Jim Lowell of Lowell & Blake Associates; Mary Camper-Titsingh of the Ford Foundation; and Andrew Duncan of the Foundation for the Study of Philanthropy all gave generously of their time and research. Dorian Yates and Tom Kinder gave us many hot leads and were a continuing source of excellent research ideas. Seth Klarman of the Baupost Group not only provided excellent advice on research points but gave an early draft of the manuscript a thorough critical review. Mary Ann Badessa always had the answer at her fingertips. George Bristol, Kate Lorenczi, C. C. Colt, Adrianne Landsman, Frank Urbanowski, and Steve Bennett made helpful suggestions on the manuscript.

However, without excellent support personnel we could never have finished this book. Mary Rogier, M. Suzanne Stoner, Alix Coulter, and Celia Popper did the 1001 tasks which would have tied us up endlessly had we had to do them ourselves. We also had terrific support and assistance from David Miller, Lori Snell, Joyce Copland, Jessica Berman, and Theresa Burns of Addison-Wesley. Amanda Heller did an excellent job editing and Gabriel Weiss did an excellent job proofreading a difficult manuscript.

Last but far from least, we wish to thank Holly Grano. Without her patience, hard work, and ability to figure out where all the arrows went, we could never have succeeded.

Amy L. Domini
Peter D. Kinder
April 1984

THE YEAR: 1898.

THE SETTING: The office of the *New York Inquirer.* Walter Thatcher has just stormed into its publisher's office demanding the paper stop exposing corruption in a streetcar company. The publisher is Thatcher's ward, Charles Foster Kane.

THATCHER: I think I should remind you, Charles, of a fact you seem to have forgotten. You are yourself one of the company's largest shareholders.

KANE: The trouble is, Mr. Thatcher, you don't realize you're talking to two people. As Charles Foster Kane, who has eighty-two thousand, six hundred and thirty-one shares of Metropolitan Transfer — you see, I do have a rough idea of my holdings — I sympathize with you. Charles Foster Kane is a dangerous scoundrel, his paper should be run out of town and a committee should be formed to boycott him. You may, if you can form such a committee, put me down for a contribution of one thousand dollars.

On the other hand — I am the publisher of the *Inquirer.* As such, it is my duty — I'll let you in on a little secret, it is also my pleasure — to see to it that the decent, hardworking people of this city are not robbed blind by a group of money-mad pirates because, God help them, they have no one to look after their interests.

— Herman J. Mankiewicz and Orson Welles in *The Citizen Kane Book*[1]

PROLOGUE

S HOULD YOUR ETHICS play a significant role in what you do with your money? Unlike Charles Foster Kane, perhaps you refuse to separate your ethics from your investments. If so, this book is for you. Today many people recognize the dilemma of profiting from enterprises whose goals, methods, or products they know are inconsistent with their personal philosophy. What environmentalist, for instance, wants to profit from dioxin? What parent wants to benefit from sponsors of television violence?

Getting rid of investments is an immediate solution, but it does nothing about the root problem: where can you put your money without facing the *Citizen Kane* dilemma? You have to make a positive choice, but you should make that choice only after a careful analysis of an investment's ethical and financial merits. That is why I've structured this book as a financial guide. The methods I describe are proven. However, *Ethical Investing* is unlike any other investment book because it shows you how to factor your ethical concerns into a positive, systematic money management strategy. Its charts and lists give you starting points for locating compatible investments.

This book stands on three assumptions.

1. Every investment — whether in stocks or savings accounts or savings bonds — has an ethical dimension.
2. Investors can and should apply their ethical standards to potential investments.
3. Investors who apply their ethical criteria to investments are more successful than those who do not.

Assumptions 1 and 2 are philosophical and moral. They are not subject to proof. Assumption 3 is.

Wall Street wisdom has it that anything unrelated to financial criteria which limits your investment choices limits your return. That is the conventional reaction to ethical investing, but it is not true. The performance of ethical portfolios flattens the limited choice argument. One money manager, Joan Bavaria, president of Franklin Research and Development Corp., put it this way: "I started running money along ethical guidelines more out of personal interest than in response to requests, although there was that too. After about two years, I realized that my ethical accounts were doing significantly better than our average account." Franklin's ethical accounts were up over 50% from mid-1982 through mid-1983, while the Dow was up 44%.

U.S. Trust Co. of Boston provides another example. For the last several years it has run Socially Sensitive Accounts separately from its regular accounts. Figure P-1 compares the results, which speak for themselves. A major New York bank analyzed the *Fortune* 500 between 1977 and 1982, comparing the performance of those companies invested in

FIGURE P-1   United States Trust Company of Boston, Massachusetts Performance Comparisons

	Socially Sensitive Accounts United States Trust Company[a]	United States Trust Company[b]	Dow Jones Industrial Average	S&P 500	90-Day Treasury Bills	Corporate Bonds (Salomon Brothers High Grade Index)	Inflation (GNP Deflator)
1980	22.4	19.7	19.8	32.3	12.4	−2.2	9.3
1981	8.4	10.7	−3.6	−5.0	14.7	−1.0	9.4
1982	27.7	26.2	27.2	21.4	10.7	43.7	6.0
1983[c]	15.9	16.2	22.1	20.7	6.5	4.8	3.0
Annual, 1980–1983:							
	19.7	19.4	16.9	17.7	11.8	10.6	7.4
Growth of $1,000,000 Invested, 1980–1983:							
	$1.964	$1.943	$1.794	$1.842	$1.520	$1.458	$1.306

a. Median discretionary account. Prior to 1980, socially sensitive accounts are included in the median discretionary accounts of United States Trust Company. Asset allocation actively managed among stocks, bonds, & money market instruments.
b. Median discretionary account through 1980. UST pooled pension and profit sharing account, thereafter. Asset allocation actively managed among stocks, bonds, & money market instruments.
c. Through the Third Quarter of 1983.

Source: U.S. Trust Co., Asset Management Division, PO Box 373, Boston, Massachusetts, 02101.

South Africa with those which were not. The former portfolio outperformed the latter in 18 out of 20 quarters. Not long ago, the *New York
Times* compared the stock performance of nuclear versus nonnuclear electric utilities. As Figure P-2 shows, nonnuclear won hands down.

These examples involve the application of a nonfinancial criterion to
a particular group of stocks. In each instance the investor would have been
better off simply segregating companies according to that criterion without
looking for positive investments among the remaining companies. But even
without the empirical data, the experience of people who advise clients
on financial matters validates the use of nonfinancial criteria. Every day
clients tell them, "I'm not interested in that industry." Or, "I don't like
that company." Or, "Find me something in widgets and I'll consider it."
Those statements reflect the investors' instincts to look toward vehicles
they know, like, and understand.

In fact, no approach is as widely accepted as the positive approach:
put your money in companies you know and understand. Wall Street has
no qualms about other limiting approaches to stock selection. All mutual
funds, for example, adopt specific investment criteria governing which
securities they will buy. Some pick only technology stocks; others buy only
high-quality bonds; still others only blue chips.

When I became interested in ethical investing, the vehemently negative responses shocked me. When I asked one top trust officer how often
he had been requested to apply ethical criteria to a client's portfolio, he
said, "Look, I just tell them, 'O.K. You don't want to buy companies in
South Africa. Get me a list of them and I won't buy them. But don't
expect me to run around looking for termites in the woodpile.'"

At the moment I didn't realize it, but that trust officer had put his
finger on the two central problems faced by ethical investors: how to find
the termites, and, much more important, how to identify the good wood.
The problem the ethical investor faces is one of information. The principal
reason money managers reject the concept lies in their ignorance and
reluctance to learn. A strong secondary reason is that ethical concerns
might make a Wall Street gunslinger look soft.

Ironically, the termites are a lot easier to find than the good wood.
An astonishing number of groups monitor corporations. Their goals vary
widely. Morality in Media focuses on companies that sponsor sex-laden
TV shows. The Council on Economic Priorities monitors the nuclear
industry, among others. A number of groups, including the American
Friends Service Committee, keep tabs on the defense industry. I've included many lists developed by organizations like these, even though some

FIGURE P-2 Electric Utilities' Nuclear Dependence and Stock Market Performance

	1982 Revenues ($ billions)	1982 Electricity Sales*	Nuclear Power As Percent of Total Output	Stock Price		
				52-Week High	52-Week Low	May 6, '83 Close
American Electric Power	$4.18	97.5	10%	20	15⅞	19⅜
Commonwealth Edison	4.13	59.2	44%	28¾	20	27¼
Consolidated Edison	5.07	27.3	18%	23⅛	16⅜	22½
Duke Power	2.24	51.4	27%	24	20¼	24
Middle South Utilities	2.90	49.4	18%	16⅜	12¼	16
New England Electric	1.21	16.4	15%	38	26½	37⅞
Niagara Mohawk Power	2.39	32.6	5%	17⅞	13	17¾
Public Service Electric and Gas	3.87	31.6	34%	24⅝	19⅛	24⅛
Southern California Edison	4.30	59.3	1%	39¼	29½	37⅜
Virginia Electric and Power	2.36	42.9	41%	15⅞	12	15⅝

* In billions of kilowatt-hours.

Nuclear dependence is measured by the percentage of electricity sales generated by nuclear power in 1982.

Source: Thomas J. Lueck, "Problems Mount for Utilities: Electric Utilities' Nuclear Dependence and Stock Market Performance," the New York Times, 9 May 1983, p. D1. Copyright © by the New York Times Company. Reprinted by permission.

FIGURE P-3   Companies Appearing in Environmental Action's "Filthy Five,"
1980–82

Environmental Action, based in Washington, D.C., annually rates the *Fortune* 500 in terms of major pollution violations and political contributions to antienvironmental candidates. Using the Freedom of Information Act to discover violations, and Federal Election Commission records for political contributions, it establishes its "Filthy Five." This is their list for 1980–82.

Dow Chemical (1980–82)   Standard Oil of Indiana (1980–82)
Republic Steel (1980–82)   Weyerhaeuser (1981–82)
Occidental Petroleum (1980–82)

Source: Environmental Action.

don't reflect my own philosophy. I've tried to write this book so that persons with quite diverse ethical concerns will find it useful.

Identifying good wood is the key to ethical investing. Many companies merit investment because of their contributions to their communities and the country. Others have enormous potential to benefit both society and their investors. Finding sound companies is not easy. Good news is no news, so achievements rarely find their way into print.

This book will help you find the good wood. It is not *Everything You Ever Wanted to Know About Ethical Investing* because the ethical element initially requires a subjective appraisal of your own values. Rather, it provides a starter kit for ethical investors containing the following tools:

- A primer on investing principles.
- A guide to investing vehicles.
- Ethical and financial self-assessment forms.
- Methodologies for identifying companies meeting your ethical criteria.
- A simplified approach to portfolio management.
- Some basic retirement planning guidelines.
- Guidance on banks, insurance companies, and money market funds.
- Lists and other examples involving hundreds of companies.
- A directory of resources available to the ethical investor.

A client once told me, "I've always had to separate money matters from the rest of me. I didn't know there was any other way to do it. I care about a lot of things, but I feel I just have to try not to think about them when I invest. If you can show me how to invest successfully without violating my principles, of course I'll do it!"

This book is for her and for all of us who are like her.

1 ETHICAL INVESTING:
THE WHYS AND THE HOWS

A T A RECENT SEMINAR on socially responsible investing, one of the speakers suggested that the participants tell everyone present what they'd earned in the last year. I caught my breath. A minute later we realized her suggestion was rhetorical. I looked around and saw the same relief I felt in the others' faces. But she had made her point. Money is a deeply personal matter. Our finances are so intimate we can share them only with our spouses and our tax accountants.

Ethical investing takes this feeling that our finances are a reflection of ourselves and carries it to a logical conclusion. You know how you feel about various issues. If you use your natural concerns wisely, they can be your greatest advantage in making your money grow.

GETTING INVOLVED

Think of the uses of the word *invest*. "I've invested years in this project." "She invested every ounce of strength she had." The word means something far beyond just buying something. Too often the investor forgets this simple truth. When you invest, you put a part of yourself into a corporation. In return, you own a piece of it.

Your options for investing are broad. Whether your investments are as simple as a money market account or as complicated as a portfolio of sophisticated investment vehicles, you can make a statement about your

1

commitment to your principles. For example, a simple act like relocating your savings account can positively change the lives of others by making possible the loans they need. If you deposit your savings at the South Shore Bank of Chicago, they will lend your investment to neighborhood redevelopment programs. Your local bank probably makes loans in your community.

Before ethical investing became as popular as it is today, most brokers and investment counselors were not interested in ethical accounts. Investors could either forget about their ethics or do the research themselves. Now, the field has attracted some excellent brokers and financial planners, and newsletters and reporting services supply research to help with your investment program. But don't stop relying on your own thoughts and instincts. No one knows it all. I relearned that lesson recently from a retired elementary school teacher who began taking computer courses and following the industry. One afternoon in the spring of 1982 she called me about Seagate Technology, a disk drive manufacturer. I tried to talk her out of buying the one hundred shares she wanted, pointing to the company's lack of earnings, its tough competition, its youthful management, and the stock's sky-high price ($5 per share). She ignored my advice, and sold a year later at $15. There are two lessons here. First, use your judgment and experience in life. Second, no matter who advises you on your investments, ultimately you are responsible for the decisions.

Ethical investing emphasizes quality. Whether you are buying stock, life insurance, government bonds, or tax shelters, the questions you should ask about the institutions which will use your money are much the same. When you discover a vehicle with *both* ethical and financial quality, then you've found an investment.

THREE APPROACHES TO ETHICAL INVESTING

Before dealing with financial quality, let's make a quick survey of the three approaches to ethical investing.

First, the avoidance approach: you refuse to invest in companies you dislike — companies that make products you don't support or whose services offend you or whose way of doing business seems wrong to you. Second, the positive choice approach: you actively invest in companies with products or services or ways of doing business that you do like. Third, the activist approach: you invest in companies you want to change and exercise your ownership rights to make those changes.

Avoidance

Ethical investors who follow the avoidance approach would prefer not to benefit from business activities they don't support in other areas of their lives. By avoiding investments in "bad" companies, you're saying, "Not with my money, you don't." Walter Burrage, managing partner of the Manchester Fund, an investment company in Boston, puts it this way, "I don't drink much, and I don't like to smoke. It doesn't strike my fancy to invest there with so many other areas of interest."

Starting to invest using this approach is very simple. Just name the industries and companies you want to avoid. Then give your current investments a quick review for any inconsistencies.

Recently I reviewed a church portfolio. The rector felt some of its investments were not consistent with the congregation's principles. He was right. I found, among others, stocks of two weapons manufacturers and a casino operator. The church finance committee's lack of awareness of the ethical dimensions of their investments not only compromised the church, but in this case also reduced its potential return on investment.

Perhaps the best-known example of avoidance is the current movement, especially among universities and pension funds, toward divestiture of stocks or bonds of companies with operations in South Africa. Divestiture focuses public attention on a political or economic situation. While the unlikely event of a total withdrawal of U.S. corporations from South Africa would dramatically affect that country's economy, the divestiture movement's immediate goal is to help educate the public.

In most cases the argument for the avoidance approach is less to draw attention to something than to refuse to profit by it. Also, it's the easiest of the ethical investment approaches. Avoiding companies — a strip mine company, a DDT manufacturer — is easier than finding ones that do things right. I've inserted various charts and lists throughout the book to help investors who want to use the avoidance approach. These include lists of defense contractors, nuclear utilities, and major polluters. Figure 1-1, for example, lists the Environmental Action "Filthy Five." The public interest groups that develop some of these lists tend to be against one specific activity or product.

Still, the avoidance strategy can be only a part of an ethical investing program. The sums most of us can afford to invest will not, if withheld, cripple an industry or even put a crimp in a company's stock price. Selling stock in a publicly traded corporation has no real effect on the company.

Avoidance is a good but limited first step in ethical investing. But,

FIGURE 1-1   The Filthy Five Stagger Along. . . .

Company	1974			1981			1974–1981 % Change In:		
	Average Stock Price	Earnings Per Share	Dividends Declared	Average Stock Price	Earnings Per Share	Dividends Declared	Stock Price	Earnings	Dividends Declared
Dow Chemical	$29.95	$ 3.18	$ .60	$31.20	$3.00	$1.80	+4	−6	+200
Occidental Petroleum	11.00	3.77	.25	28.25	7.55	2.43	+157	+100	+872
Republic Steel	24.45	10.55	2.80	27.30	11.75	2.25	+12	+11	−20
Standard Oil of Indiana	22.45	3.43	.83	63.65	6.56	2.60	+184	+91	+213
Weyerhaeuser	34.95	2.17	.80	32.45	1.67	1.30	−7	−23	+63
5-Co. Average:	$24.56	$4.62	$1.06	$36.57	$6.11	$2.08	+49	+32	+96
Yearly Change:							+5	+4	+11
Dow Jones Industrial Average							+42		

Source: *Good Money*, 28 Main Street, Montpelier, VT 05602, July/Aug. 1983, p. 10.

knowing where you're not going to put your money doesn't help you decide where to invest it.

The Positive Approach

The positive approach complements the avoidance approach. Those adopting it seek investments in companies that enhance the quality of life. These companies produce goods or services of high quality and have good relations with their employees and the communities in which they operate. This approach assumes that all these positives indicate the probability of a superior investment return — which it does. As Dr. Robert Schwartz, vice president of Shearson/American Express and one of ethical investing's earliest advocates, has said, "It's been my experience that a company that is aware of its community responsibilities, aware of its responsibility to its employees, is also a company that is progressive in its thinking, and this cannot help but carry over into its overall business acumen."[1]

Enlightened Self-Interest. A degree of enlightened self-interest regulates this pattern of corporate involvement. The good you do others can be good for you, too. Take the case of Julius Rosenwald. Around 1910 he recognized that many farmers were too poor to buy goods from his mail order house, Sears, Roebuck & Company. Rosenwald set out to help farmers by advocating the county agent system, which helped farmers adopt improved agricultural methods such as contour farming, and by setting up 4-H Clubs to train young people to be better farmers. Agriculture prospered. And Rosenwald's sales showed that what was good for the farmer was good for Sears.[2]

For the ethical investor, Rosenwald's positive approach has numerous advantages. You live your life according to your interests and beliefs, and you try to be consistent. You should invest in the same manner. How, for example, can you demonstrate your commitment to the environment? Give money to groups lobbying for conservation. Build passive solar heating into your home. Loan your money to a cooperative that recycles waste products. Recycle your own garbage as much as possible. Buy stocks in companies that demonstrate respect for our natural environment. There are many more possibilities, but you can see the pattern. Using Figure 1-2 you can begin identifying the areas that interest you.

If you choose your investments with this sort of benevolent self-interest, you will enjoy keeping track of your investments and will pay

FIGURE 1-2   Ethical Assessment Form

	I want to stress this area	OK to buy	I don't care
Negatives			
Alcohol	_____	_____	_____
Tobacco	_____	_____	_____
Gambling	_____	_____	_____
Asbestos litigants	_____	_____	_____
Agent Orange litigants	_____	_____	_____
Weapons	_____	_____	_____
Nuclear energy	_____	_____	_____
Nonunion	_____	_____	_____
Flagrant environmental abusers	_____	_____	_____
Poor product safety records	_____	_____	_____
Poor worker safety records	_____	_____	_____
Doing business with Soviet bloc	_____	_____	_____
Doing business with South Africa	_____	_____	_____
Doing business with _____	_____	_____	_____
Other products or services I wish to avoid _____	_____	_____	_____
Other ways of doing business I wish to avoid _____	_____	_____	_____

more attention to them. Investment advisers agree that an informed and careful investor does better.

A Time to Buy, a Time to Sell. Positive ethical investing is not just buying the right security at the right time. It's selling it at the right time too. The ethical merits of investments change just like the financial merits. Suppose your favorite solar energy company began to bid on Department of Defense contracts for space weaponry. It would be time to sell.

All the ethical mutual funds use the positive investment approach, as do many religious organizations. Consider a few of the criteria established by the National Council of Churches for measuring the positive nature of a potential investment:

FIGURE 1-2   *(continued)*

	I want to stress this area	OK to buy	I don't care
Positives			
Solar energy	_____	_____	_____
Companies meeting needs of elderly or disabled	_____	_____	_____
Alternative energy	_____	_____	_____
Basic human needs (food, shelter, clothing)	_____	_____	_____
Health care	_____	_____	_____
Recycling	_____	_____	_____
Education	_____	_____	_____
Alternative food sources	_____	_____	_____
Energy conservation	_____	_____	_____
Civic commitments	_____	_____	_____
Equal opportunity employment	_____	_____	_____
Environmental record	_____	_____	_____
Product safety record	_____	_____	_____
Worker safety record	_____	_____	_____
Good work environments	_____	_____	_____
Others	_____	_____	_____

- Do products meet government standards?
- Is their labeling adequate and easily understood?
- Will the products last for a reasonable amount of time?
- Does the company actively recruit women and minorities?
- Is the company pioneering safe alternative energy sources or studying ways to reduce demand for resources?
- Is the company researching the development of new products or means of production which will enhance the quality of life?[3]

Choices. Positive ethical investing often requires hard choices. Do you put Standard Oil of Indiana on your OK list because it supports low-income housing or eliminate it as one of the Environmental Action "Filthy Five"? You must follow your own standards and research each company well.

You also have to choose from a range of company types. Standard Oil of Indiana is a blue-chip, old-line corporation with a long track record of steady returns. It's the kind of stock often recommended for the most conservative investor. If big oil companies don't fit your ethical criteria but alternative energy corporations do, and you can afford to speculate, you can do very well. For instance, between August 1982 and June 1983 stocks of three far from blue-chip solar companies made spectacular gains. BESI Corp. was up 2908%, American Solar King was up 1342%, and Chronar was up 1202%. The Dow Jones Industrial Average did just fine during that period too — up 44% — but the investors in these speculative solar stocks obviously did far better.[4]

If speculative stocks aren't your style, then consider electric utilities. According to one study, nuclear utilities increased their dividends by 30% between 1974 and 1982, while nonnuclear utilities had dividend gains of 81%. Taking dividend income and stock price gains into account, the nuclear group had total gains over the period of 124% while the nonnuclear did more than twice as well, with total returns of 269%.[5]

The positive approach makes the Citizen Kane dilemma — fighting with one hand what you're supporting with the other — impossible. All the pieces, your finances and your principles, fit together. This consistency adds satisfaction far beyond what profitable investment alone brings.

Activist Approach

Some ethical investors want to do more than avoid bad companies and invest in good ones. They want to change the bad into the good. For these investors there is the activist approach.

A woman I know was so angry about the needless death of a young friend that she organized a local chapter of Mothers Against Drunk Drivers. She dedicates many hours a week to it, running workshops and lobbying for stricter laws. She doesn't just complain about drunk drivers to her friends; she works for change.

Activist investors take a similar approach to political and moral issues — trade with the Communist bloc or South Africa, product safety, equal employment, nuclear power. Depending on the issue, the activists may concentrate on corporations that influence national policy on these matters. Or they may target companies that have particularly poor records.

Gadflies. The activists start from one basic fact: shareholders own the company. Supposedly management works for them. At least once a year shareholders have the right to elect directors, and to propose and vote on resolutions relating to corporate policy. If the owners fail to exercise their power to direct corporate policy, they waive a powerful means for change.

Corporations operate on a one-share one-vote system, not one-share-holder one-vote. Still, someone holding even 10,000 shares of, say, IBM will not have much influence on the voting because IBM has another 299,990,000 shares outstanding. Nevertheless, since the early 1960s individuals like Louis Gilbert and small organizations like the Sisters of Loretto have used shareholder resolutions and participation at annual meetings as mechanisms to educate and expose.

According to their many opponents, these activists are "corporate gadflies." The dictionary says gadflies include horseflies, botflies, and others which bite or annoy livestock. The critics of the corporate species claim that they are an ineffective, expensive annoyance. But over the last ten years, corporations have spent millions on lobbying, lawsuits, and regulatory actions attempting to limit the gadflies' influence. They must have bitten someone.

The Institutions' Role. Although a recent change in the Securities and Exchange Commission's regulations will make it considerably more difficult for the gadflies to function, they have shown other, much more powerful investors how to influence corporate policy. To contrast them with individuals, these investors are called *institutions.* They include banks, trust companies, union and corporate pension funds, mutual funds, money market mutual funds, college endowment funds, and other poolings of money.

The institutions have enormous fiscal clout. In 1980 private pension funds alone held over $400 billion. By 1995 they will grow to over $3 trillion.[6] So when a union pension fund with millions of dollars in a company wants to know what its equal employment policy is, the company responds.

Corporations respond because the corporate gadflies have taught the institutions that management doesn't always know best. Until this decade institutions automatically voted with existing management. In the wake of constitutional support for challenges to management at corporations like Superior Oil and Trans World Corp. (hotels and vending machines, and at that time, an airline), no company can take their support for granted.

Since the Trans World battle involved purely financial issues — dissident shareholders wanted to "spin off" the airline — its importance to ethical investors might not seem large. However, people run the institutions, and they can be influenced — particularly by other institutional investors. Money definitely talks when one message it carries is that it may walk elsewhere.

Institutional investors sometimes determine who runs a company. Where they bank their billions can determine who sits on the board of a corporation or what loans the bank makes. For example, J. P. Stevens (textiles) continued fighting the Amalgamated Clothing & Textile Workers Union long after its employees had voted to join. So the union led a campaign to isolate the company from the investment community. By threatening to remove hundreds of millions of dollars in union accounts away from Manufacturers Hanover Trust, it forced Stevens's chairman to resign from the bank's board of directors.[7]

Corporations are themselves becoming activists. They have begun taking a role in referenda. For instance, in 1982 a California referendum question that would have required a deposit on beverage containers lost by a vote of 56% to 44%. Various businesses spent over $5 million to defeat the bill, while those in favor raised only $750,000. Figure 1-3 lists companies that contributed to another 1982 California referendum — this one in support of gun control.

FIGURE 1-3   Selected Corporate Contributors In Favor of California's 1982 Gun Control Referendum

The following corporations contributed at least $1,000 in support of California's 1982 referendum which would have controlled hand guns. The antis prevailed, 63% to 37%.

A&M Records	Bank of Beverly Hills
Blue Chip Stamps	Carter, Hawley, Hale Stores
City National Bank (Beverly Hills)	Clorox Co.
Collins Food International, Inc.	Dart & Kraft Industries
Estee Lauder	First City Properties
Grey Advertising, Inc.	The Hechinger Co.
Hotel Systems International	ICN Pharmaceuticals
Kaufman & Broad	Lincoln National Corp.
MCA Inc.	Moana Corp.
Natomas Corp.	Occidental Petroleum
Pacific Mutual Life Insurance	Republic Supply Co. (Fluor Corp.)
Jos. Seagrams & Sons	Shapell Industries
Southern California Edison	TAT Communications
TICOR	Twentieth Century-Fox
Whittaker Corp.	Wilsey Foods, Inc.

Data courtesy of Carl Olson, Chairman, Stockholders for World Freedom, P.O. Box 7273, Alexandria, VA 22307.

FIGURE 1-4   NAACP Fair Share List

These companies have signed agreements with the National Association for the Advancement of Colored People (NAACP) stating that they will do their fair share in seeking out minority-owned contractors, suppliers, transportation companies, and marketing firms to do business with.

The Kroger Co.	Georgia Power Co.
Brown & Williamson Co.	MGM/UA Entertainment Co.
Washington Gas Light Co.	BI-LO Food, Inc.
Mississippi Power & Light Co.	Walt Disney Productions

Source: Fred H. Rasheed, NAACP, New York City, NY; August 1983. Reprinted by permission.

More troubling than corporate participation in referenda is the increasing power of corporate political action committees (PACs). Their emergence is one of the great unintended consequences of the effort to clean up campaign financing in the wake of the Nixon debacle. PACs were intended to provide corporations with a legitimate means of participating in elections. What no one foresaw was the enormous amount of money corporations would funnel into the election campaigns of legislators. PACs are not unique to large corporations. Dairy farmers, lawyers, doctors, and many other groups have strong political programs.

How You Can Participate. How does the individual investor get to wield some of this clout? If your pension plan or your college endowment fund is active in these battles, or if you invest in an ethical mutual fund, you will contribute to this growing force for social responsibility. You may express your views to the investment managers responsible for these funds. Your money will talk louder as pension funds grow in size and sophistication, and managers of other large pools of money realize the power of activist investing. Of course, indirect involvement through institutions is just one activist route. You may choose to buy stock in objectionable companies and support the gadflies.

FIGURE 1-5   Some Asbestos Defendants

These companies are among the 200 defendants in the over 10,000 asbestos-related lawsuits filed on behalf of more than 25,000 people.

Armstrong World Industries	Johns Manville Corporation
ASARCO, Inc.	Owens-Corning Fiberglas Corporation
Asbestos Corporation Limited	Owens-Illinois, Inc.
Jim Walter Corporation	Raymark Corporation

Where from Here?

The three approaches to ethical investing are compatible with each other. The avoidance and positive approaches necessarily go together. The activist approach takes a different tack altogether and requires, I think, a greater commitment by the investor.

In the succeeding chapters, I will treat the avoidance and positive approaches together as I describe an ethical approach to money management. The book will close with a long look at the methods used by the activists.

2 MAKING YOUR
MONEY WORK

I START EACH of my ethical investing seminars by asking how many of the participants would like an overview of investment basics. Never fewer than three-quarters of them raise their hands. For that reason, this chapter defines the basic concepts of investing, while Chapter 3 describes how to research particular opportunities. Chapters 4 through 12 show how to apply the rules developed here to particular investment situations. But note: ethical criteria apply to *every* form of investment because they usually appraise the issuer, not the particular vehicle.

THE BASIC CONCEPTS

Investment opportunities come in many forms. Most people have heard of bank accounts, stocks, bonds, mutual funds, and money market funds. However, significantly fewer know about opportunities in, say, limited partnerships.

Because money-making opportunities are so diverse, investors refer to them generally as *vehicles*. This book deals exclusively with common investment vehicles, like the ones listed above. I have not dealt with vehicles like *commodities* (grain and oil futures, for example) or precious metals, which require enormous, specialized expertise, while posing ethical problems for many investors.

Debt and Equity

Debt and equity are the two basic categories of investments. You either make a loan to a company or a government unit (*debt*) or you buy a part of a company (*equity*).

When you buy debt (bonds, commercial paper, bank notes), you make a loan or acquire someone else's loan at a stated interest rate until a specific date when you expect your money back. If you buy a Citizens' Utilities (an innovative Connecticut utility holding company) 8⅞% bond maturing in 2005 for its *par* (face) *value* of $1000, you receive $88.75 each year until 2005, when Citizens' Utilities will return your $1000.

When you buy equity (*common stock* or *shares*), you purchase a part of the ownership of a corporation. The value of your interest depends on the company's success. You have a right to share in the profits, but only after debt holders receive their interest and principal repayments. Unlike debt, your ownership interest entitles you to a voice in the company's affairs.

Capital Gains and Income

The terms *capital gains* and *income* describe how you make money on investments. If you sell for a profit, the difference between what you paid and what you get — after deducting brokers' *commissions* (fees for handling the transaction) — is a capital gain. The formula for calculating a capital gain or loss is: sale price minus purchase price, commission or service fees on purchase, and commission or service fees on sale equals capital gain (or loss). For example, suppose you bought 100 shares of American Solar King (solar heating systems) for $2 per share in August 1982, sold it at $20 in June 1983, and your brokerage commissions totaled $85. Your capital gain was $1715. (I should stop to explain here that stock prices are *quoted*, or stated, in eighths of a dollar, or $.125, with the dollar sign customarily omitted. Thus, a stock selling at 2⅜ carries a price of $2.375 per share.)

Because you held American Solar King for less than a year, the capital gain was short term, which the IRS treats as *ordinary income* (income taxed like your salary). If you had held it for a year and a day or longer, you'd have had a long-term capital gain. (At this writing, Congress appeared headed toward changing the capital gains holding period to six months — a period that belies the descriptor "long-term.") The highest tax rate you can pay on such a gain is 20% of its amount. The chances are you will pay a lot less than that. For example, if you are in the 30% bracket you pay 12%; in the 20% bracket, 8%.

Any interest, whether paid on a bond or a bank account, or *dividends* (a company's distributions of its profits) you receive are also ordinary income. You can get both income and capital gains from most, but not all, investments. Intermedics, Inc. (cardiac pacemakers), for instance, has not paid a dividend since it went public more than 12 years ago. This company retains its profits for reinvestment in the company's future growth. Investors buy Intermedics, which ranged from 13¼ to 37¾ in 1982, for capital gains. By contrast, Minnesota Power & Light (a nonnuclear electric utility) ranged from 17½ to 24, but its shareholders received $2.28 per share in dividends.

DEBT

The balance of this chapter examines various forms and aggregations of debt and equities. There are many more forms of debt than of equities.

Corporate Bonds

Corporate bonds represent a loan. Corporations usually issue bonds in $1000 denominations (their *par value*). They pay a stated rate of interest semi-annually until the bonds *mature* (come due) on a certain date. For example, AT&T has a bond which matures February 15, 2001, with a *stated yield* (the amount the company promises to pay) of 7% per year. Box 2-1 explains the concept of yield.

Bond Prices. Bonds normally *trade* (change hands) on the basis of current interest rates. However, because on maturity they pay $1000, as that maturity date approaches, the price gets closer and closer to $1000, regardless of interest rates.

The AT&T bond is still a long way from maturity. You wouldn't pay $1000 for that 7% bond when you could get 12% elsewhere. But you would pay a price for the bond on which your *return* is 12%. That's why at certain points some bonds sell at a lot less than their par value. In fact, on June 10, 1981, that AT&T bond sold at $575. At that price the *current*

BOX 2-1   Bonds: Three Types of Yield

Pay close attention to the differences among the three types of yields when you consider buying bonds.

The *stated* or *coupon yield* is the percent of $1000 the company promises to pay each year. In the case of the AT&T bond, the coupon is 7%.

The *current yield* is the amount of the coupon divided by the current price. You know that that AT&T bond may sell at $575. On a purchase price of $575, $70 per year (the coupon) gives a current yield of 12.17%.

The *yield to maturity*, also called *basis yield*, takes into account the fact that the AT&T bond holder will have a capital gain in the year 2001, when the bond bought for $575 will be redeemed for $1000. And, the interest should be earning interest. This calculation is complicated. Have your broker do it for you. (In this example it is 13.17%.)

---

yield was 12.17%. So it's possible to lose money on even the highest quality bonds, if you buy before a steep rise in interest rates. But if you buy before interest rates fall, you may receive significant capital gains.

A confusing aspect of bonds is that both the newspapers and brokers quote their prices at one-tenth the actual price. You would not read in the newspaper that the AT&T bond sold at $575 but rather at 57½. This number actually represents the percentage of par paid for the bond: 57½% of $1000 = $575.

Quality Ratings. Two rating services, Standard & Poor's and Moody's, monitor the financial condition of corporations issuing bonds and evaluate the financial quality of each debt issue. When a bond's quality rating changes, it immediately affects the bond's price. In 1982, when Citizens' Utilities received a AAA rating from Standard & Poor's, it became the only utility besides AT&T to achieve the highest rating. As a result, Citizens' 8⅞% of 3/01/05 (the interest rate and maturity date as they are usually expressed) rose about $20 in value. Figure 2-1 reproduces Standard & Poor's rating system and definitions.

Call Features. Most corporations (and municipalities too) issue bonds with a call feature. The corporation has the right to *call* (buy) the bond back from you at its discretion. When you are thinking about buying a particular bond, you should check Standard & Poor's *Corporation Records* for the call price (which is usually over par) and the year of the first call. If interest rates drop and the company can borrow at a rate lower than it is paying on a bond issue, that issue is a prime candidate for a call. If the bond's market price is below par, the corporation probably won't call your bond. When interest rates drop, investors who hold bonds bearing high coupon yields may not anticipate a call with pleasure.

For example, Citizens' Utilities could have called its 8⅞% on March 1, 1982, at 106.54. The call price dropped to 106.25 in 1983 and will continue to drop each year until it reaches par. If the bond sells in the market at 80, and Citizens' wants to retire part of its debt, it will buy bonds there. But you can be sure that if the market price were 110, Citizens' would exercise its call rights.

Municipal Bonds

Municipal bonds ("munis") are loans to state or local government units. Like corporates, munis usually have call features. They come in $1000 denominations but, unlike corporates, are sold generally in lots of five bonds.

Muni bond quotes are always on a yield-to-maturity basis, called *basis yield* by brokers. (See Box 2-1.) The market operates on basis yield, not dollar bids. Ask your broker what this means in dollars and cents on particular issues. Also, you'll have to ask your broker for approximate quotes on the bond's value. Muni prices don't appear in newspapers.

Types of Municipal Bonds. Some ethical investors favor munis as an opportunity to invest in something they really care about: school construction, water supply systems, or elderly housing. The entities issuing bonds include states, municipalities, local housing authorities, port authorities, and even state parks. The most common types are:

1. *General obligations,* which are backed by the issuers' taxing powers. This makes it critical to check an issuer's tax base. For example, are you buying bonds issued by a city with a declining tax base?
2. *Revenue bonds,* which are paid out of the issuer's revenues.
3. *Housing bonds,* which are secured by mortgages on single family or multifamily housing and underwritten by the issuer.
4. *Authority* or *agency bonds,* which are issued by entities created by states to perform special functions, such as operating airports, turnpikes, tunnels, and the like.
5. *Insured bonds,* which are guaranteed by either the Municipal Bond Insurance Association (MBIA) or the American Municipal Bond As-

FIGURE 2-1   Standard & Poor's Corporate and Municipal Debt Rating Definitions

A Standard & Poor's corporate or municipal debt rating is a current assessment of the credit-worthiness of an obligor with respect to a specific obligation. This assessment may take into consideration obligors such as guarantors, insurers, or lessees.

The debt rating is not a recommendation to purchase, sell or hold a security, inasmuch as it does not comment as to market price or suitability for a particular investor.

The ratings are based on current information furnished by the issuer or obtained by Standard & Poor's from other sources it considers reliable. Standard & Poor's does not perform any audit in connection with any rating and may, on occasion, rely on unaudited financial information. The ratings may be changed, suspended or withdrawn as a result of changes in, or unavailability of, such information, or for other circumstances.

The ratings are based, in varying degrees, on the following considerations:

I.   Likelihood of default-capacity and willingness of the obligor as to the timely payment of interest and repayment of principal in accordance with the terms of the obligation;

II. Nature of and provisions of the obligation;

III. Protection afforded by, and relative position of, the obligation in the event of bankruptcy, reorganization or other arrangement under the laws of bankruptcy and other laws affecting creditors' rights.

AAA   Debt rated AAA has the highest rating assigned by Standard & Poor's. Capacity to pay interest and repay principal is extremely strong.

AA   Debt rated AA has a very strong capacity to pay interest and repay principal and differs from the higher rated issues only in small degree.

A   Debt rated A has a strong capacity to pay interest and repay principal although it is somewhat more susceptible to the adverse effects of changes in circumstances and economic conditions than debt in higher rated categories.

BBB   Debt rated BBB is regarded as having an adequate capacity to pay interest and repay principal. Whereas it normally exhibits adequate protection parameters, adverse economic conditions or changing circumstances are more likely to lead to a weakened capacity to pay interest and repay principal for debt in this category than in higher rated categories.

BB, B, CCC, CC   Debt rated BB, B, CCC and CC is regarded, on balance, as predominantly speculative with respect to capacity to pay interest and repay principal in accordance

Source: Standard & Poor's Corp., *Monthly Bond Guide.* Reprinted by permission.

surance Corporation. Standard & Poor's gives insured bonds its highest rating. For example, MBIA insures North Kingston Rhode Island's 8.45% due in 1983. Moody's rates this bond A, but because of the insurance Standard & Poor's rates it AAA. Its market value is somewhat lower than a "real" AAA but higher than a Moody's A, and the insurance enabled North Kingston to borrow at a low interest rate. Box 2-2 compares Standard & Poor's and Moody's ratings.

Bond Ratings. Quality ratings mean a lot to a municipal bond's price. If you've ever seen a state or municipality faced with a down-rating, like New York City in the mid-1970s, you know what a disaster it can be for a public treasury. However, ratings don't mean everything. Moody's, for instance, rates Chicago general obligations as A and New York's two steps

FIGURE 2-1   *(continued)*

with the terms of the obligation. BB indicates the lowest degree of speculation and CC the highest degree of speculation. While such debt will likely have some quality and protective characteristics, these are outweighed by large uncertainties or major risk exposures to adverse conditions.

C   The rating C is reserved for income bonds on which no interest is being paid.

D   Debt rated D is in default, and payment of interest and/or repayment of principal is in arrears.

Plus (+) or Minus (−):   The ratings from "AA" to "B" may be modified by the addition of a plus or minus sign to show relative standing within the major rating categories.

Provisional Ratings: The letter "p" indicates that the rating is provisional. A provisional rating assumes the successful completion of the project being financed by the debt being rated and indicates that payment of debt service requirements is largely or entirely dependent upon the successful and timely completion of the project. This rating, however, while addressing credit quality subsequent to completion of the project, makes no comment on the likelihood of, or the risk of default upon failure of such completion. The investor should exercise his own judgment with respect to such likelihood and risk.

NR   Indicates that no rating has been requested, that there is insufficient information on which to base a rating, or that S&P does not rate a particular type of obligation as a matter of policy.

Debt Obligations of issuers outside the United States and its territories are rated on the same basis as domestic corporate and municipal issues. The ratings measure the creditworthiness of the obligor but do not take into account currency exchange and related uncertainties.

Bond Investment Quality Standards: Under present commercial bank regulations issued by the Comptroller of the Currency, bonds rated in the top four categories (AAA, AA, A, BBB, commonly known as "Investment Grade" ratings) are generally regarded as eligible for bank investment. In addition, the Legal Investment Laws of various states impose certain rating or other standards for obligations eligible for investment by savings banks, trust companies, insurance companies and fiduciaries generally.

lower at Ba-1. Yet in mid-1982 both traded on a 12% basis. Meanwhile Boston, a Ba, traded on a 13¼% basis. The difference: Boston and Chicago don't have city income taxes; New York does. The added revenues give stronger backing to the Big Apple's bonds.

Taxes on Interest. Brokerages often advertise munis as "tax free." The federal government does not tax the interest munis pay. If you are a resident of the state in which the bond is issued, it will not tax it either. This favorable taxation makes it easier for governmental units to borrow and enables them to borrow at a lower rate than corporations. In Chapter 10 I'll discuss the impact the tax-free feature should have on an individual's investment decisions.

Coupon vs. Registered Form. Before July 1983 most municipal bonds were sold in *coupon* form. ("Clipping coupons" doesn't always refer to grocery

---

BOX 2-2   The Rating Services Compared

Standard & Poor's	Moody's
AAA	Aaa
AA	Aa
A	A
BBB	Baa
BB	Ba
B	B
CCC	Caa
CC	Ca
C	C
D	

---

store ads.) These bonds have what appear to be pages of individually dated green stamps attached. On the appropriate date, holders clip the appropriate coupons and deposit them in their bank accounts. The bank collects the interest payment from the municipality.

Coupons indicate *bearer* bonds, meaning a purchaser may presume the holder to be the owner. If you lose one, your chances of getting it back match those of recovering your money after a mugging.

All municipal bonds issued after June 1983 must be *registered*. Like a stock certificate, a registered bond certificate has the owner's name printed on its front. The issuer mails interest payments to the bond owner. Corporations have issued only registered bonds for years.

U.S. Treasury Issues

The United States government borrows more than anyone else — $90 billion in the second half of 1982 alone. Because the government's taxing power backs them, Treasuries have the highest quality rating. The federal government taxes the interest on Treasury issues, but the states do not.

For the ethical investor concerned about particular government programs, U.S. Treasury issues (*Treasuries*) pose a problem. Their proceeds go into the government's general fund, so they may just as soon end up in tobacco subsidies or B-1 bombers, mass transit construction or hazardous waste clean-up programs. Neither the government nor the investor can say what a particular issue will do.

Treasury Bills. Every Monday the U.S. Treasury auctions its three-month and six-month *Treasury bills* (*T-bills*). About once a month it offers a nine-

FIGURE 2-2   Corporations in Support of Public Television

In 1983, in the face of massive cutbacks in federal support for public television, twelve large companies joined to form Corporations in Support of Public Television in order to seek greater business support for PBS.

Atlantic Richfield	Ford Motor Company
American Telephone & Telegraph	General Electric Company
Chevron (Standard Oil of California)	Gulf Oil Corp.
The Chubb Group	Mobil Oil Corp.
Danskin (a subsidiary of Esmark)	Xerox
Exxon	

Source: San Francisco Chronicle, 13 April 1983.

---

month or twelve-month bill. T-bills require an initial minimum investment of $10,000, after which $5000 increments are available. Unlike most other bonds, T-bills sell at a discount from their face value. For example, on March 22, 1982, an investor would have paid $9682.70 for a $10,000 T-bill due three months later. The $317.30 difference between the face value and its cost represents the purchaser's interest. Because of their short life, T-bills are *book entry*, meaning the buyer does not receive an ownership certificate. The Treasury just records the purchaser's interest on its books.

Treasury Notes. The Treasury offers *Treasury notes* (*T-notes*) at auction almost every month. Their maturity dates range from two to seven years after purchase. The Treasury issues T-notes at full face value ($1000) and the purchaser must buy a minimum of five notes. The Treasury issues certificates for T-notes.

Treasury Bonds. *T-bonds* differ from T-notes only in their maturities, which are always greater than five years.

U.S. Government Obligations

For ethical investors choosing to avoid Treasuries, *U.S. agency obligations* offer a good alternative. They are only slightly less safe than Treasuries and yield slightly more. The proceeds go for particular projects. For instance, the Student Loan Marketing Association (Sallie Mae) issues debt to finance educational loans, while the Federal Farm Credit System finances loans to farmers.

Transactions in agency issues usually require the services of a broker. You can purchase Treasury obligations through your broker or a bank, or you may buy new issues directly from a Federal Reserve Bank. You can follow Treasury and most agency issues in the *Wall Street Journal,* which quotes their prices every day.

Commercial Paper

Commercial paper represents a short-term — 30, 60, or 90 day — loan to a corporation. Usually issued in $100,000 denominations, these loans help issuing corporations meet short-term cash requirements. A toy company like Mattel must build large inventories in the summer in order to have stock for Christmas. They often sell commercial paper to meet short-term cash needs. Commercial paper can be a good choice for the wealthy investor seeking an alternative to T-bills or a money market fund. And commercial paper often carries higher interest rates than government issues.

Certificates of Deposit

Certificates of deposit (CDs) are term loans to banks. In November 1983 a typical bank offered the following CDs:

7 to 90 days	$5000 minimum investment
	8.5% annualized fixed rate
91 to 180 days	$2500 minimum investment
	8.6% annualized fixed rate
180 days to 30 months	$1000 minimum investment
	8.75% annualized fixed rate
31 months plus	$500 minimum investment
	9.5% annualized variable rate

The interest on CDs usually paces the rate of inflation, so you won't lose or make much. And the interest is taxable. Severe interest penalties apply to early withdrawals. The Federal Deposit Insurance Corporation (FDIC), a government agency, insures CDs up to $100,000.

Money Market Funds

Money market funds are a specialized type of mutual fund designed for investors who want ready access to their money but also want to earn as

FIGURE 2-3   The Ten Best Places for Blacks to Work

According to *Black Enterprise,* these ten companies offer blacks the best opportunity for hiring, promotion, and pay.

American Telephone & Telegraph Co. (the old company)
The Equitable Life Assurance Society
Exxon Corp.
Gannett Co., Inc.
General Electric Co.
General Motors Corp.
Hewlett-Packard Co.
International Business Machines Corp.
Sea-Land
Xerox Corp.

Source: Black Enterprise, February 1982, p. 44.

much interest as possible. The value of a share is always $1. Many allow you to write checks on your account.

A money market fund typically invests in short-term debt: T-bills, commercial paper, and CDs. The interest, which compounds daily, flows through to the investors minus a fee of .5% to 1%. Every day some of the fund's investments come due and are reinvested. Therefore, the fund's yield fluctuates daily.

This rapid turnover generally poses difficulties for ethical investors because at any given moment they can have very little idea what their money is in. A short-term loan (CD) to Norstar (an Albany-based bank with no overseas loans) might be replaced by one to Citibank (a major lender to the Eastern bloc countries).

Federal insurance does not cover money market funds. The banking industry's collapse could mean your holdings would drop in value. However, some money funds purchase only U.S. Treasury obligations and so lessen the already slight risk.

Bank Accounts

Bank accounts are not normally considered debt, but they are. A bank borrows depositors' money and loans it to others. The bank makes money by charging more for its loans than it pays for deposits. It is virtually impossible to find out what kinds of loans a bank makes because loan portfolios change daily. So some ethical investors prefer to limit their accounts to those few banks run along ethical guidelines. Others restrict their banking to small banks that loan primarily to local businesses and homeowners.

EQUITIES

Equities are common and preferred stocks. This is where the most inno-vative ethical investors operate. Stocks offer everything: ethical invest-ments, high current income, and growth. See Box 2-3 for some basic information on stocks.

Common Stock

Common stock represents shares of ownership in a company. Each stock-holder, or *shareholder*, owns a percentage of the corporation determined by dividing the number of shares held by the number of shares outstanding. The rights accompanying stock ownership include:

- The right to vote for corporate directors and on proxy issues.
- The right to financial disclosure in the forms of quarterly income statements and balance sheets and an annually audited financial re-port.
- The right to participate in profits in the form of dividends to the extent of your proportionate ownership.

BOX 2-3   Stock: Some Essential Definitions

Earnings per share — profits per share, calculated by dividing the company's profits by the number of shares outstanding.

Dividend — the amount of the earnings distributed to shareholders. Earnings and dividends are not the same. Gerber Products (baby foods and accessories) had profits (*earnings*) per share of $2.92 in 1982 and paid $1.333 per share in dividends. Dividends may also come in the form of stock. Missouri Public Service has paid a 2% stock dividend twice a year for many years. For every 100 shares owned, you would receive two shares each time Missouri Public Service paid a dividend. A stock dividend has no real economic impact, because a shareholder owns the same percentage of a company as before.

Merger — the taking over of one company by another. Very often a corporation with extra cash will decide to buy another company with assets it can use by *soliciting* (offering to buy) sufficient shares in the target company to give it control. The acquiring corporation usually pays well above current stock market value for the target company's shares.

Retained earnings — that part of the earnings not paid out. They finance growth, research, and development expenses.

Stock split — increasing the number of shares outstanding by giving stock-holders additional new stock. A two-for-one split would give the owner of 100 shares of stock 200.

Why Companies Issue Stock. Not all companies have publicly traded stock. Tens of thousands of privately held corporations operate in America today. For example, Secretary of State George Schultz formerly headed Bechtel Corporation, a multibillion-dollar privately held corporation with extensive interests in Saudi Arabia.

Bechtel is exceptional. Normally, when a company grows beyond a certain point, its owners find it extremely profitable to *go public* (to sell part or all of their ownership rights). Often the company has grown to such a size that future growth requires massive outlays of capital, which the owners can't raise on their own. Many prefer to exchange some of their ownership for the necessary cash — and a healthy capital gain. Apple Computer went public for these reasons. This book discusses only *publicly traded* (i.e., on one of the national or regional stock exchanges) stock.

How Stock Changes Hands. If a corporation's stock is publicly traded, the process by which it changes hands is essentially the same whenever it is traded in an open market. After it issues stock, a corporation does not directly benefit from its sale. The corporation has sold a piece of itself, and now that piece is traded between individuals. When you buy stock in a company, you buy it usually from another individual via a broker. The demand for shares and the number of shares available for purchase determine the price. Thus, stock prices rise when buyers are more eager than sellers and fall when sellers are more eager than buyers.

Shareholders receive stock *certificates* from the corporation. When they sell stock, they endorse their certificates — much as they would checks — and turn them over to brokers, who send them to *transfer agents*, usually banks, which keep track of a corporation's shareowners. The company issues the buyer a certificate in three to five weeks.

A number of books (some of which I've listed in the bibliography) describe in considerable detail the mechanics of a trade. Though it is dated, a good place to start is Claude N. Rosenberg, Jr.'s *Stock Market Primer* (Warner Books, 1976).

Brokers and Commissions. Your stockbroker charges a *commission* (fee) for finding an individual to buy your stock or sell some to you, and the other party's broker earns a commission for locating you. If, for example, you buy some stock on the New York Stock Exchange, you will pay your broker the price per share times the number of shares plus the commission. The seller will receive a check from her broker with the commission already deducted.

Most new investors worry about the fees they will incur by doing business with a full-service firm. Usually these firms charge a minimum commission of about $30 to $40 every time you buy or sell. For trades between $2500 and $20,000 the commission charge varies between 1½% and 2½%.

Most brokerage firms will hold your stocks and bonds without charging any fee for safekeeping. However, some charge less active accounts for this service. Certainly your broker should explain any incidental fees you may incur for special services before they appear on your account. These services do not include the full-service broker's time, research, advice, portfolio review, or other information. The broker charges a commission only for selling or buying for you.

You don't have to use a broker or trade on a stock exchange. You always have the option of finding a buyer, agreeing on a price, and transferring the stock yourself. All you have to do is fill out the back of the certificate and mail it to the company's transfer agent.

Preferred Stocks

Preferred stocks — the words have a nice ring to them. However, "preferred" means only that its holders take priority over common stockholders should the company go bankrupt. Debt holders and other secured creditors would get their money first.

Brokers usually identify preferred stocks by their dividend. For instance, General Motors (a leader among companies attempting to ameliorate conditions in South Africa) issued a $3.75 preferred in 1947. Preferred stock pays a fixed dividend forever. However, the company must pay the interest and principal due its debt holders before paying dividends on the preferred. Then, if money remains, it pays dividends on the common stock.

Preferred stock has some real disadvantages. Since the dividend never changes, the preferred shareholder cannot benefit from even spectacular growth. When a company first issues preferred, its dividend is higher than the common's. But through the years, the common's may rise to more than the preferred's. AT&T issued a $3.64 preferred in 1973, when it paid a common dividend of $2.87. In 1983 the common paid $5.85; the preferred still paid $3.64.

Ordinary preferred's price has no reason to go up other than that the dividend offers a good rate of return when compared with interest rates generally. However, this should tempt you only when you think interest rates are about to fall. Like bonds, preferred stock trades against interest rates. Its prices rise as rates fall, and vice versa. Therefore, you should buy only when interest rates are very high and likely to fall, or if you need income now and are not concerned about appreciation in value.

Preferred stocks normally carry no voting rights. That means preferred shareholders do not participate in votes on company policy at the annual meeting.

Convertible Securities

Some companies issue bonds or preferred stock, which the holder can convert into shares of common stock at a fixed rate of exchange. Sometimes the convertible feature has the same life as the underlying security. Other times the holder may exercise the conversion right only for a certain period.

Convertible Preferred. With a convertible security your first question is, "What's its conversion price?" because the conversion price may be too distant from current market values to make it attractive. However, if it is only 15% to 25% above the common's current market value, purchasing the convertible security should give you higher income while you wait for conversion to become desirable. Beatrice Foods (a large contributor to the Chicago Lyric Opera) offers a $3.38 cumulative convertible preferred. Each share may be converted into 1.86 shares of common. In June 1983 the common sold for 26 and the preferred for 49. If the common sold at 26½, it would be at parity with the preferred (1.86 × 26½ = 49). However, a share of preferred pays $3.38 per year in dividends, while 1.86 shares of common paid only $2.98 in 1983. Even at parity conversion is not attrac-

FIGURE 2-4   Top Ten Sponsors of Sex, Violence, and Profanity on TV

RCA	Beecham
Mazda	Pabst Brewing
Tampax	Denny's
I.C. Industries	Esmark
Helene Curtis	Warner Lambert

Source: Report of the Spring 1983 Television Monitoring Program of the Coalition for Better Television, Prime-Time Viewing, January 30–June 15, 1983. Reprinted by permission.

tive, since you would receive more in dividends by sticking with the preferred. In fact, you would never convert a preferred unless its dividend were less than that of the underlying common stock. See Figure 2-5 for a list of some convertible preferred stocks.

Convertible Bonds. Occasionally a corporation issues a bond that holders may convert into common stock. The issuer often wishes to reduce its debt over the bond's life and convert that debt into ownership. Usually conversion is fixed at a point where the common would have to rise 15% to make it worth considering. Thus, the corporation can reduce its debt in the future while avoiding issuing stock at an unfavorable price.

Kinder-Care Learning Centers (day care) has some convertible bonds due in 1998. In 1982 its common stock paid only $.10 a share. Its convertible bonds are of a low quality, but they are certainly safer than the common. They pay $110 per year in interest. Thus, you can buy the bond, receive high income, and if the common skyrockets, convert your bond. One Kinder-Care bond converts into 55.94 shares of common stock.

Unlike ordinary bonds or straight preferred stock, the conversion feature of a convertible bond will drive the bond's price higher as the common stock's price increases. For that reason, with a convertible bond you do not depend exclusively on interest rates going your way to make money.

FIGURE 2-5 Selected Convertible Preferreds

	S&P Rating/Moody's Rating
Arvin Industries $2.00 Cv.	BB/NR
Chemical New York $1.875 Cv.	NR/Aa
Cooper Industries $2.90 Cv.	BBB/Baa
Emons Industries $1.1875 Cv.	B/NR
Hawaiian Electric $1.44 Cv.	A/A
Hesston $1.60 Cv.	NR
Indianapolis Power & Light 6¼% Cv.	AA/Aa
Liberty National $2.125 Cv.	NR
MCI Communications $1.80 Cv.	B/B
MCI Communications $1.84 Cv.	B/B
Potomac Electric Power $2.44 Cv.	A/Aa
Southern California Edison 5.20% Cv.	A/A
Southwest Florida Banks $2.1875 Cv.	NR
Transco Companies, Inc. $3.875 Cv.	B/Ba
U.S. Air, Inc. $1.875 Cv.	BB-/Ba
Washington Gas Light $4.36	NR/Baa
Western Air Lines $2.00 Cv.	BB-/B
Western Union 4.60% Cv.	BB-/NR
Western Union 4.90% Cv.	B/NR

Mutual Funds

Mutual funds pool investors' money to buy a portfolio of securities. They offer the advantages of diversification by allowing the investor to own an interest in a greater variety of stock than most individuals can afford. They also provide professional management of the investor's assets. In addition, liquidity may be greater and transaction costs lower than with a diversified individual portfolio.

Buying and Selling Fund Shares. All ethical mutual funds are *open ended,* which means they have no set number of shares. When you buy shares, the fund creates new ones for you. The price per share is the *net asset value* per share (total value of stocks held by the fund at yesterday's market price, divided by the number of shares outstanding yesterday) plus a *load* (commission), if any. Load funds are sold by stockbrokers. *No-load* (commissionless) funds are sold directly by the mutual funds. Some mutual funds have begun to sell directly to shareholders with a small sales charge (2%–3%). These are commonly called *low-load* funds.

None of the ethical funds are *closed-end* funds. These funds have a fixed number of shares and are not priced at net asset value. Their shares trade on exchanges like stocks.

Mutual Funds and the Ethical Investor. Ethical investors have an easier time evaluating mutual funds than they do money market funds. Every mutual fund has a particular stated investment concept. Dreyfus Third Century

FIGURE 2-6   Selected Beer and Alcohol Stocks

Amdisco	Imperial Group
American Brands, Inc.	Iroquois Brands Ltd.
Archer-Daniels-Midland Co.	Kane-Miller Corp.
Bacardi Corp.	Nabisco Brands, Inc.
Brown-Forman Distillers Corp.	National Distillers & Chemical Corp.
Canadaigua Wine Co., Inc.	Norlin Corporation
Carling O'Keefe Ltd.	Norton Simon, Inc.
The Coca-Cola Company	Olympia Brewing
Adolph Coors Co.	Pabst Brewing Co.
Di Giorgio Corp.	Pfizer, Inc.
Early California Industries, Inc.	Philip Morris, Inc.
Falstaff Brewing Corporation	Publicker Industries, Inc.
Flanigan's Enterprises, Inc.	The Seagram Company Ltd.
Foremost-McKesson, Inc.	Sonoma Vineyards
Genesee Brewing Co., Inc.	Univar Corp.
Glenmore Distilleries Co.	U.S. Tobacco Co.
G. Heileman Brewing Co.	

Fund invests only in companies meeting its social responsibility guidelines, while Wisconsin Income invests in high-interest corporate bonds regardless of their ethical qualifications. United States Gold Shares, which would satisfy few ethical investors, invests in gold mining companies. Also, mutual funds hold stocks for considerably longer than money funds can hold the short-term instruments they buy.

One of the great virtues of ethical funds, like the Pax World Fund, is that they sometimes perform the activist shareholder's role by aggressively participating in proxy campaigns focusing on social and moral issues. Also, Pax notifies the boards of companies it divests of the reasons for its actions.

Conclusions: Making Choices

The ethical investor can choose from many investment vehicles: stocks, bonds, mutual funds, government issues, bank accounts, and the many subgroups of each. I've known a number of socially conscious investors who feel completely comfortable investing in defense or nuclear energy. Sometimes their major concern is that companies show a strong commitment to local communities and workers. International Business Machines (IBM) suits them because it strongly supports inner-city development; it pays its employees well and provides an open system for complaints; and it has had no layoffs in 40 years. However, IBM is a top defense contractor and has automated apartheid in South Africa.

As for the drug industry, the head of a highly successful investment firm acknowledges that some of its companies have bad environmental and consumer product histories but says, "We can live with the problems in the drug industry. It's a relative point of view. These companies are generally constructive and socially responsible." One investment adviser learned just how relative ethical concerns can be when she advised a client to drop Eli Lilly from her portfolio because of its South African interests. "I won't drop Lilly," the client responded. "They make my insulin!"

Concerned investors must deal with these conflicts, deciding what to insist on and what to accept in order to foster what they care most about. However, before you can make informed decisions about investments from either a financial or an ethical standpoint, you must define your goals. The next chapter will guide you in evaluating yourself and in making the hard decisions required by ethical investing.

3 MANAGING THE
   ETHICAL PORTFOLIO

A NCIENT GREEKS traveled to Delphi, paid the Oracle to cut open a chicken, and listened to what augured. Most should have saved their money and heeded the sign outside the Oracle's temple: "Know thyself." That's also excellent advice for investors, particularly ethical investors. No matter how good the company or investment vehicle, it must fit your ethics, financial needs, and personality. This chapter describes how to go about the self-analysis required to become a successful ethical investor.

GROWTH AND INCOME

The two most common investment goals for investors are growth and income. In my trade's jargon, *growth* describes investments held for their appreciation in value rather than the income which they produce. Investors do not expect to profit from a growth investment until they sell it.

When I use the word *growth*, I mean long-term growth. *Long-term* refers to the amount of time the investor holds the vehicle. Because the Internal Revenue Code discriminates in its treatment of long-term and short-term capital gains, the definition of *long-term* follows the Internal Revenue Code's.

Many growth investors are not long-term investors. *Traders* look for

31

short-term appreciation in the vehicle's value and then sell. In a book of this scope, I couldn't begin to introduce their sophisticated strategies. More important, you can't be an ethical investor and trade.

While an investment for income may produce a profit on sale, its purpose is to produce income currently. Income investors can expect that their profits on sale will be significantly smaller than what the growth seeker would consider adequate. Keep in mind, however, that only investors on the extreme ends of the growth-income spectrum limit their choices to one class of vehicle. Most seek a balance that reflects their personality. You should decide where you fit on the spectrum. This chapter will help you appraise yourself, and so will your broker or investment adviser. But before they can help, you need to know what you have now — what's in your portfolio. See Appendix A for forms to help you make your evaluation.

YOUR PORTFOLIO

Your *portfolio* holds all of your *liquid assets* — the assets you can turn into cash easily. These include cash, stocks, bonds, and money market and mutual fund shares. When you make decisions about these resources — how they will be invested, when they will be sold — you must also think about your *non-liquid assets*. These include your house, pension plan, antiques, fine art, or insurance, which will become part of your estate. These play a direct role in how you evaluate your portfolio.

Your stage in life also influences portfolio management. If you have just received your first big promotion and can look forward to a significant year-end bonus, you should be considering vehicles other than money market and mutual funds. If your children are about to head for college, you're going to have more liquid assets in the coming year than in the past. If retirement looms in the next five years, you will be shifting your investments to compensate for your decline in earnings. In short, you cannot separate how you manage your portfolio from what is going on in your life.

Portfolio management begins with a review of your financial position. Whether it takes the form of an annual look at your investments with your investment adviser or your own well-thought-out analysis, this review permits you to compare what you own against your current standards and encourages you to fine tune your criteria in light of your needs, market conditions, and industry developments.

The vast majority of investors lack any unified approach to their

FIGURE 3-1   Companies Doing Business in South Africa Which Are Not Signatories to the Sullivan Principles (1983)

The following is a list of publicly traded companies which have *not* signed the Sullivan Principles and have more than ten employees in South Africa. Appendix D contains a list of those companies which have, and rates them.

A.M. International Inc.
AccuRay Corporation
Air Express International Corp.
Alexander & Alexander International Corp.
Allegheny International Inc.
Amdahl Corp.
BBDO International Inc.
The Badger Company, Inc.*
Baker International Corporation
Bausch & Lomb, Inc.
Bell & Howell Co.
The Black and Decker Manufacturing
    Company
Blue Bell Inc.
Buckman Laboratories, Inc.
Bucyrus-Erie Co.
Bundy Corporation
Champion Spark Plug Co.
Chesebrough-Ponds Inc.
Chicago Pneumatic Tool Company
Chrysler Corp.
City Investing International Inc.
Collier Inc.**
Computer Sciences Corp.
Crown Cork & Seal Co., Inc.
Dresser Industries Inc.
Dun & Bradstreet International Limited
Eaton Corporation
Echlin Manufacturing Co.
Foster Wheeler Energy Corp.
Fruehauf International Ltd.
Fuller Co.
GATX

J. Gerber & Co.
Grolier Incorporated
Frank B. Hall & Co., Inc.
Harnischfeger Corporation
The Harper Group
IMS International Inc.
Ingersoll-Rand Co.
International Flavors & Fragrances Inc.
Kimberly-Clark Corp.
Leeds & Northrup Co.***
Loctite Corporation
Lubrizol Corporation
Martin Marietta Corp.
Mohawk Data Sciences
Newmont Mining Corp.
A. C. Nielsen Company
Parker Hannifin Corp.
Pepsico International
Phibro-Salomon Inc.
Pizza Inn Inc.
Revlon, Inc.
A. H. Robins Co., Inc.
G. D. Searle International Co.
Sedco Inc.
Simplicity Pattern Co., Inc.
The Singer Company
Smith International
Sybron Corp.
Timken Co.
United States Industries
West Point-Pepperell
Westin Hotels****

*Subsidiary of Raytheon Co.
**Subsidiary of MacMillan, Inc.
***Subsidiary of General Signal Corporation
****Subsidiary of UAL, Inc.

Source: International Council for Equality of Opportunity Principles, Inc., 1501 North Broad Street, Philadelphia, PA 19122 (copies of full report available for $15.00).

assets. For the ethical investor this approach will not work. You can't achieve your goals — ethical or financial — this way any more than you can train for the New York Marathon by jogging occasionally. Developing a financial strategy provides a structure with which you can feel comfortable. It reduces the number of choices you have to make. That is a major reason why your financial adviser or broker should play a role in your review and be fully informed of your strategy.

PLANNING FOR PORTFOLIO MANAGEMENT

Managing an ethical portfolio requires focused, disciplined thought. By the end of the planning phase you should have answered three questions: 1. What is your appraisal of yourself as an ethical investor, and how does that appraisal affect the way you want to manage your portfolio? 2. What do you need from your assets in both the short and long range? 3. Where are you starting from? The guidelines in the sections below will make the planning process much simpler.

Appraising Yourself

Spend some time thinking carefully about yourself, your needs, and your environment. Do this with pen in hand. Putting things on paper will focus your effort. Here are the factors to consider:

Your Ethical Screens. The emphasis on financial strategy in this chapter in no way implies downgrading ethical concerns. Your ethical objectives require careful inventory as well. Chapter 1 contains a form to get you started. I can't tell you what your ethical criteria should be and how to rank them. But I can tell you that the more clearly you can define your ethical goals, the easier it will be to create a universe of potential investments.

Your Financial Resources. Many people think all they should consider is the money they have to spend on stocks or bonds. That is far too limited. Identify all of your resources, including Social Security, the money you keep in savings, passive sources of income, and so on.

Your Time. If you are inclined to manage your own portfolio, do you have the time to do it right? If not, will your broker or someone else help you? Can you afford to hire someone to manage your money in accordance with your criteria? I'll have more to say about this decision later.

Your Feelings About Investments. What kind of investor are you? What degree of security do you require in your investments? Do you feel comfortable knowing your money is at risk? Are you capable of dealing with daily swings in your asset value?

Your Advantages. What in your daily life has changed which might give you an advantage in investing? What field do you know well enough to evaluate claims made about products?

Setting Your Goals

Once you've worked through a self-appraisal, list your short-, medium-, and long-range financial goals. Organize them chronologically according to when you will look to your portfolio to produce a given result.

Your Outlook. What do your earnings look like this year? How secure is your job? How will changes in the national economy affect you? Do you live in a house carrying a variable-rate mortgage? If interest rates stay high, what will that do to your net income? Are you in a sector where another recession could endanger your job?

Your Immediate Needs. What do you need from your assets between now and your next review? Are you looking at land? Do you have a child heading for school this fall? Will you need higher income next year than usual? Are you taking maternity leave from your job?

Your Long-Range Needs. What expenses will you have to rely on your portfolio to meet? Retirement? Children's education? Second home? When will you incur those expenses?

Evaluating Your Assets. Before you begin to plan your portfolio, you have to know where you are. That can take some real work. Here are the questions I have my clients answer:

Liquidity. Are all of your assets liquid? Are they in savings accounts, money market funds, banks? Or are your assets land, furniture, an interest in a new software package, or other property that is not easily turned into cash? If not all, then what percentage is liquid? Can you buy one investment vehicle without selling another? If all your assets are liquid, draw up your portfolio management plan and begin investing deliberately. If they're not, you should proceed through this list.

Your Present Portfolio. Is a substantial portion of your assets in a portfolio now? Was the portfolio developed before you decided to invest along socially responsible guidelines? If so, before proceeding further you must evaluate what you now hold for both financial and ethical implications.

Assets Not in Your Control. Do you have an interest in assets which you do not control? For example, if you are the beneficiary of a trust fund, you probably have no control over its assets. But you must take them into account as you make investments for yourself. In most cases you should not duplicate the holdings already in the trust. Instead, take the opportunity to diversify your holdings. From an ethical standpoint, as a trust beneficiary you should ask your trustees at least to apply some avoidance guidelines. Often they will do so if you provide them with specific information on companies you do not want.

Funds Available for Investment. How much do you have to invest? Suppose you have between $2000 and $10,000 available for investment which you want to build slowly into a portfolio. You face a difficult planning task. You will have to sketch the outline of your portfolio and pick an initial investment. If someone in this category insists on picking a single vehicle, I recommend a safe holding, like the AAA-rated Citizens' Utilities bonds mentioned in Chapter 2. Although safety ranks high, younger investors tend to look for capital gains, not income. So I look for relative safety among growth investments. I think ethical mutual funds make much more sense for them than a tax-exempt issue. As your assets available for investment grow above $10,000, your range of choices will increase, too.

Thinking of Everything

Before plunging into planning your portfolio, go back to square one. Have you thought of *everything* that might affect your investment decisions? For instance, have you weighed your risk in developments such as significant changes in the Internal Revenue Code? (You should discuss possibilities like these with your lawyer or accountant.) Could the deregulation of an industry affect one of your current holdings? What types of emergency planning have you done for yourself? Do you own a summer house you could rent for the winter? Have you got money tucked away in certificates of deposit which you could spend if you had to? These are the kinds of questions you should ask yourself as you review your preparations for planning your portfolio.

PLANNING A PORTFOLIO

When you've finished thinking about where you are and where you want to go, it is time to begin developing your financial strategy. First, identify your position on the growth-income spectrum. As you do, keep in mind that it refers to a general philosophy, which almost always demands a mix of the two categories. One of the key decisions you have to make is how far into either category you fall. For that reason, as we look at growth and income portfolios, I'll give you a broad band of percentages for each investment category.

The Growth Seeker's Portfolio

Emergency Reserve. Make sure you have enough cash in a very safe but accessible place (e.g., a bank or a money fund) to maintain your standard of living through six months without any income. Only the truly blessed encounter layoffs or serious illness at the top of a market. These always seem to coincide with recessions and bear markets. But you *never* want to be forced to sell something.

Debt. The growth seeker will want between 5% and 40% in debt — 5% if your sources of income other than your portfolio are steady and secure, 40% if you think the interest rate cycle is peaking. Those are the extremes. Consider the opportunities the stock market offers. If the market looks promising and you put too much into safe income vehicles, you may cost yourself opportunities.

You should spread the percentage of your portfolio that is in interest-bearing vehicles among those offering variable interest rates, such as money

FIGURE 3-2   1982 Ballot Questions. Campaigns Affecting Corporate Interests

Measure	Spending*	% Vote**
(won/lost)	Business backed/ other side	Business backed/ other side
Arizona Deposit on beverage containers (L)	$681,000/59,000	68/32
California Hand gun registration (L)	5,116,000/2,275,000	63/37
Deposit on beverage containers (L)	5,172,000/755,000	56/44
Colorado Deposit on beverage containers (L)	770,000/498,000	76/24
Maine Shut down nuclear power plant (L)	801,000/185,000	56/44
Massachusetts Deposit on beverage containers (W)	840,000/147,000	40/60
Restrict nuclear waste disposal (W)	25,000/100,000	33/67
Michigan Elect Public Service Commissioners (L)		63/37

Preliminary figures as of late October from state Elections Commisssions. Final figures will probably be higher.

**No figures available from state Elections Commissions. This figure is an estimate provided by the campaign committee itself. Source: *Initiative News Reports*, Washington, D.C.

Source: Council on Economic Priorities Newsletter, February 1983, p. 4.

market funds or *floating rate bonds*. A floating rate bond is like other bonds except that its rate can vary. Chase Manhattan offers some floating rates due on June 15, 1999. The interest rate changes at every payment and is always 1% above the current Treasury bill rate. When you think interest rates are low, put up to 90% of your debt money into variable-rate debt. When interest rates seem very high, reduce this to only 10%.

The balance of the money you have to invest in debt should go into fixed-incomes, even if you think interest rates are about to go up. In case you're wrong, you should put some portion into fixed incomes spread over a number of different maturities.

FIGURE 3-2   *(continued)*

| Measure | Spending* | | % Vote** | |
(won/lost)	Business backed/ other side		Business backed/ other side	
Regulate fuel adjustment (citizen-backed) (W)	on all 3 measures 5,500,000/175,000*		49/51	
Regulate fuel adjustment (business-backed) (W)			60/40	
Missouri Establish Citizens Utility Board (L)	208,000/19,000		61/39	
Nebraska Ban corporate purchase of farmland (W)	463,000/33,000		44/56	
Ohio Elect Public Utilities Commissioners (L)	790,000/663,000		67/33	
Oregon Abolish Land Conservation Commission (L)	109,000/125,000		45/55	
Property Tax Reform (L)	400,000**/113,000		51/49	
Washington Deposit on beverage containers (L)	833,000/249,000		71/29	
Limit consumer credit interest rates (L)	1,179,000/237,000		66/34	
Remove food sales tax (L)	92,000/22,000		66/34	

Your choices of debt investments also depend on how much you have to spend. If your total portfolio amounts to $25,000 and you're putting only $6000 into bonds, you cannot economically invest in more than two issuers' bonds. Most brokerage houses charge a minimum transaction commission well above what the commission on one bond would be otherwise. The commission costs of buying one bond each of six companies are prohibitive because each counts as a separate transaction. Even two different issues by the same issuer count as separate transactions. You might put the entire $6000 into one issue. In this situation, if there were any ethical bond mutual funds, they would be the ideal choice.

Common Stocks and Diversification. The remaining 60% to 95% of your liquid assets should be in common or convertible preferred stocks. Here, the key rule, as in portfolio management generally, is diversify. Large corporations diversify in order to protect themselves against bad times. You should follow their example.

Most people diversify according to industry groups like lumber, office equipment, aero-space, and food products. Some investment advisers use their own categories, such as companies influenced by changes in interest rates or companies dependent on natural resources. I prefer to group them by trends, like corporations influenced by consumer borrowing. But however you categorize stocks, you want to avoid a situation in which the same factors affect all your stocks in the same way. You will not want a portfolio filled with companies catering to new mothers and newborns when the baby boomlet ends.

The Calvert Social Investment Fund works on the basis of industry groups and does not concentrate more than 25% of the value of its assets in any single industry. Some analysts recommend that regardless of how you categorize companies, you should pick one stock per industry group and exceed that limit only when you feel particularly strongly about a certain stock. Diversification also protects you against the worst. If you happen to be dead wrong about a particular stock, you lose only what you have in it.

You should also diversify into companies at different stages of development. While Johnson & Johnson is an appropriate investment for the growth seeker, it is a far more mature and far larger company than Hybritech, a medical technology company that makes monoclonal antibodies. Both pass most ethical investors' screens, though Hybritech's business — genetic engineering — may nix it for some.

Limiting your investments helps ensure that you know as much as possible about the companies you've bought. Jim Lowell of Lowell & Blake Associates told me, "Our core list is about 15 stocks. At any time we might be buying five or six. We add one or two major companies a year." If you have less than seven hours a month to spend actively managing your portfolio, I usually recommend against holding shares in more than ten companies.

Two final points about diversification. First, suppose you already hold as many stocks as you can readily monitor, but then you discover another very strong candidate. You must always be prepared to sell the weakest vehicle in your portfolio to make way for investments with greater promise. If you feel Wang Laboratories is too good to miss, you might sell your Apple Computer, whose earnings are slumping. Second, while you should diversify your portfolio, you should buy stock in amounts of not less than

$1000. Most brokerages charge you a minimum commission on smaller lots that is the same as that on a $1000 transaction.

The Income Seeker's Portfolio

Emergency Reserve. In this category, the standard is identical for growth and income seekers alike.

Interest-Bearing Vehicles. If you are an income seeker, your portfolio should hold between 30% and 70% interest-bearing vehicles. You should diversify your holdings with both floating-rate and fixed-income debt with diversified maturities. Also consider varying the quality of the debt. If you can afford to take the risk, you can get higher interest rates. For instance, in August 1983 AAA-rated General Electric's (defense and nuclear power) 8½% due in 2004 sold at 73¾ for a current yield of 11.53% and a yield to maturity of 11.95%. BBB-rated W. E. Heller's (real estate development) 8¾% due in 2002 sold at 68¼ for a current yield of 12.82% and a yield to maturity of 13.44%.

Common Stocks. The balance of your portfolio ought to be in high-yield common or convertible preferred stocks. In almost every case the income seeker who ignores common stocks makes a serious mistake. The reason: most income seekers need higher income in the future than they do now. Common stocks can, and often do, raise their dividends. For instance, Black Hills Power & Light (a nonnuclear utility) has a five-year dividend growth rate of 15.7%. If possible, buy a couple of stocks with lower yields but which have good dividend records and a real chance for capital appreciation. And don't forget that the best type of income is long-term capital gains, since it is taxed at a maximum rate of 20%. Inflation can seriously erode your portfolio if it isn't replenished by well-timed capital gains.

Income seekers should diversify their stock holdings for the same reasons as the growth seekers. The same caveats apply too.

Putting Your Plan into Effect

Few investors can develop a plan and immediately put it into full effect. Instead, you should develop a timetable for putting your ideas to work, and stick to it.

Portfolio management has two constants. The first, ironically, is change. Events occur which require the investor to review the plan and the portfolio. The second is deliberateness, a characteristic you must develop. If you practice, say, sticking to your investment timetable on the easy parts of portfolio management, you'll become disciplined enough to master the hard part — doing what you set out to do. Most important, you must exert the will power to avoid tips, ignore fads, and disregard what everyone else is doing.

Adding to Your Portfolio

Most people hope to add to their portfolios from time to time. When the opportunity comes, you have some decisions to make. Basically, you apply the same rules to this decision that you applied to formulate your investment plan. Think the entire situation out carefully. For instance, what expenses are coming up? Where are the economy and interest rates going? What portfolio balances do you want to maintain?

Having answered these questions, consider next how this addition affects your portfolio management strategy. Where are the opportunities for reaching your goals? Which companies you've researched are ripe for purchase? Should you ignore certain opportunities because they would create an imbalance in your portfolio? These are the kinds of questions you should be asking yourself and your broker or investment adviser.

What to Add. Though your plan may call for you to acquire a certain vehicle next, you cannot always get what you want when you want it. If you're looking for investments that give you high income at the bottom of an interest rate cycle, not only are you going to have a hard time finding high income, but you run the risk of capital loss as interest rates drop. For example, in the early summer of 1982 you could have bought Louisville Gas and Electric's (a nonnuclear utility) AA-rated 7½% bonds due 7/1/ 2002 at 50 (or $500 a bond). A year later that bond sold at 64. If you were adding to the fixed-income portion of your portfolio in the summer of 1983, you were settling for current yields of 11.7% on the same quality bonds you could have gotten 15% on a year earlier. With bond yields dropping, the income investor must look elsewhere, i.e., stocks, perhaps to a fast-growing environmental protection manufacturer. How about Betz Laboratories or Thermo Electron? Or a railroad which passes most social screens, such as Soo Lines? What about a growth utility that is paying dividends as well as growing fast, like Tucson Electric Power?

In short, your plan has to be flexible. Buy your second or even third priority if the first does not make financial sense at the moment.

Time to Sell. While considering portfolio acquisitions, check to see if your needs are changing. If so, you may want to change the balance in your portfolio. You could add to an area which seems to hold particular promise or, if that would create an imbalance, spread the purchases across the portfolio while emphasizing the promising area. Or let's say you have another $15,000 to add to your growth-oriented portfolio, but next year you're going to take a six-month sabbatical and won't have any money coming in. Put the money into a money fund. Growth is not your short-term goal. Money to live on is.

It may seem strange, but the time when you are considering portfolio acquisitions is an excellent time to consider what you should sell. Selling brings you full circle. If you sell, treat the proceeds as funds for additions to the portfolio.

The Capital Gains Trap. In evaluating what you should sell for either ethical or financial reasons, be sure to consider the tax implications of each sale, but avoid the capital gains trap.

On the whole, people are too concerned with taxes on their long-term capital gains. They have had a good shelter from taxes while value built up. If they had had to declare paper gains along the way and pay income taxes on them at the same rate as ordinary income, they would be in much worse shape. Psychologically it is hard to face the prospect of having less to reinvest than the appreciated value of the stock on paper. That difficulty prevents people from realizing the dangers of developing a death grip on investments. In 1972 those holding Polaroid might have felt they couldn't afford to take a profit when it hit $125 per share. Perhaps they regretted their caution when Polaroid bottomed at $19 per share in 1974. The discussion of capital gains in Chapter 2 illustrates how foolish it is for many investors not to take their capital gains when they have them. You should sell because the price per share of a company in which you have a profit has gotten ahead of its prospects for the future.

YOUR ROLE IN MANAGING YOUR PORTFOLIO

The preceding sections may give the impression that all individual investors should manage their own portfolios. Let me correct that impression. At the extremes, my clients fall into two types. Some absorb news instantly.

FIGURE 3-3 Annual Dividend Payments Since the 19th Century

Began in	Stock	Began in	Stock
1784	Bank of New York Co., Inc.	1883	Chesebrough-Ponds Inc.
1784	First National Boston Corp.	1883	Exxon Corporation
1791	Fleet Financial Group, Inc.	1885	Consolidated Edison Co.
1804	Norstar Bancorp Inc.	1885	Eli Lilly and Company
1813	Citicorp	1885	UGI Corporation
1813	First Nat'l State Bancorporation	1886	Hackensack Water Co.
1827	Chemical New York Corp.*	1889	West Point-Pepperell, Inc.
1840	Morgan (J. P.) & Co. Inc.	1890	American Brands, Inc.
1848	Chase Manhattan Corporation	1890	Boston Edison Co.*
1850	Connecticut Energy Corp.	1890	Commonwealth Edison Co.*
1851	Connecticut Natural Gas Corp.*	1890	Hydraulic Company
1851	Manhattan National Corp.	1890	Procter & Gamble Co.*
1852	Bay State Gas Co.*	1891	Southern New England Tel. Co.*
1852	Manufacturers Hanover Corp.	1892	Times Mirror Company
1852	Washington Gas Light Co.*	1892	Westvaco Corporation*
1853	Cincinnati Gas & Electric Co.	1893	Coca-Cola Co.
1853	Continental Corporation	1893	Fidelity Union Bancorporation
1856	Scovill Inc.	1894	Rexnord Inc.
1863	Pennwalt Corporation	1894	Standard Oil Co. (Indiana)
1863	Singer Company	1895	Burroughs Corp.*
1865	Irving Bank Corp.*	1895	Colgate-Palmolive Co.
1866	First Atlanta Corp.	1895	Mellon National Corp.*
1866	Travelers Corporation*	1895	Raymark Corporation
1867	CIGNA Corporation	1896	Castle & Cooke, Inc.
1868	American Express Co.	1898	General Mills, Inc.
1875	InterFirst Corporation*	1898	"Shell" Transport & Trading
1877	Stanley Works*		Co., Public Ltd. Co.
1879	Cincinnati Bell Inc.*	1898	Springs Industries, Inc.
1880	Bancal Tri-State Corp.*	1899	Borden, Inc.
1881	American Tel. & Tel. Co.*	1899	General Electric Co.*
1881	Corning Glass Works	1899	Nabisco Brands, Inc.*
1881	Security Pacific Corp.	1899	PPG Industries, Inc.*
1882	Bell Canada*	1899	Washington Water Power Co.
1883	Carter-Wallace, Inc.		

*Unbroken quarterly record since the 19th century
Source: New York Stock Exchange Fact Book, 1983.

They see it on TV or read it in an advisory service. This type of client knows a company's stock is going to split before management does. The other type finds out about the split when stock arrives in the mail. Both groups have the best of intentions about their portfolio. But those in the second group just never get around to doing the homework and making the decisions. They shouldn't even try. Instead, they should find a broker or investment adviser they trust who will do part of the work for them.

The point is not who does the work but rather that the planning gets done.

Brokers and Investment Advisers

Where to Look for Help. Don't start with the Yellow Pages. They're your last resort. Instead, ask people you trust to make recommendations and referrals. Start by asking other ethical investors or investment professionals you know and respect. Accountants, bankers, and lawyers are logical persons to ask. As an ethical investor, you may have difficulty finding the right person if you are not part of a network of like-minded people or if you live outside a major metropolitan area. For those who live in cities, you may use the resource groups discussed below to meet other ethical investors and learn who they use.

Brokers. There is no sense in paying for unnecessary financial services. For that reason the first step in finding a broker is to determine whether you need a full-service broker or a discount broker. The *full-service brokerage* offers investment advice on a wide range of vehicles: stocks, bonds, tax-advantaged investments, retirement plans, life insurance, mutual funds, and a host of others. At this type of firm you can receive at no charge — beyond the commissions on your transactions — research on companies that brokers recommend to you. You can expect to be contacted by the broker when it is time to sell or buy.

If you plan to control the research and you do not want advice, a *discount broker* may be right for you. They handle transactions for significantly reduced commission rates because these streamlined operations do not provide the personal attention and services a full-service broker does.

If you decide the advice and service are worth the cost, the next step is to find a broker with a positive outlook on socially responsible investing. You should shop around before settling on a particular broker. Listen carefully to brokers' responses to your objectives. Find out if they can fill your needs. Be specific. Ask, for example, if they have access to information such as who the top defense contractors are, who does business in South Africa, or who is into nuclear power technology. Find out if they have any purchase recommendations that they can give you on companies whose products or policies enhance the quality of life. If they can't respond to questions of this sort, look further.

Once you find the right broker, your most important task is to let her know precisely what you expect. Too many people tell me, "Just make money for me!" That isn't enough. To do my job I have to know whether you need money today in the form of high income on your investments or whether you are investing in preparation for sending your child to college in ten years. Also, what kinds of reserves do you have for emergencies? What is your need for safety? You should give your broker the information about yourself that you develop in the self-appraisal I outlined earlier in this chapter.

Investment Advisers. Writing in the *New York Times*, Leonard Sloane defined *investment advisers* as "money managers who invest their clients' funds in accordance with predetermined goals. . . . Some counselors handle accounts on an advisory basis . . . but most insist that accounts be discretionary, and that they be empowered to make transactions without advance consultation."[1] Among the thousands of investment advisers, a few specialize in ethical investing. Networking and this book are the best ways to find them.

When a person's financial situation gets beyond a certain level of complexity, it is time to consider an investment adviser. A $200,000 portfolio is my benchmark. However, this decision often turns on the degree of control investors want over their investments. Cost must be considered, too. An adviser's fee will usually range from 1% to 2% of the funds managed annually. Since investment advisers are not brokers, you must pay for both their advice and the brokerage fees on your transactions.

The Periodic Review

All investors should take an active interest in their portfolios. Periodic portfolio reviews — quarterly if your temperament can stand it, otherwise

FIGURE 3-4   Some Corporations with Business Ethics Programs

Allied Corp.	The Equitable Life Assurance Society
Avco Corp.	Honeywell, Inc.
BankAmerica Corp.	Levi Strauss & Co.
Cummins Engine Co., Inc.	Northwest Bank, Bloomington
Dart & Kraft, Inc.	The Prudential Insurance Company of
Dayton-Hudson Corp.	America

Source: Adapted from Porian S. Moskal, "Corporate Responsibility: Putting Your Act Together," *Industry Week,* July 26, 1982, pp. 51–56.

•

annually — are not optional. As an ethical investor you have an obligation to know what your money is doing. If brokers or money managers have not done a good job, their performance may escape notice for a long time unless the client insists on periodic reviews. If after two or three years they're not doing the job to your satisfaction, fire them and find people who will.

The best time to conduct your annual review is in the spring or early summer, when annual reports appear and your taxes are due. At no other time of the year are you so aware of your financial conditions and of opportunities in vehicles such as individual retirement accounts.

Dozens of reasons for an annual review come to mind. For instance, on June 27, 1983, while I was working on this chapter, Fort Howard Paper acquired Maryland Cup (paper and plastic cups for McDonald's, Wendy's, and 7-11 Stores). For some ethical investors Fort Howard's acquisition marked a significant deviation from its old strategy of recycling paper into numerous products, including power for its factories and trucks. Many dropped Fort Howard from their portfolios. (I couldn't help wondering why Fort Howard had changed its focus. Earnings over the past ten years had soared 616%.) The decision to sell rests with the investor. But the point is that periodically the ethical investor must address questions like those posed by Fort Howard's acquisition. Investing along socially responsible lines means controlling money and what happens to it.

Periodic reviews also encourage the refinement of your ethical criteria. If you are prepared to go beyond the veto approach and look for positive investments in a field, the periodic review is the time to broach the subject with the person handling your portfolio.

Furthermore, the financial picture may have changed since you last looked at your portfolio. Suppose you invested for growth in Dynascan when CB radios were hot. If you reviewed your holdings quarterly, you'd have sold when the CB boom busted. You might have bought it again two years later when it began making freedom phones.

Periodic reviews do not involve wholesale revisions of your strategy. Instead, you are formulating tactics for reaching your goals. When I do periodic reviews with clients, I focus on four elements of their plans.

1. *Emergency Reserve.* Is your emergency reserve still sufficient? Has anything happened in your life — like the arrival of a new child — which means more should be set aside?
2. *Income-producing Assets.* How can you increase the income portion of your portfolio? Perhaps the value of a stock has increased to a point where you could take a profit, reinvest the proceeds, and end up with

FIGURE 3-5   Top 25 Black-Owned Businesses

Only one of the top 25 is a publicly traded company. Shares of Johnson Products Co., Inc., trade on the American Stock Exchange.

Company	Type of Business	1982 Sales in Millions
Motown Industries	Entertainment	104,300
H. J. Russell Construction Co.	Construction/ development/ communications	103,060
Johnson Publishing Company, Inc.	Publishing, cosmetics, and broadcasting	102,660
Fedco Foods Corporation	Supermarkets	85,000
Wardoco, Inc.	Commercial fuel oils	84,393
Thacker Construction Company	Construction/ engineering	77,300
G & M Oil Company, Inc.	Petroleum sales	62,096
Soft Sheen Products, Inc.	Manufacturer and distributor of hair care products	55,000
Vanguard Oil and Service Company	Petroleum sales	53,000
The Jackson Oil Company	Petroleum sales	50,801
M & M Products Company, Inc.	Manufacturer and distributor of hair care products	48,000

Source: Black Enterprise, June 1983, pp. 79–80.

more income than you had before. You should also review income investments for possible dangers. For instance, if rising interest rates are a strong possibility, consider selling at least some of your fixed-income bonds.

3. *Growth Assets.* Are there any recent changes in outlook for a company? Sell a company if its earnings seem to be flattening out or sliding downward. Also, watch for better opportunities. If an area you expected to show good growth lets you down, look for a better idea rather than let assets dwindle. For instance, if you thought food stocks would be making money by now but see no increase in sight, sell them.

FIGURE 3-5   *(continued)*

Company	Type of Business	1982 Sales in Millions
Johnson Products Company, Inc.	Manufacturer of hair care products and cosmetics	42,400
Dick Griffey Productions	Entertainment	41,200
The Smith Pipe Companies, Inc.	Oilfield pipe and supply sales	35,000
Systems and Applied Sciences Corporation	Computer and electronic data systems	34,000
Wallace & Wallace Enterprises, Inc.	Petroleum sales	32,000
Grimes Oil Company, Inc.	Petroleum sales	31,906
Housing Innovations, Inc.	Real estate development/construction	29,230
Teleport Oil Company	Petroleum sales	28,000
L. H. Smith Oil Corporation	Petroleum sales	27,000
Inner City Broadcasting Corporation	Radio and TV communications	24,600
Community Foods, Inc.	Retail foods	23,000
Robinson Cadillac-Pontiac, Inc.	Auto sales & service	22,379
American Development Corporation	Manufacturing	21,000
Restoration Supermarket	Retail grocery	21,000

4. *Portfolio Balance.* What balance do you want to maintain in your portfolio? What if long-term interest rates drop dramatically and you, an income seeker, see a sudden large gain in your bonds? The bond portion of your portfolio might be worth more than the percentage of your assets you wanted in long-term bonds. Consider selling off some of the income-producing bonds and putting the proceeds into an area which has room to grow.

If you are one of those individuals for whom even a periodic portfolio review has the appeal of a root canal, you owe it to yourself at least to make sure that the person handling your money has a good track record in your areas of interest. Seriously consider having your lawyer or your accountant review your position at least once a year.

FIGURE 3-6   Top Ten Sponsors of Profanity on TV

RCA Corp.	Polaroid
Visa USA	Mazda Motors of America
Tampax	Mastercard
Vidal Sassoon	Volkswagen
K-Mart	IBM

Source: Report of the Spring 1983 Television Monitoring Program of the Coalition for Better Television, Prime-Time Viewing, January 30–June 15, 1983. Reprinted by permission.

Portfolio management is no science. No magic formula does it all for you. Instead, it requires hard work, focusing on your ethics and your needs. No one can guarantee you success if you observe these guidelines, but you will have a significant advantage over other investors.

4 EXPLORING THE CORPORATE UNIVERSE

E THICAL INVESTING is fascinating, engrossing work. Leave aside for a moment its serious purpose and the financial analyses. Because of the research it requires, ethical investing appeals to the detective in all of us. What companies have consistently run afoul of the antitrust laws? Which companies have found the glitter of casinos impossible to resist? Where do old CIA spooks tend to pop up? See Appendix F for more of the kinds of questions you ought to be asking about corporations.

Companies often give the ethical investor conflicting signals as to their values and ethics. For instance, Crown Zellerbach and another company agreed to pay $750,000 in civil fines for clean water violations at a paper mill they jointly operated in Eureka, California. Two weeks later it received the American Paper Institute and National Forest Products Association's annual environmental and energy achievement award for air pollution control at its Antioch, California, mill.[1]

Your research will also provide insights into social and political life which directly affect investments. For instance, in January 1981 an hour's thought about the corporate affiliations of President Reagan's kitchen cabinet would have told you he would take a benign attitude toward corporate acquisitions, regardless of their size. Because of his advisers' regional orientation and their views on organized labor, you could have surmised that his tax program would ignore the smokestack industries in the North and Midwest. Look around you. Economics, politics, cultural changes, new patterns in the fabric of everyday life — all these affect the financial world. Understanding the interrelationship between social and political action and investment gives ethical investing its focus and makes ethical investors good investors.

Finding companies and investments that will further your social and ethical views takes work. In this chapter we'll begin looking at how to implement a positive ethical investment program.

PUBLICATIONS

Every day I'm swamped with information at work. Magazines stack up at home; newspapers seem to have doubled in size. Each mail brings offers to sell me every conceivable type of information service. But when I want to know about an industry or a company, the information glut works to my benefit. As an ethical investor I can use not only all the traditional sources but also a number tailored to my special needs. I will be mentioning only a few of the publications available in this chapter. Other sources, including many designed for the ethical investor, are listed in Appendix B.

Two places to go for information are a full-service brokerage or a public library. Each has its advantages. The brokerage may have unpublished research reports on companies. The public library offers more general publications which may do features on particular companies. For example, the British weekly *The Economist* often runs first-rate analyses of American businesses.

Investment Data

Several publications provide the raw information investors need to appraise stocks. These publications are particularly useful in winnowing out companies that do not pass your ethical screen.

Moody's and Standard & Poor's. Moody's and *Standard & Poor's (S&P)* have a reputation for providing unbiased information. They supply key financial data that allow the ethical investor to determine whether a company merits further investigation. Most libraries carry one or the other.

The two services provide "tear sheets," so called because users can easily tear out pages from the volumes. They are available for all companies on the New York and American Stock Exchanges and for many whose stock is sold over the counter. The tear sheets contain a chart of the price

FIGURE 4-1 A Standard & Poor's Tear Sheet

Super Valu Stores 2169

NYSE Symbol SVU

Price	Range	P-E Ratio	Dividend	Yield	S&P Ranking
Oct. 24'83 32 1/8	1983 37-25 1/2	16	0.60	1.9%	A+

Summary

Super Valu is the nation's largest food wholesaler, serving some 2,200 independent food stores in 28 states. Other activities include retail specialty shops, discount department stores, and insurance services for the supermarket industry. An expanding market share, reflecting in part the acquisition of several small food wholesalers in fiscal 1982-3, plus a boost from increased consumer spending in nonfood areas, enhance prospects for another worthwhile earnings gain in 1983-4.

Current Outlook

Earnings for fiscal 1983-4 should rise to about $2.20 a share from the $1.85 of 1982-3.

The quarterly dividend was raised to $0.15, from $0.14, with the September, 1983 payment.

Sales for fiscal 1983-4 should benefit from the acquisitions of several small food wholesalers during 1982-3 and greater unit volume at existing wholesale outlets; expansion of other segments will contribute to growth. Operating efficiencies and increased contributions from general merchandise retailers would bolster profitability.

Net Sales (Million $)

Period:	1983-4	1982-3	1981-2	1980-1
16 Wks. Jun.	1,711	1,489	1,365	1,170
12 Wks. Sep.	1,333	1,172	1,071	929
12 Wks. Dec.		1,250	1,093	1,011
12 Wks. Feb.		1,286	1,093	1,093
		5,197	4,622	4,204

Sales for the 28 weeks ended September 10, 1983 advanced 14%, year to year, reflecting increased volume in all divisions. Led by strength at the nonfood retail stores, net income rose 19%. Share earnings increased to $1.05, from $0.89.

Common Share Earnings ($)

Period:	1983-4	1982-3	1981-2	1980-1
16 Wks. Jun.	0.61	0.51	0.49	0.42
12 Wks. Sep.	0.44	0.38	0.37	0.30
12 Wks. Dec.		0.45	0.41	0.35
12 Wks. Feb.		0.52	0.50	0.45
		1.85	1.77	1.52

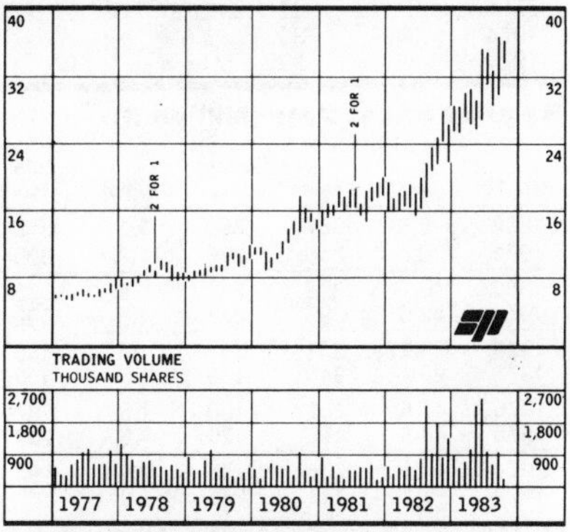

Important Developments

Oct. '83—SVU acquired a distribution facility in Miami, Fla. from Pantry Pride, Inc. The unit will continue to supply Pantry Pride's Miami-based retail stores with merchandise and support services. SVU also obtained an option to buy a second distribution outlet in Jacksonville.

Jun. '83—The company planned to add seven new franchised Cub Food stores, 10 County Seat outlets, and three ShopKo stores (three more were subsequently planned). Wholesale operations were expected to benefit from the projected addition of 50 independently-owned County Market units (spin-offs of Cub). In all, capital expenditures for fiscal 1983-4 were projected at $185 million, most of which was to be generated internally.

Next earnings report due in late December.

Per Share Data ($)

Yr. End Feb. 28[1]	1982	1981	1980	[2]1979	1978	[2]1977	[3]1976	1975	1974	1973
Book Value	**8.76**	7.43	6.12	5.08	4.13	3.34	2.96	2.49	2.11	1.86
Earnings	**1.85**	1.77	1.53	1.25	1.03	0.84	0.63	0.45	0.36	0.30
Dividends	**0.54**	0.46	0.38 3/8	0.31 1/2	0.25 5/8	0.24 1/2	0.11 3/4	0.13 1/8	0.10 5/8	0.09 5/8
Payout Ratio	**29%**	26%	25%	25%	25%	29%	19%	33%	30%	32%
Prices[4]—High	**28 1/8**	20 1/8	17 7/8	12	10 1/8	8 1/8	6 1/8	3 1/2	2 1/2	3 1/8
Low	**15 1/2**	14 1/4	9	7 3/4	6 7/8	5 3/8	3 1/8	1 7/8	1 1/2	1 5/8
P/E Ratio—	**15-8**	11-8	12-6	10-6	10-7	10-6	10-5	8-4	7-4	10-5

Data as orig. reptd. Adj. for stk. div(s). of 100% Aug. 1981, 100% Aug. 1978, 100% Aug. 1976. **1.** Of fol. cal. yr. **2.** Reflects merger or acquisition. **3.** Reflects accounting change. **4.** Cal. yr.

Standard NYSE Stock Reports
Vol. 50/No. 210/Sec. 17

October 31, 1983

Standard & Poor's Corp.
25 Broadway, NY, NY 10004

FIGURE 4-1   (continued)

2169

Super Valu Stores, Inc.

Income Data (Million $)

Year Ended Feb. 28	Revs.	Oper. Inc.	% Oper. Inc. of Revs.	Cap. Exp.	Depr.	Int. Exp.	Net Bef. Taxes	Eff. Tax Rate	Net Inc.	% Net Inc. of Revs.
1982	5,197	178	3.4%	105	44.8	19.7	¹126	46.0%	68.0	1.3%
1981	4,622	169	3.6%	69	38.2	10.6	¹121	46.5%	64.7	1.4%
1980	4,204	147	3.5%	75	35.3	12.1	¹101	45.1%	55.6	1.3%
²1979	3,475	120	3.4%	72	28.3	8.6	¹ 84	46.0%	45.3	1.3%
1978	3,033	101	3.3%	79	24.4	7.6	¹ 70	47.1%	36.9	1.2%
²1977	2,594	84	3.2%	50	19.3	7.5	¹ 58	48.1%	30.1	1.2%
³1976	2,134	54	2.5%	27	10.0	2.4	¹ 42	47.4%	22.3	1.0%
1975	1,823	39	2.2%	19	7.9	3.5	¹ 28	48.7%	14.3	0.8%
1974	1,642	33	2.0%	7	7.1	4.4	¹ 22	49.5%	11.1	0.7%
1973	1,448	23	1.6%	12	6.9	3.4	¹ 17	46.3%	9.1	0.6%

Balance Sheet Data (Million $)

Feb. 28	Cash	Current Assets	Current Liab.	Ratio	Total Assets	Ret. on Assets	Long Term Debt	Common Equity	Total Cap.	% LT Debt of Cap.	Ret. on Equity
1982	0.8	387	360	1.1	858	8.8%	169	328	497	34.0%	22.4%
1981	0.7	346	296	1.2	685	10.1%	111	277	388	28.6%	25.4%
1980	0.7	302	247	1.2	593	9.8%	114	232	346	33.0%	26.4%
1979	42.5	297	231	1.3	534	9.3%	113	189	301	37.5%	26.5%
1978	20.2	241	183	1.3	435	8.9%	98	154	251	38.8%	26.4%
1977	29.1	240	179	1.3	393	9.1%	88	124	213	41.5%	26.1%
1976	47.6	202	130	1.6	267	8.8%	28	106	134	21.0%	23.0%
1975	43.8	195	120	1.6	238	6.2%	28	88	117	24.2%	17.5%
1974	17.5	158	86	1.8	193	6.0%	41	65	106	38.8%	18.2%
1973	5.1	141	75	1.9	177	5.5%	44	57	101	43.6%	17.0%

Data as orig. reptd. 1. Incl. equity in earns. of nonconsol. subs. 2. Reflects merger or acquisition. 3. Reflects accounting change.

Business Summary

Super Valu is the nation's largest food wholesaler, serving some 2,200 independent stores in 28 states, primarily in the central U.S. At fiscal 1982–3 year end, the company also was operating 68 supermarkets, 43 convenience stores, 265 County Seat casual apparel stores, and 36 ShopKo general merchandise department stores.

Fiscal 1982-3	Sales	Oper. Earns.
Wholesale foods	78%	75%
Retail foods	12%	1%
ShopKo	3%	7%
County Seat	7%	17%

Wholesale deliveries generally are made from one of 16 distribution centers on company-owned trucks. Sales typically are on a cost or adjusted cost-plus-fee basis, with a weekly fee based on volume. Products sold under Super Valu private labels accounted for about 12% of 1982–3 wholesale volume. Retailers are offered a variety of promotional, managerial and financial services, usually for additional fees.

County Seat stores, located in 33 states, sell men's, women's and children's casual wear; some 50% of sales are derived from "Levi's"

brand merchandise. ShopKo units sell various general merchandise in medium-sized cities in Wisconsin, Minnesota, South Dakota and Michigan.

Risk Planners, Inc., markets insurance to food retailers from 12 offices. Unconsolidated SUVACO Insurance International (Bermuda) and Excel Insurance Co. are in the property/casualty reinsurance business.

Dividend Data

Dividends have been paid since 1936.

Amt. of Divd. $	Date Decl.	Ex-divd. Date	Stock of Record	Payment Date
0.14	Dec. 15	Feb. 23	Mar. 1	Mar. 15'83
0.14	Apr. 20	May 24	May 31	Jun. 15'83
0.15	Jun. 27	Aug. 24	Aug. 30	Sep. 15'83
0.15	Oct. 19	Nov. 25	Dec. 1	Dec. 15'83

Next dividend meeting: mid-Dec. '83.

Capitalization

Long Term Debt: $167,984,000, incl. $105,273,000 of capital lease obligations.

Common Stock: 36,883,534 shs. ($1 par).
Institutions hold some 49%.
Shareholders of record: 6,323.

Office—11840 Valley View Rd., Eden Prairie, Minn. 55344; P.O. Box 990, Minneapolis, Minn. 55440. Tel—(612) 828-4000. Chrmn & Pres—M. W. Wright. Treas—R. O. Erickson. VP-Secy—C. D. Dugan, Jr. Investor Contact—R. Simmer. Dirs—W. S. Bailey, J. J. Crocker, S. I. D'Agostino, V. H. Heath, M. Lewis, Jr., R. D. McCormick, J. P. McFarland, J. E. Morrissey, H. Perlmutter, A. R. Weber, A. R. Whitman, M. W. Wright, J. T. Wyman. Transfer Agents—Morgan Guaranty Trust Co., NYC; First National Bank of Minneapolis. Registrars—Chemical Bank, NYC; Northwestern National Bank of Minneapolis. Incorporated in Delaware in 1925.

Information has been obtained from sources believed to be reliable, but its accuracy and completeness are not guaranteed.   Barbara Ingrassia

action in the stock for the last ten years; tabulated stock information for the last ten years; income and balance sheet information for the same period; and a brief description of the company — what it does, what it sells, and what makes it tick. They identify the major shareholders; give the address of the company's headquarters; and if the company has a shareholder relations department, tells how to contact it. (See Figure 4-1.) *Standard & Poor's* and *Moody's* also rate the financial stability of companies' investments.

These services are good starting places for the concerned investor. If you like what you read, you can contact the company directly for more information. Your broker can provide you with tear sheets for any company you are considering.

The Value Line Investment Survey. Value Line provides investment advice. This service reviews the performance of approximately 1700 companies and updates the information regularly. It reveals when company insiders trade in their company's stock and when the pension funds, mutual funds, and other institutions are active in it. *Value Line* also gives the company's cash flow, the date of its next annual meeting, and a myriad of other information beyond standard income statement and balance sheet data. And it forecasts the stock's price performance. Many investors subscribe to *Value Line*. However, it is expensive. Your local library or your broker will probably have copies.

Concerned Investors Guide. The *Concerned Investors Guide* (Resource Publishing Group, Inc., P.O. Box 390, Arlington, VA 22201) will save you hundreds of hours of research into the ethical aspects of your investments. In an easy-to-read format (see Figure 4-2), it reports on over 1400 companies listed on the New York Stock Exchange. It shows the companies' performance in the areas of environment, product safety, occupational safety and health, labor practices, nuclear issues, and South Africa.*

Brokerage Reports

All full-service brokerage firms offer their clients investment reports on recommended companies. These reports can be quite brief — perhaps only a page — and cover only the highlights of a company. Or they can go on

---

* I am a member of Resource Publishing's board of directors.

FIGURE 4-2   Sample Page from the Concerned Investors Guide

SHELLER-GLOBE CORPORATION
1505 Jefferson Avenue, Toledo OH 43697

Principle Business: Manufactures automotive parts and equipment, office supplies and equipment, nuclear radiation measurement instruments
S.I.C.: 3714, 3069, 3079, 3465, 3469, 3471, 3544, 3621, 3694
Stock Exchange: NYS, MID

Employees: 9,000

COMPANY		S/D	DATE	INFORMATION

ENVIRONMENT
There was no information reported on this company under this heading.

FAIR LABOR
There was no information reported on this company under this heading.

OCCUPATIONAL SAFETY AND HEALTH

COMPANY		S/D	DATE	WILLFUL	SERIOUS	REPEATED	CONTESTED
Sheller-Globe	Lima OH		09/07/78	3	1	0	yes
Sheller-Globe	Gainesville GA		11/22/77	0	10	0	no

PRODUCT SAFETY

COMPANY		S/D	DATE	INFORMATION
Bohn Rex-Rotary	Englewood NJ	D	01/03/77	Desk photocopier RR 4040. Possible shock hazard. Corrective insulation added.

ANTITRUST
There was no information reported on this company under this heading.

CIVILIAN NUCLEAR INDUSTRY

COMPANY		S/D	DATE	INFORMATION
Victoreen Inc. (Material Licensee)	Cleveland OH	S	01/06/83	Improper papers and labels for radioactive shipment. Paid $625 penalty.

SOUTH AFRICA
There was no information reported on this company under this heading.

WEAPONS CONTRACTORS
There was no information reported on this company under this heading.

SHELL OIL COMPANY
One Shell Plaza, Houston TX 77001

Principle Business: Produces oil, gas and chemicals.
S.I.C.: 1311, 2819, 2821, 2822, 2879, 2911
Stock Exchange: NYS, BOS, MID, CIN, PSE, PAC, TOR, MON

Employees: 37,273

ENVIRONMENT

COMPANY		S/D	DATE	INFORMATION
Shell Oil Co.	Bedford Park IL		10/17/79	Clean Air Act, Stationary Source
Shell Oil Co.	Arlington Heights IL		10/17/79	Clean Air Act, Stationary Source
Shell Oil Co.	Harristown PA		10/17/79	Clean Air Act, Stationary Source
Shell Oil Co.	Dayton OH		03/14/80	Clean Air Act, Stationary Source
Shell Oil Co.	Toledo OH		03/14/80	Clean Air Act, Stationary Source
Shell Oil Co.	Cleveland OH		03/14/80	Clean Air Act, Stationary Source
Shell Chemical Co.	Geismar LA	S	12/02/77	Clean Water Act
Shell Chemical Co.	Geismar LA	S	07/08/78	Clean Water Act

FAIR LABOR

Shell Oil Co.	USDC	TX		01/17/79	#75-H-1557 & 76-H-1000 CRA 1866 and 1964 Racial discrimination. Judgment for company.
Shell Oil Co.	USCA	6th		07/07/78	#77-3238 ADEA. Vacated and remanded USDC judgment for company.
Shell Chemical Co.	USDC	AL	S	05/18/81	#80-06-5014 CRA 1866, 1964 and U.S. Constitution Racial discrimination. Judgment for company.
Shell Oil Co.	USCA	9th		01/23/81	#79-4053 ADEA. Affirmed USDC granting summary judgment motion.

OCCUPATIONAL SAFETY AND HEALTH

			WILLFUL	SERIOUS	REPEATED	CONTESTED
Shell Oil Co. .... Wood River	IL	04/05/79	0	5	0	no

PRODUCT SAFETY
There was no information reported on this company under this heading.

ANTITRUST
There was no information reported on this company under this heading.

CIVILIAN NUCLEAR INDUSTRY
There was no information reported on this company under this heading.

SOUTH AFRICA
There was no information reported on this company under this heading.

WEAPONS CONTRACTORS
There was no information reported on this company under this heading.

SHELL TRANSPORT & TRADING COMPANY P.L.C.   Shell Centre, London England SE1 7NA

Principle Business: Holding company: oil, gas, nuclear energy and coal.
S.I.C.: 6711
Stock Exchange: NYS, BOS, MID, PSE   **Employees:** not available

There was no information reported on this company under any heading.

SHERWIN-WILLIAMS COMPANY   101 Prospect Avenue, N.W., Cleveland OH 44115

Principle Business: Manufactures paints, varnishes, chemicals, sealants and painting accessories.
S.I.C.: 2816, 2819, 2851, 2869, 2891, 3411, 3991, 5231
Stock Exchange: NYS, MID, PSE   **Employees:** 23,507

COMPANY	S/D	DATE	INFORMATION

ENVIRONMENT
There was no information reported on this company under this heading.

FAIR LABOR

Sherwin-Williams	USCA	4th	06/15/82	#80-1879 ADEA. Affirmed USDC judgment for company.
Sherwin-Williams	USDC	MI	07/18/80	#75-718336 CRA 1964 and 1866 Racial discrimination. Judgment for company.

OCCUPATIONAL SAFETY AND HEALTH

			WILLFUL	SERIOUS	REPEATED	CONTESTED
Sherwin-Williams	Elgin IL	02/15/80	0	32	0	yes
Sherwin-Williams	Cleveland OH	08/20/81	0	8	0	no
Sherwin-Williams	Chicago IL	10/16/78	0	5	0	yes

for 50 pages, giving you an in-depth analysis of the company, its industry, and its competition.

All brokerage firm reports are basically optimistic. Wall Street firms compete to find established companies whose financial condition and management are impeccable but whose stocks have not peaked. They generally recommend a purchase after the stock has proven itself by rising well above its low. But they also want stocks that will double in the two years following the report. Since the report is often issued after the stock has come close to doubling, that's a tall order to fill. Also keep in mind what John Train recently wrote:

> Don't expect much from market letters and brokers' inspirations, or the economic "overviews" put out by trust companies. Generally they subsist by reenforcing the public's instincts, which are usually wrong. As a practical matter, I find, one cannot successfully use economic theory in the daily business of investing. However, if there is a consensus as to the economic outlook — lower interest rates ahead, recession impending — the long odds, and therefore the safer bet, will probably be on the other side."[2]

One sage I know put it more simply. "Don't bother me with brokerage reports or anything in magazines. The *Wall Street Journal* is all I need. That way my mind doesn't get all cluttered up with a lot of opinions."

Periodicals and Newspapers

When you have a particular company in mind, always start with *Moody's* or *S&P* or *Value Line* and brokerage reports. After all, why do lots of research on a company which may not qualify on its face?

Once you have found a company which appears to pass your screen, you may want to do some library research. Use the *Reader's Guide* or particular periodical indices to spot stories about the company. Many times you'll find nothing, but when there is an article, its view often differs from the services' or the brokerages'. I once researched publicly owned day care chains because they seemed to fit my concerns as a working mother and an ethical investor. I found some likely prospects in the services. But an article I found pointed out that child care chains operated on the assumption that their customers wanted convenience first, low cost next, and finally quality. The article and my own experience indicated that parents put quality last only because they lack alternatives. Further, the teachers, who earn the minimum wage, routinely work 11-hour days with no break.

The average staff-to-children ratio is 1 to 10. Investing in these chains was inconsistent with my beliefs about child care.

Research of this type is not just a glorified avoidance screen. As often as I discover negatives, I find positives. For instance, I learned Quaker Oats, a favorite company of mine, has a chemical business. This made me very nervous until I discovered where the chemical business came from. Quaker Oats recycled oat hulls, a waste product of cereal manufacturing, into furfural, a solvent used in oil refining. Ironically, furfural sales add more to its bottom line than oatmeal.

Develop a Reading Routine. Successful ethical investing depends on knowledge of the financial markets and their environment. I mean that in the broadest sense. For example, if you invest for income and favor corporate bonds, you must not only grasp the mechanics of bond trading but also the state of our economy. Your portfolio's value depends on what interest rates are doing, and those in turn depend on questions like how much money the Treasury is going to borrow over the coming months, because high borrowing demands cause an increase in interest rates.

Research on a particular issue or company is not enough. As an ethical investor you should make reading about financial issues a daily habit. But don't limit your reading to publications catering to your ethical concerns. They have far too narrow a focus. Successful investors need a good grasp of what is happening around them. A basic reading list includes both dailies — the *Wall Street Journal,* the *New York Times* Business Day section, and your local paper's business pages — and periodicals — *Barron's, Forbes, Business Week, Inc.,* and *Fortune.* At a minimum you should read the *Wall Street Journal* and another paper's business section every day as well as one of the weeklies and one of the biweeklies or monthlies. These periodicals contain information you can use to shape your investment strategy.

Many people think that by the time a story appears in the paper, it is too late to act on it. That notion is wrong. Look especially at your local newspaper's business section. Many times the *Boston Globe* beats the *Wall Street Journal* on stories about companies with interests in New England. On January 24, 1980, the *Globe* carried a long story on the likelihood RKO General (a General Tire Division) would lose its Boston TV license. The next day, the *Wall Street Journal* picked it up. General Tire's stock did not drop until the *Journal* story appeared, and Boston readers had a chance to get out the day before, at 22⅝. The day the *Journal's* story appeared, the stock's high was 18⅞.

FIGURE 4-3   "Abreast of the Market"

Rally Fades Despite Brief Surges By Industrials in Moderate Trading

By VICTOR J. HILLERY

1.   The stock market rally ran out of steam yesterday and prices turned down for the first time in five sessions. Trading was moderately active, at more than 49 million shares.

2.   Technology issues, which had been in the forefront of the rally, were prominent on the casualty list. They were joined on the downside by the airline, drug, auto, paper and machinery issues.

3.   The Dow Jones industrial average, which spurted 30.82 points in the previous four sessions, showed small gains briefly early yesterday and again at 2 p.m. EST but finished at 823.34, down 3.33 points. The transportation and utility indexes also lost ground.

4.   New York Stock Exchange losers nosed out the gainers about seven to six.

Continental Illinois National Bank & Trust reduced the fee it charges on loans to brokers to 14¾% from 15¾% and Southwest Bank of St. Louis cut its prime, or base, lending rate to 16% from 16½%. But most short-term interest rates moved up.

"The recent four-session advance was a technical rally," asserted Stephen S. Weisglass, president of Ladenburg, Thalmann & Co. "It could move up further, but we expect to see another down phase with the industrial average probably bottoming in the mid-700s between now and June."

Judith Corchard, senior vice president of Wright Investors Service, Bridgeport, Conn., asserted that "we view the gains as short-lived and are continuing to maintain cash reserves of 50% in our equity portfolios." She added: "The high interest rates and expected very unfavorable earnings reports for the March quarter not only will keep the market from going up, but probably will send it down,

MARKET DIARY

	Wed.	Tue.	Mon.	Fri.	Thu.	Wed.
Issues traded	1,865	1,919	1,872	1,854	1,853	1,872
Advances	663	972	1,210	848	1,021	674
Declines	763	528	303	573	406	779
Unchanged	439	419	359	433	426	419
New highs	21	33	29	11	7	7
New lows	22	19	19	45	49	102

DOW JONES CLOSING AVERAGES

	---- Wednesday ----		Yr. Ago		--Since--	
	1982	Change	%	1981	% Chg.	Dec. 31	%
Ind	823.34	- 3.33	-0.40	1015.22	-18.90	- 51.66	- 5.90
Trn	337.21	- 2.13	-0.63	433.56	-22.22	- 43.09	- 11.33
Utl	108.41	- 0.08	-0.07	108.55	- 0.13	- 0.61	- 0.56
Cmp	324.14	- 1.36	-0.42	391.67	-17.24	- 23.66	- 6.80

OTHER MARKET INDICATORS

		1982	-Change-		1981
N.Y.S.E.	Composite	65.00	- 0.30	-0.46%	78.82
	Industrial	72.94	- 0.39	-0.53%	92.37
	Utility	38.93	- 0.11	-0.28%	38.18
	Transp.	56.37	- 0.39	-0.69%	80.56
	Financial	70.01	- 0.05	-0.07%	75.33
Am. Ex. Mkt Val Index		259.94	- 2.21	-0.84%	362.03
Nasdaq OTC Composite		174.84	- 0.11	-0.06%	209.31
	Industrial	197.67	- 0.37	-0.19%	263.26
	Insurance	187.72	+ 0.17	+0.09%	185.83
	Banks	136.61	+ 0.34	+0.25%	127.79
Standard & Poor's 500		112.97	- 0.58	-0.51%	137.11
400 Industrial		125.34	- 0.73	-0.58%	155.60
Value Line Index		125.36	- 0.15	-0.12%	153.80
Wilshire 5000 Equity		1,160.549	- 5.173	-0.44%	1,405.353

Market value, in billions of dollars, of N.Y.S.E., Amex and actively traded OTC issues.

TRADING ACTIVITY

Volume, of advancing stocks on N.Y.S.E., 18,503,900 shares; volume of declining stocks, 24,982,500. On American S.E., volume of advancing stocks, 1,484,200; volume of declining stocks, 1,886,200. Nasdaq volume of advancing stocks, 8,284,200; volume of declining stocks, 7,365,200.

possibly to the 750 level, as long as the Federal Reserve continues its present monetary policies."

However, Donald Trott, investment policy committee chairman at A. G. Becker Inc., contended that "the time has come to move back into equities" and recommended that "50% of cash reserves be shifted into equities." He said "we believe that essentially the recent major market retreat has been completed" and that those investors waiting for one more extended drop will be caught in "a bear trap" as the rally unfolds with more potency than had been anticipated.

"If the Fed gives up now, or permits immediate fears to dominate broader policy, the problems will be even worse when they recur—as they surely will," said Alan

Abreast of the Market

FIGURE 4-3 *(continued)*

C. Lerner, senior vice president at Bankers
Trust.
5. Big Board volume slowed to 49,380,000
shares from 67,130,000 Tuesday. Reduced
but still heavy institutional activity was reflected in the 901 trades of 10,000 or more,
down from 1,119 the prior session.

6. **Technology Issues Slide**

Among the technology issues, Storage
Technology slid 1⅜ to 25⅞ in active trading. Digital Equipment slipped 1½ to 78¼;
Teledyne, ⅞ to 117⅜; Texas Instruments,
1⅝ to 80; Honeywell, 1¼ to 67½; Motorola,
1⅛ to 56⅝; Data General, 1½ to 31; Prime
Computer, ⅝ to 19¾, and National Semi-
conductor, ⅜ to 21⅝.
7. However, Scientific-Atlanta, an active
issue, rebounded 1¼ to 18⅞ after dropping
3⅜ Tuesday when the company said its
earnings for the third quarter ending
Wednesday essentially will equal those of
the year-earlier period.
8. Other losers included American Standard, down 1⅞ to 26⅛; the company expects to report first quarter per-share net
of about 25 cents, down from a restated
9. $1.37 a year earlier. Tosco skidded 1⅜ to
9¼; federal officials are reconsidering
terms of $1.1 billion in loan guarantees
granted to Tosco, which is building an oil-
shale project with Exxon.

Kane-Miller, which Tuesday closed at
12, up ¾, didn't trade yesterday pending a
company announcement today.

Some Gainers

10. On the plus side, NL Industries climbed
1¼ to 25½; it expects to report record net
for the first quarter and plans to purchase
up to five million of its common from time
to time in the open market or in private
transactions.

Canal-Randolph advanced 1⅞ to 26⅞; 11.
Warburg Investment Management Ltd. acquired 11.5% of Canal-Randolph's common.
Foremost-McKesson, which plans to divest 12.
its home building operations, gained 1⅛ to
31⅝.

Chesebrough-Pond's slipped ⅜ to 33½; 13.
two blocks totaling 420,100 shares were
handled over the counter by Jefferies & Co.

Echlin Manufacturing rose ⅜ to 12⅝; a
250,000-share block handled by Paine Webber, Mitchell Hutchins moved at 12½.

Diamond Shamrock slipped ⅝ to 19⅞; a
200,000-share block handled by Salomon
Brothers traded at 20⅛.

The American Stock Exchange index 14.
fell 2.21 to 259.94 as losers edged winners
283 to 276. Turnover slackened to 3,920,000
from 4,430,000 Tuesday.

Amex gainers included Forest Labora- 15.
tories Class A stock, up 1⅛ to 23¾; the
company's British subsidiary received approval to market a drug for the treatment
of angina and for aborting angina attacks.

In over-the-counter trading, the Nasdaq 16.
composite index fell 0.11 to 174.84. Gainers
outpaced the losers 628 to 473. Turnover
slowed to 29,558,100 shares from 29,859,500
Tuesday.

Franklin Electric dropped ¾ to 15; it 17.
said a small first quarter loss is possible.

Note: The numbers correspond to the discussion in the text on pages 62–64.

Source: Reprinted by permission of the *Wall Street Journal,*

How to Read Financial Columns. Let's take a look at a *Wall Street Journal* column and see what it can tell you. "Abreast of the Market" (keyed in Figure 4-3 to the following discussion) appears daily on the *Journal*'s next-to-last page. Just reading "Abreast of the Market" every day will give you a feel for Wall Street's dynamics. What makes professional investors bid up the price of a stock? Why do they suddenly sell? And what sort of price movements are big for a day? Read this column faithfully and you will know more about the market's workings than 90% of all investors. But beware: don't follow the Wall Street herd!

1. Forty-nine million shares traded on the New York Stock Exchange, a volume now considered very light. Twenty years ago 10 million shares swamped the NYSE.

2. The prices of companies in an industry group, like automobiles, tend to move together. Ford does not go up if Chrysler is down and American Motors remains unchanged. Often good news for one company may be bad news for its competitors, yet the buying spreads. One morning IBM announced a new mainframe computer and price reductions on older models — bad news for the competition. Yet at the end of the day, all the mainframe manufacturers were up.

3. The Dow Jones Industrial Index is made up of 30 stocks, called the Dow Jones 30 Industrials (see Figure 4-4). These stocks are *blue chips* (stocks the market has regarded over the years as high-quality investments). Here the Index is down 3.33 points, which is not a big drop. Although not a broad market indicator, it sometimes reflects what the market as a whole is doing. During the 1982–83 bull market, the Dow Jones Industrial Average outperformed the very broad averages, such as *Standard & Poor's* 500, because the blue chips, faced with less antitrust enforcement from the Reagan administration, were perceived as safer investments.

   Dow Jones also publishes indexes based on companies in transportation (airlines, rails, trucking) and on utilities (electric and gas primarily). These often confirm the market's major trend and, occa-

FIGURE 4-4   The Dow Jones 30 Industrials

Allied Corp.	General Foods	Owens-Illinois
Aluminum Co. of America	General Motors	Procter & Gamble
American Brands	Goodyear	Sears, Roebuck
American Can	Inco	Standard Oil of California
American Telephone & Telegraph (AT&T)	IBM	Texaco
Bethlehem Steel	Int'l. Harvester	Union Carbide
Du Pont	Int'l. Paper	United Technologies
Eastman Kodak	Manville Corp.	US Steel
Exxon	Merck	Westinghouse Electric
General Electric	Minnesota Mining & Manufacturing (3M)	Woolworth

sionally, by moving in a different direction from the industrials, disprove an apparent trend.

4. The column's next five paragraphs describe what happened yesterday and why. Here experts air their opinions and make predictions. After reading this column for a few weeks, you'll become familiar with the experts and identify those whose opinions you value.

5. The "Big Board" is the NYSE. Institutions dominate market activity, often accounting for 75% to 80% of its volume.

6. The rest of the column notes the performance of particular stocks. These comments reveal what excites professional traders and causes price changes. When you read that Storage Technology (a computer peripherals manufacturer) slid $1\frac{3}{8}$ to $25\frac{1}{8}$, it means that the price per share had been $27.25 the previous day and that anxious sellers caused the price per share to drop to $25.875.

7. Scientific Atlanta (a communications company whose U.S. government contracts accounted for 10% of its 1981 sales) bounced back because it had sold down dramatically the previous day.

8. American Standard (transportation and building products) dropped on the expectation of lower earnings.

9. Tosco (an independent gasoline refiner) dropped because a major loan was under reconsideration.

10. N. L. Industries (a major supplier of petroleum services) rose on two pieces of news: its earnings would set a record for the company, and the company thought its own shares were such a good investment that it was going to buy some from the public.

11. Canal-Randolph (real estate management and stockyards) rose because an investment company bought a large amount of their stock.

12. Foremost-McKesson (a diversified company in drugs, foods, spirits, and chemicals) rose because it was getting rid of an unprofitable subsidiary.

13. The news on Chesebrough-Pond, Echlin Manufacturing, and Diamond Shamrock may not interest you, but brokers like to gnash their teeth and wonder how the competition got those big orders.

14. The volume of trades on the American Stock Exchange (called the AMEX or the "Curb") is much smaller than that on the Big Board. Fewer companies' stocks are listed on this exchange, and the average firm is considerably smaller than the average company listed on the New York Stock Exchange (NYSE).

15. Forest Laboratories (a pharmaceutical manufacturer and distributor) was up because of news that Great Britain would allow the company

to market a drug for treating heart ailments. New product developments, especially when they have large market potential, often cause
stocks to rise.

16. Over-the-counter (OTC) trading provides investors with a third marketplace, but unlike the exchanges it is a telephone network among
brokerages which maintain inventories in certain stocks. They sell
these shares to each other and the public. *Nasdaq* refers to the National
Association of Securities Dealers Automated Quotations, which are
reported on the computer systems at the brokerage firms. These are
"Nasdaq-listed shares."

17. Franklin Electric (a manufacturer of water system motors) dropped 75
cents per share on the news that earnings might be lower.

If you read "Abreast of the Market" regularly it won't be long before
you have a good understanding of stock price changes and what sorts of
information interests Wall Street experts. It doesn't take much time and
is an extremely valuable tool.

Trade Journals and Issue-Oriented Publications

One key to investing success is to invest in areas you know something
about. If you read trade journals as part of your job, don't assume that
everyone knows what you know. You are definitely ahead of the investing
crowd. As Oliver Rogers of the American Friends Service Committee's
investment advisory committee pointed out, "How are different companies
doing on minority issues or safety? It used to be easy. You used to read all
about it in the *Wall Street Journal.* Now there's no government reporting
to read. So I go to the trade journals. In every industry there's a gossipy
weekly. There you'll find the dirt on companies. You find the better
companies by eliminating the weaker ones."

Rogers further suggests that you "read literature by people concerned
with an issue. Certain companies will predominate. From them you can
easily end up with a list of the lower half of the companies. Our policy is
to try to stick with the other half, the top half, in all issue areas." Issue-
oriented newsletters appear in virtually every field.

An invaluable source for researching large corporations is Moskowitz,
Katz, and Levering, eds., *Everybody's Business: An Almanac* (Harper &
Row, 1980), and its 1982 update. This remarkable, witty volume sum-
marizes the histories of 317 of America's largest companies and provides

insights into their corporate personalities. Another fine resource book by the same authors is *The 100 Best Companies to Work for in America* (Addison-Wesley, 1984), with profiles of the top companies in the country based on management style, corporate culture, and mobility.

Investment Newsletters

Pick up any issue of *Barron's* and you'll find dozens of advertisements for investment newsletters. A few not routinely advertised in *Barrons* cater to the ethical investor.

The Corporate Examiner. (Interfaith Center on Corporate Responsibility, 475 Riverside Drive, Room 566, New York, NY 10115.) This letter examines corporate policies and practices with regard to labor, environment, consumerism, equal employment, genetic engineering, minorities, women, agribusiness, military production, and foreign investment, among others. It targets activist shareholders as its audience. Its coverage of new publications — including investments — is particularly good.

Council on Economic Priorities Newsletter. (The Council on Economic Priorities, 84 Fifth Avenue, New York, NY 10011.) This monthly newsletter examines corporate activity, generally devoting the entire issue to a single concern. A recent edition examined "The Defense Department's Top 100."

Good Money. (Center for Economic Revitalization, Inc., Box 363, Calais Stage Road, Worcester, VT 05682.) This folksy bimonthly covers events of interest to responsible investors and offers background on investment vehicles (such as tax shelters or municipal bonds). It also reports on some events of interest to activists but it focuses primarily on investments, often of an alternative nature. Of special interest is *Netbacking*, a bimonthly supplement in which subscribers make announcements, share ideas, and network.

Insight: The Advisory Letter for Concerned Investors. (Franklin Research and Development Corporation, 222 Lewis Wharf, Boston, MA 02110.) Every issue of *Insight* features companies recommended for purchase and includes in-depth studies of corporations that meet various social criteria. It contains an ethical shopping list and rates the companies. While it is bimonthly, *Insight* sends a barrage of investor updates, industry reports (such as renewable energy), and alternative investment recommendations. As Figure 4-5 shows, *Insight's* ratings of financially qualified companies on eight social criteria makes it an excellent guide for considered investment decisions. *

Investor Responsibility Research Center News for Investors. (Investor Responsibility Research Center, Inc., 1319 F Street, N.W., Washington, D.C. 20004.) This monthly serves primarily activist shareholders, keeping them informed of proxy battles and legislative initiatives affecting shareholders' rights. It also covers corporate actions on shareholder and union initiatives. The *IRRC NEWS* does not advise on investments. However, it is an invaluable source of information on corporate activities.

Mutual Funds

If you find yourself bereft of investment ideas, write to the ethical mutual funds discussed in Chapter 9 and ask for their prospectuses, which list their portfolios. If the fund meets your criteria, then the stocks it holds are essentially prescreened for you. All you have to do is study them and select the companies that fit your needs. Appendix C contains several recent portfolios.

INFORMATION FROM THE COMPANIES

For reasons of self-protection and self-interest, publicly traded companies must supply investors with much information.

The self-protective aspect arises from the requirements of various state and federal securities laws. Compliance with these laws never guarantees the quality of an investment. To the contrary, they assume that investors with accurate information are in the best position to evaluate a security. So while the Securities Exchange Commission (SEC) takes action against companies defrauding the public, it does not tell investors that a vehicle is a risky investment. The key protections offered by the federal Securities Acts (state laws are similar) are the reports required from companies which offer their securities to the public. The three most important are the annual report, the proxy statement, and the prospectus.

In their self-interest, publicly traded companies voluntarily supply a

---

* I am a member of *Insight's* board of directors.

FIGURE 4-5 *Insight:* What Would We Buy?

Symbol	Stock Name	Social Screen Rating								Earnings per Share			Dividends per Share	Price/Earnings Ratio		Risk/Reward
		AF	LA	MK	EN	NE	DE	AE	AG	1982	'83E	'84E		'83E	'84E	
AFGN	AFG Industries	2	2	3	3	1	2	1	2	1.61	1.35	1.75	.48	13.4	10.4	FV at $18 1/8
AMI	AMI International	2	3	3	–	2	2	–	3	1.69	2.05	2.55	.48	14.4	11.6	UV at $29 1/2
BETZ	Betz Laboratories	2	–	–	2	2	2	3	2	1.93	2.10	2.54	.88	18	14.9	UV at $37 3/4
CMPH	Comprehensive Care	2	2	2	3	2	2	2	2	0.80	1.23	1.60	.32	20.3	15.6	UV at $25
DEC	Digital Equipment	2	2	2	–	2	–	3	2	7.53	5.10	7.10	nil	20.3	14.6	UV at $103 5/8
FHP	Fort Howard Paper	2	1	–	1	2	2	1	2	3.43	3.80	4.45	1.32	13.9	11.8	UV at $52 3/8
MRK	Merck and Company	5	2	3	2	2	2	2	3	5.61	6.25	7.20	2.80	14.8	12.9	UV at $92 1/4
PBI	Pitney Bowes	2	–	–	–	2	2	3	3	2.18	2.75	3.20	.92	10.1	8.7	UV at $27 3/4
OAT	Quaker Oats	2	2	2	3	2	3	3	2	4.53	2.66	6.65	2.00	17.3	6.9	FV at $46
SGN	Signal Companies	2	2	3	2	3	4	1	3	1.56	1.25	3.40	.90	28.3	10.4	FV at $35 3/8
SX	Southern Pacific RR	2	3	3	3	2	2	2	3	2.15	9.15	4.00	1.42	4.35	10	FV at $39 7/8
STBK	State Street Bank	2	2	2	3	2	2	3	2	3.78	4.05	4.85	1.40	8.6	7.2	UV at $35
TMO	Thermo Electron	2	3	–	1	2	2	–	2	.60	.55	2.30	nil	53	13	FV at $29
WANG	Wang B	2	–	2	2	2	2	3	2	.88	1.20	1.60	.10	27	19.9	FV at $31 7/8
WMX	Waste Management	2	3	3	3	2	2	3	3	2.40	2.70	3.90	.68	17.6	12.2	UV at $47 1/2
ZRN	Zurn Industries	2	–	–	2	2	2	1	2	3.75	3.45	2.55	1.32	7.2	9.75	FV at $24 7/8

The risk-reward column is a judgment of the value of the stock at the price quoted, relative to the return required by the stock market for all stocks of a similar risk class. The judgment is based on projected earnings one year out. This is not a necessary indication of future performance but may be an aid to informed security selection.
UV means that the stock is likely to outperform other stocks of its risk class.
FV means that the stock is likely to perform at or near the median of other stocks of its class.
OV means over-valued.

Stocks recommended for purchase in this advisory letter are to be considered long-term investment commitments. Because we are not in touch with investors on a daily basis, turns in the fortunes of the companies, short term, will be impossible for us to report. However, we will certainly follow within the time constraints of our publishing schedule. We advise subscribers to seek timely advice from qualified investment professionals.

Social Screen Key: AF = South Africa. LA = Labor. MK = Marketing. EN = Environment. NE = Nuclear Energy. DE = Defense. AE = Alternate Energy. AG = Aggregate Ranking. 1, 2 = above average; 3 = average; 4, 5 = below average, needs improvement; – = no information.

Source: Insight's Insights, supplement to *Insight,* Franklin Research and Development Corp., 222 Lewis Wharf, Boston, MA 02110. Reprinted by permission.

tremendous amount of information about themselves. They spend millions of dollars preparing reports to inform their public of how they view their business, civic activities, and administration. While they aren't completely objective, a critical analysis will tell you much about a company's philosophy.

Annual Reports

The annual report to the shareholders is the most accessible company document. It is usually available free upon request. If you are a stockholder you will receive one automatically. If you cannot find the company in *Moody's* or *Standard & Poor's,* your library or stockbroker will have a directory of company addresses.

I like to have annual reports for a company going back at least two or three years. I don't want them for their raw financial information; *S&P* gives you that in a concise tabular form for the preceding ten years. I want reports because they reveal much about the company's character. Where else will you find up to 40 pages describing the company, its product lines, its management's concerns, and its policy on a variety of issues?

Annual reports are extraordinarily valuable resources both for their face value and for their subtler message. MASCO Corp. (plumbing fixtures) produces one of my favorites. Like most, it features many pictures. The pictures of its personnel are dominated by men in business suits or rolled-up oxford cloth shirt sleeves looking seriously at charts or discussing something with other men. However, the pictures of its products emphasize women in bathrobes or in the kitchen, or both. There's even a girl in a bubble bath. By contrast, Herman Miller, Inc. (office furniture) puts out an annual report that encourages further investigation by the ethical investor. The company's concern for the work environment of its customers' employees clearly extends to its own workers. Herman Miller appears regularly on Franklin Research & Development's buy lists.

Accountant's Opinion. After I skim the annual report for a quick sense of the company, I begin studying it. The first thing I turn to is the accountant's opinion. The accountant has performed the company's annual outside audit of its books. An accountant's opinion should look like the one in Fig. 4-6. The certification simply means the company has presented its figures in accordance with generally accepted standards. Accountants apply generally accepted accounting standards because they provide uniformity.

FIGURE 4-6   An Accountant's Certification of a Financial Report
(Worthington Industries 1983)

Report of Independent Accountants

Shareholders and Board of Directors
Worthington Industries, Inc.
Columbus, Ohio

We have examined the consolidated balance sheets of Worthington Industries, Inc. and subsidiaries as of May 31, 1983 and 1982, and the related consolidated statements of earnings, shareholders' equity and changes in financial position for each of the three years in the period ended May 31, 1983. Our examinations were made in accordance with generally accepted auditing standards and, accordingly, included such tests of the accounting records and such other auditing procedures as we considered necessary in the circumstances.

In our opinion, the financial statements referred to above present fairly the consolidated financial position of Worthington Industries, Inc. and subsidiaries at May 31, 1983 and 1982, and the consolidated results of their operations and the changes in their financial position for each of the three years in the period ended May 31, 1983, in conformity with generally accepted accounting principles applied on a consistent basis.

Columbus, Ohio
June 15, 1983

Ernst + Whinney

Source: Worthington Industries, Inc., 1983 Annual Report. Reprinted by permission.

By law accountants must qualify their opinions by inserting a sentence or two drawing attention to any use of numbers which does not meet generally accepted accounting standards. If the certification contains a statement that the accountant will not take responsibility for the way in which the company is handling something — say, reserves in case they lose a big lawsuit — treat it as a serious warning. However, an accountant's certification does not mean the corporation is healthy. It only means that the statements are accurate — as far as the accountant can tell.

CEO's Letter to Shareholders. Once I've checked the accountant's opinion, I turn to the front of the annual report. There, by tradition, appears the chief executive officer's (CEO) letter to the shareholder. I find this letter critical to my appraisal of the company because it is as close as I am likely to come to having a strategic planning discussion with the company's top management.

Often the CEO's letter describes changes in the board of directors, new civic activities undertaken by the corporation, and the like. The way the letter deals with the company's employees is often a good indication of management's attitude toward them.

Board of Directors. Next I study the list of board members. I want to see who they represent—creditors, opinion leaders, suppliers. Usually, the annual report contains their photographs too. I check to see how many women and minorities serve on the board — another good test of management's attitude.

Description of Corporate Activities. Next I read the pages describing the company's activity and products. The reporting laws do not require a company to go into detail in this section, but almost all do. This section often reveals whether a prospective investment meets an ethical investor's criteria. But here especially keep in mind that much in the annual report is puffery, written to make shareholders feel proud of their investments and to create interest in the company among other investors. Still, this section usually does review concisely the company's operations. For example, H&R Block's report reveals that it runs a chain of drop-in legal clinics in addition to its tax offices. CACI, Inc., tells you that this fast-growing software house counts the defense industry as its most important customer.

One reason I particularly like this section is that I lack training in engineering and science. It gives me a clear picture of a company's products and its customers. For instance, I had no idea that Nicolet Instrument's spectrum analyzers assessed smokestack emissions until I read their annual report. In fact, I didn't know what a spectrum analyzer was.

Social Issues. Either in the section describing the company or at the very end of the annual report, you may find a section addressing social issues. The 1982 annual report for Johnson Products Co., Inc. (personal care

FIGURE 4-7   Who Owns the Land

Figures as to who owns most land in the United States are deceiving. The oil companies' vast holdings include acreage under the ocean and land on which they own only the rights to oil and gas beneath the surface. Therefore they are listed separately from those companies which have whole surface rights to their land.

Mineral Rights	Total Acreage	Full Surface Rights	Total Acreage
Exxon	40,200,000	Kimberly-Clark	12,500,000
Standard Oil of Indiana	29,700,000	Burlington Northern	8,600,000
Gulf Oil Corporation	15,300,000	Union Pacific Corporation	7,900,000
Mobil Oil Corporation	12,300,000	International Paper	8,200,000
Texaco	12,000,000	Weyerhaeuser	6,200,000
Shell Oil Company	9,500,000	Boise-Cascade	6,000,000
Phillips Petroleum	9,200,000	Southern Pacific Company	5,200,000
Standard Oil of California	7,500,000	Georgia Pacific	5,100,000
Continental Oil (Conoco)	5,300,000	St. Regis Paper Company	4,500,000
Union Oil	4,900,000	Crown Zellerbach	2,800,000

Source: © *Town & Country,* June 1983, The Hearst Corp., p. 95. Reprinted by permission.

products for the ethnic market), for example, includes a statement of philosophy.

> At Johnson Products we regard and treat others as we wish to be regarded and treated. We also have a deep concern for quality — quality of products and methods of doing business, and the quality of life as it affects all of us. We operate daily with a strong sense of corporate responsibility, and since our founding 28 years ago, have been greatly involved in programs and with organizations working to improve the quality of life for all Americans. Our officers and employees serve on boards and committees of governmental commissions as well as important civic and charitable groups, nationally and locally. We contribute through active leadership and financial giving. We have been called "Company with a Conscience." We are proud of that and will earnestly strive to maintain our commitment to serve our fellow human beings.[3]

In its 1981 and 1982 annual reports, Sears, Roebuck & Company included a unique report on its equal opportunity efforts. In addition to describing its achievements, Sears provided a chart showing the percentage of female and minority members in each of the nine Equal Employment Opportunity Commission categories. A most impressive report — and performance.

The Financials. The last section I look at is the numbers. As I mentioned earlier, you can get the basic financial information in *Moody's* and *S&P*, although this report is always their source. Here I focus on the footnotes, which the tear sheets don't reproduce. Among many other things they reveal the company's unfunded pension obligations and pending litigation, both of which may affect the company's future performance. Figure 4-8 shows a footnote to Northwest Energy's (natural gas) annual report. Note that the report does not discuss all pending litigation but only what might have a material effect on its balance sheet.

Just by reading three or four annual reports of companies in a single industry you will learn an astonishing amount about it. But don't check your skepticism. Judge annual reports like statements by candidates for public office.

Proxy Statements

If you are a shareholder, you will receive a proxy statement with your annual report. Proxy statements list the company's directors, their principal occupations now and for the previous five years, their other directorships,

FIGURE 4-8   Footnote on Law Suits
(Northwest Energy Co. 1982)

Legal Matters
In February 1983, in a lawsuit brought in the Circuit Court of the State of Oregon, Umatilla County, by Banister Continental Corporation against Pipeline regarding inspection procedures for construction of certain of Pipeline's facilities used for the importation of natural gas from Alberta, Canada, the lower court awarded plaintiffs approximately $12.8 million in damages. Pipeline believes the lower court decision was in error and will appeal that decision. Pipeline further believes that if, after exhaustion of all appeals, plaintiffs prevail, there should be no adverse impact on income of future periods, since such costs could probably be capitalized as additional gas transmission property, the construction of which gave rise to the lawsuit.

Pipeline is also a party to a lawsuit which pertains to the alleged miscalculation of amounts previously applied to a carried interest in certain gas production properties. At issue is the determination of the payout date and the possible reversion of working interests to one of the defendants in the action. Management believes that the resolution of this matter will not have a material adverse financial impact on Pipeline.

The Company is a party to various other lawsuits. Based on presently available facts, as well as available defenses, management believes that such suits are not material to the operation or financial condition of the Company as a whole.

Source: Courtesy Northwest Energy Company, 1982 Annual Report, footnote 6 to Financial Statement (excerpted). Reprinted by permission.

and their ages. The proxy also reveals how many shares they and each officer hold in the company, as well as senior management's compensation.

This section should give you a sense of management's commitment to its company. I've seen proxy statements issued by struggling companies with $20 to $25 million in sales whose managers were collecting salaries in excess of $100,000, thus wiping out the shareholders' profits. By contrast, in 1982 Hybritech's chief executive officer (CEO) and president received a salary, a director's fee, and a bonus totaling $88,125 (hardly princely by biotech standards). Since he owns 205,000 shares of common stock, his interest, like mine, lies in the stock's increasing value.

Of utmost importance to the concerned investor is the proxy statement's description of the shareholder resolutions. These often refer to issues of social importance. Their perspectives can vary widely. For instance, Stockholders for World Freedom, long critical of Occidental Petroleum's trade with Communist countries, proposed a resolution which would require each Occidental shareholder meeting to open with the Pledge of Allegiance. At the other end of the spectrum, three religious orders requested J. P. Morgan (investment banking) to report on its Chilean loans (see Figure 4-9). Note that Morgan's board of directors opposed the resolution. The SEC rules permit a board to express its opinion of a resolution

FIGURE 4-9   A Shareholder Resolution
(J. P. Morgan & Co., Inc. 1983)

5

*Stockholder
Proposal Relating to
Loans to the
Republic of Chile*

The Sisters of Charity of Nazareth on behalf of The Nazareth Literary and
Benevolent Institution, Inc., Nazareth, Kentucky 40048, which owns 750 shares of
Common Stock of Morgan; The Sisters of Saint Francis of the Congregation of Our
Lady of Lourdes, Box 4900, Assisi Heights, Rochester, Minnesota 55903, who own
300 shares of Common Stock of Morgan and The Sisters of Saint Dominic, Siena
Center, Racine, Wisconsin 53402, who own 700 shares of Common Stock of Morgan,
have indicated that they will introduce the following resolution at the meeting:

"WHEREAS: Since 1973, Chile had been ruled by a military dictatorship responsible
for the torture, murder, disappearance and exile of thousands of innocent people.

"Amnesty International (Nobel Peace Prize recipient) reported in September 1981
that arbitary arrest, abduction, and murder continue in Chile. Torture is a systematic
part of official policy, using electric shock, and rape, for example. Opponents of the
government continue to be exiled, or condemned to international banishment, while
trade unionism is severely repressed.

"A US court has linked the Chilean government with the Washington assassination
of Orlando Letelier and US citizen Ronnie Moffitt—an act of international terrorism.

"In October 1981 the US Senate unanimously agreed to withhold military or security
assistance to Chile, unless and until there is 'significant progress' in the
government's compliance with internationally established principles of human rights.

"The economic situation in Chile continues to deteriorate and alarm international
bankers: eg:

· more than 945 industries have gone bankrupt since January 1981, including CRAV,
  the ninth largest Chilean company;
· a sky-rocketing trade deficit;
· the largest per capita foreign debt in the world.

"JP Morgan has made numerous loans to Chile since 1973. We believe foreign
loans are a vote of confidence in an economically unstable and repressive regime.

"RESOLVED: Shareholder request the Board of Directors to issue a report available
by September 1983 (preparation cost shall be limited and proprietary information
respected), to include:

· For the years 1972-1982, a report by category of all loans to the government of
  Chile, its agencies, or instrumentalities;
· An evaluation of how these loans contribute to the majority population's well-being;
· A description of the human rights sources, in Chile and the US, which the
  corporation uses to gain information about the situation in Chile."

In support of the foregoing resolution, the proponents state:

"As church investors we believe loans to Chile provide legitimacy to an
economically unsound and repressive regime, and have not helped Chile's people
many of whom live in abject poverty. We believe loans with no social conditions on
them are a tacit approval of the status quo, which the regime interprets as support
for its repressive policies.

"JP Morgan is one of the most prominent and active American banks in Chile, and
has been lead manager of substantial syndicated loans to the Chilean government.
In May 1981 Morgan, as equal owner, opened a commercial bank in Chile, and has
made a number of recent loans to the Chilean government. By the end of 1981 the
banks assets were $392 million, larger than any foreign commercial bank in Chile.
The bank's name has been used in Chilean government advertisements, thus
lending legitimacy to this repressive regime.

"Chile's poor record on human rights and services must be carefully considered
before investing our shareholder money further in Chile. The proposed report will
help shareholders evaluate the loan criteria which our bank uses in investing our
funds."

FIGURE 4-9   *(continued)*

The affirmative vote of a majority of the shares of Common Stock of Morgan represented and voting at the annual meeting is required for approval of the foregoing proposal.

The Board of Directors recommends a vote AGAINST the above proposal.

The Board of Directors and management join the stockholders who have submitted this resolution in deploring deprivations of human rights wherever they may occur. Extending credit to a foreign government or its agencies does not imply endorsement of all the policies of that government.

We oppose the present resolution because the report it calls for would breach the confidentiality which clients expect, and to which they are entitled, in their relationships and transactions with a bank. The issuance of such a report would, in our opinion, violate good banking practice and damage the reputation of Morgan and the Bank for the proper conduct of their business.

Source: J. P. Morgan & Co., Inc. 1983 Proxy Statement, pp. 18-19. Reprinted by permission.

---

in the proxy statement. Chapter 13 discusses shareholder resolutions in more detail.

Corporate Public Relations

Companies often provide information packets about themselves. These may include a catalogue of the goods they sell — particularly if they are small — and recent newspaper articles and brokerage reports. Be sure when writing for an annual report to ask if such a packet is available. Smaller companies commonly use them to build their reputations.

If you have questions which your research has not answered, call the company and ask to speak with its shareholder relations representative. Of course they are not allowed to discuss such matters as what the company's earnings will be next year. With smaller companies you often find yourself talking to the company treasurer, as I did recently when I called a small Wisconsin company. He could not get over the fact that someone had called from Boston to inquire about his company. I quickly got all the data I wanted. One very useful service shareholder relations representatives perform is supplying lists of brokerages which have issued reports on their companies. This information can save you hours of hunting.

Some investors use the corporation's willingness to respond to ask very pointed questions. Jim Lowell of Lowell & Blake told me, "Betz Laboratories is a case in point. We contacted management and said, 'Look, aren't you just shoving toxic waste around from one place to another?' They didn't like that a bit. Management spent a lot of time with us going over what they do and how. We bought the stock, and it's been a top performer."

While not every company representative may be prepared to talk about issues, many are quite eager to point out their leadership in a particular area. For instance, many firms will not release data on their minority hiring efforts. By contrast, Digital Equipment Corp. takes pride in its record of attracting qualified black workers.

The Prospectus

The federal securities laws require a company making a new public offering of stocks or bonds to publish a prospectus. A prospectus contains information on risk factors, competitors, customers, and the offering itself which you won't find elsewhere. Ethical investors are not likely to find information of direct relevance to their ethical screens in prospectuses that is not readily available elsewhere.

This small booklet provides the same sort of information about the board of directors and officers that the proxy statement does. One recent prospectus noted that the offerer's treasurer had some experience in the field — two years as a restaurant bookkeeper. The company ran into serious trouble shortly after the offering.

Many observers complain that investors rarely read prospectuses — primarily because they do not want to be bothered but also because, frankly, most are incredibly dull. Dull or not, the prospectus provides much information an investor needs to make an informed decision. Investors who choose to ignore them do so at their own peril. Not long ago, Alan Abelson, *Barron's* acerbic commentator on the investing world, discovered the ultimate prospectus. The Lezak Group was offering 9.7 million shares to the public. The prospectus listed 19 "extremely high risk factors, not the least of which was the company's lack of a business plan."

> Sometimes the juxtapositions of warnings are pure artistry. To illustrate, the heading on Risk Factor no. 6 is "Total dependence on chief executive officer." Immediately on its heels comes Risk Factor no. 7: "No employment agreement with the chief executive officer." As it happens the chief executive officer of Lezak Group is named, by sheer coincidence, Lezak . . . .

The prospectus then noted some potential conflicts of interest.

> "The company's chief executive officer, upon whom it is dependent, is associated with numerous companies in a variety of businesses. The company rents office space in California and in Nevada from its chief executive officer.

Twenty-five percent of the stock of the transfer agent is owned by the company's chief executive officer. The underwriter is a market maker in the securities of six of the companies with which the company's chief executive officer is associated, and he is a significant brokerage customer of the underwriter. The underwriter has participated in three drilling programs with energy companies with which the company's chief executive officer is associated. Counsel for the company are general counsel for the underwriter who is being separately represented in connection with this offering."

Caveat emptor, indeed! But Abelson notes that despite the clear warnings in the company's prospectus, investors contributed $440,000.10 for 9.7 million shares in the Lezak Group. Mr. Lezak, on the other hand, bought 5 million shares for $5000.10.[4] This cautionary tale illustrates — negatively — why ethical investors who routinely scrutinize investment vehicles make better investors.

I've covered a lot of ground in this chapter. However, its lessons can be summed up in three sentences:

- Never stray from your ethical guidelines.
- Always observe the fundamentals of investing.
- Do your homework.

I can't guarantee you success if you follow these rules. But as an ethical investor you are already ahead of the competition because you care enough to research the investments you make. Knowledge and understanding are the keys to success.

5 IDENTIFYING SMALL COMPANIES

A STUDY BY *INC.* magazine indicates that as a group the *Fortune* 1000 has added no new jobs to the economy over the last several decades. Who did? Small businesses.[1] That fact alone justifies a close look at small companies by ethical investors. But why spend a whole chapter on them? Virtually all of the companies I've mentioned so far are sizable operations. Newspaper financial pages and business magazines cover them. Information on small companies is harder to find, but it's well worth the trouble. Often these are innovative companies begun by people with a dream. Apple Computers is the classic example.

When I talk about small companies, I'm not talking about their stock prices. Just because a company like Pan Am sells for under $10 a share doesn't mean it's a small company. And just because OshKosh B'Gosh sells for over $200 per share on the rare days it trades doesn't mean this maker of high-quality children's wear is a large company.

I have no clear-cut definition of a small company. An analyst I know defines them as companies with $200 million or less in revenues. A broker says revenues have nothing to do with it. *Market value* or *capitalization* (number of shares times price per share) of $500 million or less makes a company small. If that seems a huge number for a small corporation, consider Ametek, number 500 in the 1983 *Fortune* 500, which had a market value of $2.25 billion.

FIGURE 5-1   Employment Growth: Ranking the Top 20 Growth Companies

INC.'s 1979 study of the 100 fastest-growing publicly held companies in the United States shows that total employment in them soared 268% between 1974 and 1978. Ranked by percent gain in number of employees, the top 20 companies are

Volunteer Capital	Mini-Computer Systems
Geneve	Envirodyne Industries
Tandem Computers	Amdahl
FMS Management Systems	Sonic Industries
Econo-Therm Energy Systems	Data Terminal Systems
Prime Computer	Med General
Cray Research	Teltronics Services
Rolm	LRC
Galveston-Houston	Data Card
Century 21 Real Estate	Verbatim

Source: Bradford W. Ketchum, Jr., "How Growing Companies Grow New Jobs." Reprinted with permission, *INC.* magazine, July 1979, p. 64. Copyright © 1979 by Inc. Publishing Corporation, 38 Commercial Wharf, Boston, MA 02210.

WHY LOOK TO SMALLER COMPANIES?

Small companies make excellent investment vehicles for ethical investors — particularly those looking for growth. According to Bob Zevin at U.S. Trust Co. in Boston, "A lot of small, innovative companies are at the heart of socially responsible portfolios. You usually find better educated, younger management running the custom-tailored high-service areas. Most of these companies have good equal opportunity practices, good maternity policies, good promotions, high pay, no pollution." But remember: without an innovative product or marketing strategy, even the best management will not produce the kind of return investors want.

Responsive Management

Small companies tend to reflect the attitudes of management to a greater extent than larger companies. This may be because they have less bureaucracy to deflect management initiatives. For instance, Tandem Computer offers its workers flexible work schedules, on-site recreational facilities which most country clubs would envy, and generous stock option plans. Tandem has grown so quickly it may not qualify as a small company. Its revenues in 1982 were over $312 million. Youthful management, like

FIGURE 5-2   Top Corporate Salaries and Stock Performance

Corporation and CEO	1981 Salary	1980–1981 Salary Increase	1981 Corporate Earnings	1981 Stock Performance
ITT				
R. V. Araskog	$1,136,000	+15%	Down 10%	Down 1%
Revlon				
M. C. Bergerac	1,133,000	+ 5%	Down 89%	Down 43%
Exxon				
C. C. Gavin	992,000	+ 8%	Down 2%	Down 23%
Household International				
G. R. Ellis	912,000	+49%	Down 28%	Down 6%
Boeing				
T. A. Wilson	751,000	+16%	Down 21%	Down 49%
Phillips Petroleum				
W. C. Douce	715,000	+39%	Down 18%	Down 31%
Avon				
D. W. Mitchell	604,000	+10%	Down 9%	Down 12%
Reynolds Metals				
D. P. Reynolds	539,000	+18%	Down 52%	Down 32%
Bausch & Lomb				
D. S. Schuman	442,000	+13%	Down 10%	Down 16%
Ford Motor				
P. Caldwell	440,000	+10%	Loss	Down 16%
United Air Lines				
R. J. Ferris	371,000	+ 8%	Loss	Down 6%

Source: Reprinted from the May 10, 1982, issue of *Business Week* by special permission, © 1982 by McGraw-Hill, Inc.

Tandem's, often consider equal employment opportunity, day care assistance, educational benefits, and flexible working arrangements to be their employees' due. They do not see them as innovations. Larger companies tend to stick to the established rules. They resist innovation, and it takes considerably longer for younger management to reach the top.

For investors, smaller companies are often quite accessible. While researching this book, I called Tootsie Roll, Inc., to inquire about women in top management. Ellen Gordon, Tootsie Roll's president, returned my call. She gave me more than an hour, suggesting leads and outlining her active participation in networking women in business.

Still, what excites me most about small companies is that a really good product can dramatically increase their revenues overnight. If you read about an exciting product or discover that everyone you know is using something you've never seen before, find out who makes it. The company manufacturing it may be so small that this one product alone will improve its bottom line dramatically. Helionetics, Inc. hopes this will prove true for them. Its president, Dr. Rosa Young, and her co-workers have produced a single crystal silicon solar cell that is 16% efficient in the conversion of sunlight into electricity. (Most solar cells are from 12% to 14% efficient.) Helionetics is one of ARCO Solar's suppliers for its photovoltaic generating station, the world's largest, which will provide power for Southern California Edison's power grid.[2]

Pure Plays

Small companies often restrict their activities to one type of customer or one line of products. Some small companies are even more restricted than that. Called "pure plays," these companies do only one thing. Once you identify a few, you can study their histories and find out what benefited

FIGURE 5-3   Solar Age Stock Index

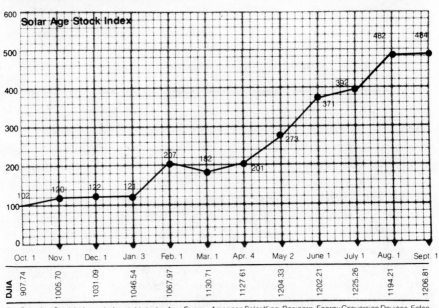

The Solar Age Stock Index includes eight stocks: Acro Energy, American Solar King, Besicorp, Energy Conversion Devices, Fafco, Mor-Flo Industries, Novan Energy, and Solaron. Stock quotes and other information for this page have been provided by Victor Macomber, Burgess & Leith, Inc., Members New York Stock Exchange.

FIGURE 5-4   Solar Pure Plays

The following companies manufacture and sell only solar devices.

A. T. Bliss & Co.	Solar water heating systems and residential heating
Acro Energy Corp.	Solar water heating systems and components
Alpha Solarco, Inc.	Solar water and space heating systems. PV desalination plants
Ambient Technology	Inflatable solar collector overseas and joint ventures
American Heliothermal	Solar water heating systems; solar appliance components
American Solar King	Residential and industrial solar hot water system components, absorber plates (OEM)
Applied Solar Energy	Space and terrestrial PVs, photosensors, contract research
Besicorp Group, Inc.	Nonmetallic collectors and systems
Chronar Corp.	PV production equipment, overseas joint ventures
Entropy Limited	Solar hot water and space heating
Equinox Solar, Inc.	Hot water heating systems, domestic and exports
Fafco, Inc.	Nonmetallic collectors, solar, pool and DHW systems
Helioscience	Commercial solar systems with third-party financing
Nationwide Power Corp.	Leasing residential DHW systems
Novan Energy, Inc.	Solar water and space heating systems, retail and wholesale alternative energy products
Olympic Solar	Collector coatings
Photovoltaics, Inc.	Photovoltaic system engineering
Piper Hydro, Inc.	Multifamily space and water heating
Servamatic Solar	Integral collector storage systems
Solaron Corp.	Solar space heating hot water systems
Solar Industries, Inc.	Solar energy collectors and systems
Suntec Systems, Inc.	Concentrating collectors for commercial and industrial applications
Thermal Energy Storage	Phase-change storage products
Wind Baron	Windmill-powered water systems

their stocks in the past. Keep a shopping list of those which pass your screens, noting what buy signals to look for.

Smaller companies generally have only one type of customer. Quite often their customers are a fragment of a type. A company like Wrigley's sells to consumers, primarily children and teenagers. Because such companies segment the market, investors can take a practical look at who buys the product. This helps them figure out whether the company faces good times or bad. General Shale (the second largest brick manufacturer) dominates the market in the South, where nearly 40% of new homes have brick fronts. They sell principally to builders and building supply houses. If their customers aren't building homes or supplying builders, General Shale's immediate prospects are bleak. When housing booms, General Shale shows strong earnings.

If a company has diversified into five or six unrelated businesses, it would be quite difficult to sort out these effects. With smaller companies you can gain the information quickly and act on it easily.

For example, an exceptionally good winter growing season in Florida means lots of cheap oranges. Orange-Co, Inc. (a pure play in orange juice) would just as soon have a slightly colder winter. Its groves are 25 years old on the average, and have greater resistance to freezing than the 10-year-old groves of their nearest competitor, American Agronomics. Orange-Co is also a superb asset play. By this I mean that their groves, processing plant, and other assets would be worth about $25 per share if assessed at market value.

But beware: pure plays in small companies may be dangerous. As Jim Lowell points out, "No solar [pure] plays for us. When the right technology comes along the solar companies will be wiped out by large companies." He may be right. It all depends on how they're wiped out — if they are. If they are taken over by larger companies, investors may make some handsome profits.

Takeover Candidates

Like small fish, small companies do tend to get gobbled by larger ones. But unlike fish, many companies choose to be swallowed. Usually an acquisition means shareholders receive a good price for their shares, often well above market. It also means realizing gains considerably earlier than shareholders might have planned.

One of the principal reasons companies buy out others is because the takeover candidate has hidden assets. As with Orange-Co., this does not mean that management has concealed the worth of the company. Standard accounting practice requires companies to list assets at cost or market value, whichever is lower. Under this rule, a building purchased on Wall Street in 1931 will appear on the company's books at its 1931 purchase price. Its 1984 market value may be exponentially greater.

While real estate is the obvious place where the asset rule comes into play, it affects other aspects of a company's business. International Bank Note Company, for example, prints food stamps, travelers checks, securities certificates, foreign currencies, and postage stamps. While it has some remarkably undervalued real estate on its books, its corporate archives — carried on its books at $1 — contain printing proofs of dozens of countries' currencies dating back two centuries.

Capital Gains Potential

Buy-outs are hardly the only way to realize a healthy capital gain on a fast-growing company. During good times, small companies' soaring revenues translate into spiking stock prices. *INC.* tracks the fastest-growing public companies in America. They recently compared the 100 fastest-growing companies' stocks versus the Dow Jones Industrial Index and found that between March 1, 1982, and March 1, 1983, the fastest-growing stocks gained 72%, while the Dow Jones gained 37%.

For ethical investors, fast growth in small companies should come as no surprise, since so many of these companies offer innovations that enhance the quality of life. Oxygen Enrichment (lightweight oxygen dispensing systems for home care) from 1978 through 1982 had a compound annual growth rate of 138%. A small company can double its revenues more easily than a large company. ASK Computer Systems, Inc., founded

FIGURE 5-5   Top Ten Sponsors of Sex on TV

Tampax	American Airlines
Helene Curtis	Thompson Medical
RCA	Trans World Corp.
Denny's	Cosmair, Inc.
Gulf & Western	Commodore International Ltd.

Source: Report of the Spring 1983 Television Monitoring Program of the Coalition for Better Television, Prime-Time Viewing, January 30–June 15, 1983. Reprinted by permission.

and headed by Sandra Kurtz, saw sales grow 4755% from 1978 through 1982 for a 164% annual growth rate.

Growth-seeking ethical investors aren't the only ones looking at smaller companies. Income seekers can find advantages here too. For instance, Chicago Rivet & Machinery (manufacturers of rivets, fasteners, machinery, and wires) sold for $15 per share in August 1983 and yielded 8%. Also, many regional banks offer good dividends and fit ethical criteria. See Chapter 7 for more bank stock ideas. However, the typical income seeker's concern with safety may make a larger, more mature company seem a safer port during times of adverse economic conditions.

Caveat Emptor

As enthusiastic as I am about small companies for the ethical investor, a few words of caution are in order. Most smaller companies are less able to weather financial storms than larger companies. When investing in smaller companies, you must consider their financial stability and resilience. If an untried company tempts you, be sure to offset that risk in your portfolio with more secure investments.

Also, when I discuss investing in small companies, I am *not* boosting *penny stocks*. These are stocks (usually priced below $5 a share) of com-

FIGURE 5-6   Largest Recipients of Corporate Largesse (1980)

	The Ten Largest Recipients of Corporate Philanthropy in 1980	Corporate Funds Received (Millions)
	American Red Cross	$40.3
	Public Broadcasting Service	$30.0
PAY	Boy Scouts	$16.3
TO	YMCA	$15.1*
THE	Massachusetts Institute of Technology	$14.0
ORDER	University of Michigan	$13.8
OF	University of Illinois	$12.7
	Harvard University	$12.4
	Salvation Army	$12.1*
	Stanford University	$11.0

*United Way estimate.

Source: Courtesy of *Fortune* Magazine, © 1981 Time Inc., 21 September 1981, p. 123. Reprinted by permission.

panies which have little more than an idea for making money. These companies are rank speculations, nothing more. During every market rally, I hear stories about fortunes being made on the Denver Exchange, where penny stocks are sold. One of the signs that a bull market has reached its top is a widespread urge among normally shrewd investors to find penny stocks. When you see these bulls running, look for a nice comfortable cave in which to hibernate.

IDENTIFYING PROMISING COMPANIES

Whether a particular company is promising depends on whether you are looking for income or growth. If income is what you are seeking, check the dividend yield first. If it isn't sufficient, you've got the wrong company. Beyond that, here are some tips for identifying promising small companies.

Stick to Basics

The key rule here as in any other area of investing is stick to the basics. A simple, logical approach will produce the best results. An investor does not need to get information faster than anyone else, but no consistently successful investor can skip doing the homework.

Newspapers and periodicals are especially good sources of information on small companies. One day I was having my hair cut. The hairdresser had the current *Vogue.* In it I found a blurb about the "Adopt a Drug Program."[3] The Pharmaceutical Manufacturers Association organized this

FIGURE 5-7   *Venture* Magazine's Top Ten Venture Capital Firms for 1982

The Hillman Co., Pittsburgh, PA	Brentwood Associates, Los Angeles, CA
Allstate Insurance, Venture Capital Division, Northbrook, IL	E. M. Warburg Pincus & Co., New York, NY
First Chicago Investment Corp. (First National Bank of Chicago)	TA Associates, Boston, MA (Tucker Anthony & R. L. Day)
General Electric Venture Capital Corp., Fairfield, CT (GE)	Security Pacific Capital Corp., Newport Beach, CA
	Citicorp Venture Capital Ltd., New York, NY
	BT Capital Corp., New York, NY (Bankers Trust N.Y.)

Source: Reprinted from the June 1983 issue of *Venture,* The Magazine for Entrepreneurs, by special permission. © 1983 Venture Magazine, Inc., 35 West 45th St., New York, N.Y. 10036.

program because some drugs designed to treat rare diseases are not produced commercially on account of their high cost and the small number of customers in need of the drug. The program encourages manufacturers to bear the cost of developing drugs not likely to pay for themselves. Merck and Abbott Laboratories volunteered, but so did Bolar Pharmaceutical Co., a small manufacturer of generic drugs. This decision would not help Bolar's bottom line, but I liked the fact that a small company was doing its share along with far larger manufacturers. This stimulated me to research Bolar, which I found passes most ethical screens and has a superb growth record.

Analyzing the High-Risk Companies

One of the great challenges of small companies lies in picking comers from among companies that have never shown a profit. For instance, in the monoclonal antibody field companies like Genetic Systems, Hybritech, and Monoclonal Antibodies have shown enormous increases in revenues but no earnings. The investor must decide which shows the most promise and whether that company has the capacity to fulfill that promise.

I have four basic rules for investing in companies without a track record of profits. First, don't invest if you don't know, or can't find out about, the company's industry. Second, give strong preference to companies that can finance expansion internally. Third, invest only in companies with strong management and boards of directors. And fourth, beware of what their auditors and lawyers say.

What Does It Sell? If the numbers look great to you but you haven't a clue as to what the company does, then you really haven't a clue as to what those great numbers mean. You must be able to evaluate a company within its micro and macro environments. Numbers rarely mean anything except in comparison to other numbers. So, stick to what you know.

Who's Paying for the Growth? Always look for companies that can finance most of their growth internally. If a company has to issue more stock, the new shares will dilute earnings. If it has to issue debt, the balance sheet picture weakens considerably.

Who's Running the Show? Especially in newly emerging industries such as high tech and biotech, the brains behind the company will make or break it, no matter it how fine a product they have.

For many years I've followed Wang Laboratories. While no longer a small company, it is still a good example of what excellent management can mean to a small company. Years ago I received conflicting reports on Wang. One set of reports said that their product was good, if pricey, but the company showed little product innovation. The other predicted great things and pointed to An Wang, a brilliant scientist and boss. He had known when to bring in professional management. His generous employee benefits, like stock option plans, an employee country club, and advanced educational training, created a loyal employee base. The years have proven the second set of reports right. In 1977, when company revenues were $163 million, you could have bought all the stock you wanted for $1 per share (adjusted for splits). Revenues in 1982 were $967 million, and the stock sold for as much as $31.

Newspapers and periodicals are perhaps your best source for learning about management. However, your brokerage may keep a file on a particular company in which you are interested. Also, I strongly recommend discussing companies with people who are in the same field.

When all else fails, a proxy or a prospectus may give you a starting point. As I indicated in Chapter 3, it lists the background of top management and how much stock they own in the company. Stock ownership is an excellent way to assess smaller companies. Who has their money at risk will tell you a great deal about who has the greatest commitment to the company's success. If those persons are not the principals, look elsewhere. I've also noted a direct correlation between commitment to social objectives and the stake management has in the company.

Pay particular attention to the members of the board of directors. Often a new company will have two or three outside board members who are principals in venture capital firms. Ask your broker about these firms' reputations. If sharp venture capitalists are backing a company, consider grabbing their shirttails.

Who's Minding the Store? When I look at an annual report, I check to see who signed the auditor's report. I want to see that it is signed by a firm I respect. (Note: I did not say a firm I have heard of.) My attitude may seem unfair to accounting firms trying to break into the big time. But all too often I've gone back to annual reports of companies which got into trouble and found either an unknown or an all-too-well-known auditor. I want to see the name of a respected, conservative firm (see Figure 5-8). If I'm going to take a risk, I want all the facts stated accurately. If I want to gamble, I'll go to the track.

Until recently I would have said another good test is the identity of

FIGURE 5-8   Big Eight Accounting Firms

Arthur Anderson	Touche Ross
Arthur Young	Deloitte, Haskins & Sells
Coopers Lybrand	Price Waterhouse
Peat, Marwick Mitchell	Ernst & Whinney

the corporation's lawyers. However, in August 1983 the American Bar Association adopted a canon of ethics which prevents lawyers from revealing a corporate client's fraudulent acts. Investors should judge accordingly any statements a company's lawyer makes.

Customer Reactions to Products

Many times investors stumble across a company because they buy its products or know their potential. Eight years ago a heart surgeon I know called me all excited about a prosthetic heart valve manufactured by St. Jude Medical. The company was then brand new and needed Food and Drug Administration approval for the essentially untried valve. The surgeon could afford the risk and felt — rightly — that the product marked an important breakthrough. Meanwhile, the company opted for slow growth based on its other medical products. Since that conversation, St. Jude's price per share has increased 4900%.

I missed a tremendous opportunity a few years ago by failing to follow my own advice. I follow telecommunications issues, including American Telephone and Telegraph (AT&T). Just at the time MCI Communications won its first court battle with AT&T over access to long-distance lines, but before the case was ultimately decided on appeal, I got a ringing endorsement of MCI from my father-in-law. He spent most of his day on long-distance calls and knew precisely what MCI was saving him. I was skeptical. MCI then had over 30 million shares outstanding. I couldn't see how it could generate enough revenue to boost earnings with that many shares outstanding. MCI's stock today is worth 20 times what it was when that conversation took place. Also, it passes most ethical investors' screens.

Investing in small companies offers ethical investors great advantages. Many look nowhere else for investment vehicles. The small company often has one basic product or service area. It usually has only one type of customer. And it offers an enormous potential for growth or income. Unlike other investors, the ethical investor may approach the small com-

FIGURE 5-9   Top Growth Companies Hiking Sales per Employee

Eighty-three of the 100 fastest-growing companies studied by *INC.* increased their productivity — measured in sales per employee — between 1974 and 1978. Excluding capital-intensive oil and gas developers and several companies with combined franchise and real estate interests, here are the top ten in sales output per employee:

Company	1978 Sales Per Employee	Percent Gain 1974–78
Rampart General	$235,907	232%*
Save-Way Industries	127,887	132
Autotrol	124,119	30
Amdahl	106,967	160*
Data Dimensions	105,416	127
Penn Virginia	93,179	46
Teleconcepts	92,957	211
Data Access Systems	89,950	100
Winston Network	88,971	319
Sonic Development	76,300	100

*Estimated
Source: Bradford W. Ketchum, Jr., "How Growing Companies Grow New Jobs." Reprinted with permission, *INC.* magazine, July 1979, p. 65. Copyright © 1979 by Inc. Publishing Corporation, 38 Commercial Wharf, Boston, MA 02210.

pany from purely logical considerations. The ethical investor looks for particular characteristics which these companies may provide.

Over the last decade small companies have offered enormous returns to investors who previously only dreamt of such rewards. Small companies, however, demand more caution and more homework than large companies because less information is readily available about them. But small companies are uniquely appropriate for the concerned investor.

6 INVESTING FOR
THE FUTURE

I N THE LAST THREE CHAPTERS I discussed how to pick companies with both ethical and financial promise. In this chapter and the next I'll focus on the criteria which go into a decision to invest. I've chosen to approach the investment decision in terms of growth and income, aims which, as I've emphasized, most portfolios should mix.

THE REWARDS AND RISKS
OF GROWTH

No other area of investment is so naturally attuned to the ethical investor as growth stocks. Because ethical investors are willing to go against conventional wisdom on investments, they are considerably more open to new ideas and concepts. It is another reason why ethical investors are successful investors.

As I noted in Chapter 2, the Internal Revenue Code taxes capital gains at an extremely favorable rate to the taxpayer — not more than 20%. If an investor's goal is to build up a significant estate, the tax code provides a further incentive for investing in growth stocks. The investor's heirs will inherit the stock on what is called a stepped-up basis — the stock's value on the date of death. In other words, the increase in value is not taxed. Another benefit of investing for growth is that the appreciation in value of your investment is not taxed until you sell. Shrewd

FIGURE 6-1   Major Players in the Gambling Industry

American Leisure Corp.	Hardwicke Companies Inc.
Bally Manufacturing Corp.	Holiday Inns, Inc.
Caesar's New Jersey, Inc.	International Game Technology
Caesar's World, Inc.	MGM Grand Hotels
Elsinor Corp.	Resorts International
Golden Nugget	Del E. Webb Corp.
Great Bay Casino Corp.	Westworld, Inc.

analyses of which companies benefit from a developing trend can lead the ethical investor toward companies whose stocks do remarkably well.

One of my favorite growth candidates is Walt Disney Productions. While intellectuals often sneer at it and environmentalists have criticized its theme parks, Disney has provided quality entertainment for fifty years. Recently the company decided to take a gamble on clean pay TV. "About 20% of the people who canceled their pay TV service did so because they don't want their children exposed to adult films," says Jim Jimirro, president of Walt Disney Productions' new cable television subsidiary. As of this writing it's too early to know if the gamble has paid off.[1]

If styles swing away from designer labels toward more casual wear, Levi Strauss & Co. (blue jeans) should begin growing vigorously again. In 1850 Levi Strauss set his goals: "a quality product, the best possible working conditions for our employees, and community service." His company still follows this credo. My favorite Levi Strauss story involves its Blackstone, Virginia, plant. In the late 1950s it could not attract enough good employees from the white population. The company decided it was time to integrate. The white workers demanded either a painted dividing line or, better yet, a wall between black and white workers. They insisted on separate drinking fountains and restrooms. The company gave the whites a choice: accept integration or lose the factory. The company won.[2]

Disadvantages of Growth Stocks

Investing for growth is far from risk free. Growth investments are often riskier than investing for income. They lack a steady dividend history. You depend on the stock market's health. While some stocks rise even in the worst markets, the growth seeker invests in the types of stock which go up most when their industry reports good earnings and many investors like its prospects. Growth stocks usually offer nothing during a bear market. But the growth seeker bets on the future because the biggest gains come in new companies untested in adverse conditions. Figure 6-2 lists *INC.* magazine's 100 fastest-growing small companies for 1983.

The larger, more established companies present less risk. However, they do not offer the same chance for spectacular growth. It is considerably easier for an emerging company with revenues of $5 million to double them than for a larger company to double $2 billion. The ethical investor must weigh the balance between stable growth companies and emerging growth companies and vigilantly watch for any indication of trouble for either the company or its industry.

The Price of Growth Stocks

Growth stocks are relatively expensive, particularly if other investors noticed them before you did and bid them up. You must carefully choose the time to buy. You may even have to pass up what initially appears to be a promising opportunity. I'm not saying that you won't have to pay more for a good company. In anything but a deep bear market you do pay more per dollar of earnings when investing for growth. More on this later in the chapter, but remember: disappointment costs investors dearly if they buy too high. For instance, analysts have finally begun looking with skepticism at the many firms competing in the personal and home computer markets. A number of former high fliers have crashed, as Osborne Computer did in September 1983.

WHO INVESTS FOR GROWTH?

When I first entered this business, I sat next to an elderly broker. I took a call for him one day when he was out sick. A client wished to sell some of her IBM (one of the top places for blacks to get ahead) and wanted to know its original cost. I called him at home and asked him where to look up that information.

"You don't have to look it up. It was 11¢ a share."

"You mean, $11 a share?"

"No, 11¢."

That day IBM sold at $265 a share. When it hit the market in the 1940s IBM was a speculative issue. Only a visionary would have put his

FIGURE 6-2 The INC. 100

Each year, *INC.* magazine assembles a list of the 100 fastest-growing small companies. Here is its 1983 list.

Rank '83	Company	Sales Growth (1978–82) Percent increase	Sales Growth (1978–82) Compound annual rate	Business description
1	**BRAE** (San Francisco)	88,970%	446%	Leasing & managing transportation equipment
2	**Altos Computer Systems** (San Jose)	33,871	329	Mfr. multi-user microcomputers
3	**Pizza Time Theatre** (Sunnyvale, CA)	28,430	311	Franchisor family entertainment restaurants
4	**ISC Systems** (Spokane)	8,850	208	Mfr. microprocessor-based terminal systems
5	**Apple Computer** (Cupertino, CA)	7,322	194	Mfr. personal computer systems
6	**Bio-Medical Sciences** (New York)	6,376	184	Mfr. thermometers
7	**Electro-Biology** (Fairfield, NJ)	6,211	182	Mfr. medical equipment
8	**Mid-America Petroleum** (Dallas)	5,983	179	Oil & gas exploration
9	**Teleco Oilfield Services** (Meriden, CT)	5,393	172	Provides oil & gas drilling data
10	**Movie Systems** (Des Moines)	5,138	169	Operates cable TV systems
11	**ASK Computer Systems** (Los Altos, CA)	4,755	164	Designs management information systems
12	**Tandon** (Chatsworth, CA)	4,594	162	Mfr. computer disk drives
13	**Biochem International** (Milwaukee)	4,447	160	Mfr. medical monitoring devices
14	**Energy Conversion Devices** (Troy, MI)	4,393	159	Designs photovoltaics, semiconductors
15	**Micom Systems** (Chatsworth, CA)	3,775	150	Mfr. data communications equipment
16	**Genentech** (San Francisco)	3,708	148	Mfr. pharmaceuticals & industrial chemicals
17	**Consul** (Eden Prairie, MN)	3,385	143	Franchises Mexican restaurants
18	**Chemical Investors** (Indianapolis)	3,354	142	Mfr. industrial tape, custom chemicals
19	**Crime Control** (Indianapolis)	3,180	139	Mfr. electronic security systems
20	**Lexidata** (Billerica, MA)	3,124	138	Mfr. graphic display processors
21	**Oxygen Enrichment** (Schenectady, NY)	3,093	138	Mfr. medical respiratory products
22	**Flare** (Midland, TX)	2,860	133	Provides seismic data services
23	**Medical Graphics** (St. Paul)	2,751	131	Mfr. computerized medical systems
24	**Healthdyne** (Marietta, GA)	2,414	124	Mfr. electronic medical equipment
25	**Data Switch** (Norwalk, CT)	2,357	123	Mfr. computer switching and control systems

Source: Reprinted with permission; *INC.* magazine, May 1983, pp. 56–57, 60–61. Copyright © by Inc. Publishing Corporation, 38 Commercial Wharf, Boston, MA 02210.

FIGURE 6-2 *(continued)*

26	Nutri/System (Huntingdon Valley, PA)	1,960	113	Owner/franchisor weight-loss centers
27	Comair (Cincinnati)	1,889	111	Commercial airline
28	KLA Instruments (Santa Clara, CA)	1,819	109	Mfr. electro-optical test systems
29	Nuclear Support Services (Hershey, PA)	1,704	106	Nuclear utility services
30	NBI (Boulder, CO)	1,702	106	Mfr. word-processing systems
31	Vector Graphic (Thousand Oaks, CA)	1,682	105	Mfr. microcomputer systems
32	Ryan's Family Steak Houses (Greenville, SC)	1,623	104	Owner/franchisor restaurants
33	Nugget Oil (Bloomington, MN)	1,554	102	Oil & gas exploration, contract drilling
34	Texas Energies (Amarillo, TX)	1,510	100	Oil & gas exploration, production
35	SPM Group (Englewood, CO)	1,486	100	Mkts. waste conversion equipment
36	LTX (Westwood, MA)	1,452	98	Mfr. computer-controlled test systems
37	Heritage Communications (Des Moines)	1,394	97	Operates cable TV systems, display communications
38	Intertec Data Systems (Columbia, SC)	1,381	96	Mfr. microcomputers
39	United States Health Care Systems (Willow Grove, PA)	1,379	96	Comprehensive health-care systems
40	Jefferson-Williams Energy (Dallas)	1,368	96	Oil & gas exploration
41	Swanton (New York)	1,362	96	Financial services, coal operations
42	M.D.C. (Denver)	1,338	95	Residential construct. & real estate develop.
43	Cetus (Berkeley, CA)	1,260	92	Microbiology research & product development
44	Godfather's Pizza (Omaha)	1,240	91	Operates pizza restaurants
45	Reeves Communications (New York)	1,232	91	Producer/distributor films & TV programs
46	Tandem Computers (Cupertino, CA)	1,184%	89%	Mfr. multiple processor computer systems
47	Nelson Research & Development (Irvine, CA)	1,169	89	Mfr. pharmaceutical products
48	Seneca Oil (Oklahoma City)	1,150	88	Oil & gas exploration
49	Gold C Enterprises (Denver)	1,147	88	Mkts. discount coupon books
50	Gulf Energy (Salt Lake City)	1,127	87	Oil, gas, coal exploration
51	Key Pharmaceuticals (Miami, FL)	1,110	87	Mfr. ethical pharmaceuticals
52	Lomak Petroleum (Hartville, OH)	1,103	86	Contract drilling of oil & gas wells
53	Oxoco (Houston)	1,098	86	Oil & gas exploration
54	Quality Systems (Tustin, CA)	1,081	85	Supplier minicomputer turnkey systems
55	Machine Technology (Whippany, NJ)	1,017	83	Mfr. systems for semiconductor manufacturers
56	Dietrich Resources (Denver)	1,006	82	Oil & gas exploration, production
57	Monument Energy (Houston)	1,001	82	Provider oil-field equipment & services
58	Shopsmith (Vandalia, OH)	984	81	Mfr. woodworking equipment
59	Phoenix American (Mill Valley, CA)	925	79	Leases data processing equipment
60	AM Cable TV Industries (Coopersburg, PA)	915	79	Constructs aerial cable distribution networks
61	St. Jude Medical (St. Paul)	913	78	Mfr. prosthetic heart valves & medical devices

62	Miller Technology & Communications (Phoenix)	875	77	Tech. training programs, computer software
63	Health Extension Services (Syosset, NY)	835	75	Prov. home health care/institutional staffing
64	Nuclear Pharmacy (Albuquerque)	830	75	Dispenser of radiopharmaceuticals
65	Compucorp (Santa Monica, CA)	816	74	Mfr. desktop & portable computers
66	Sykes Datatronics (Rochester)	807	74	Mfr. minicomputer peripheral equipment
67	Victor Kellering (Brooklyn)	803	73	Mfr. plastic vials for pharmaceutical products
68	Dysan (Santa Clara, CA)	757	71	Mfr. magnetic data storage media
69	Hadson Petroleum (Oklahoma City)	754	71	Oil & gas exploration, production
70	Barton Valve (Shawnee, OK)	752	71	Mfr. parts for oil & gas industry
71	Sea Galley Stores (Mountlake Terrace, WA)	751	71	Operates seafood restaurants
72	Service Fracturing (Pampa, TX)	745	71	Oil & gas field services
73	C. P. Rehab (New York)	743	70	Prov. mgt. services to cardiac rehab. centers
74	Cray Research (Minneapolis)	722	69	Mfr. large-scale scientific computers
75	Pengo Industries (Fort Worth)	700	68	Oil & gas field services & equipment
76	Trans-Western Exploration (Dallas)	673	67	Oil & gas exploration
77	Intergraph (Huntsville, AL)	673	67	Mfr. interactive computer graphics systems
78	Scientific Leasing (Farmington, CT)	672	67	Leases equip. to health-care providers
79	CACI (Arlington, VA)	671	67	Computer programming, management consulting
80	Plasma-Therm (Kresson, NJ)	665	66	Mfr. plasma-technology systems
81	Hadron (Vienna, VA)	642	65	Mfr. laser systems, provides computer services
82	BSN (Dallas)	623	64	Mail-order mkting. of sports equipment
83	CPT (Minneapolis)	620	64	Mfr. word-processing systems
84	Liz Claiborne (New York)	612	63	Mfr. women's sportswear
85	Matrix (Northvale, NJ)	604	63	Mfr. medical diag. sys. & graphic recorders
86	Cipher Data Products (San Diego)	596	62	Mfr. magnetic-tape drives
87	International Game Technology (Reno)	592	62	Mfr. coin-operated video games
88	Alaska Diversified Resources (Anchorage)	591	62	Operates retail consumer electronics stores & hotels
89	Immuno Nuclear (Stillwater, MN)	585	62	Mfr. medical diagnostic kits
90	ADAC Laboratories (Sunnyvale, CA)	575	61	Mfr. medical diagnostic imaging systems
91	Ventrex Laboratories (Portland, ME)	573	61	Mfr. medical diagnostic products
92	C3 (Reston, VA)	565	61	Supplier customized minicomputer systems
93	Ferrofluidics (Nashua, NH)	551	60	Mfr. ferrofluidic seals & magnetic fluids
94	Computer Associates International (Jericho, NY)	551	59	Mfr. standardized software products
95	North American Watch (New York)	538	59	Importer/distributor of watches
96	Diagnostic/Retrieval Systems (Oakland, NJ)	529	58	Mfr. signal processors & digital recording systems
97	Cullinet Software (Westwood, MA)	523	58	Provides database management systems
98	Cable TV Industries (Los Angeles)	517	58	Mfr. products used in cable TV industry
99	Xonics (Des Plaines, IL)	504	57	Mfr. medical imaging products
100	Intelligent Systems (Atlanta)	500	56	Mfr. display terminals & desktop computers

FIGURE 6-3   Top Ten Corporate Givers (1981)

Some companies did not disclose their giving for 1981. These included IBM and Sears, Roebuck. AT&T listed its contributions by constituent elements, such as Western Electric, Bell Labs, etc. Its total contributions were 44.7 million.

Exxon	$45.1 million
Atlantic Richfield	$28.3 million
General Motors	$24.1 million
Chevron	$21.7 million
Mobil	$15.3 million
Shell Oil	$13.2 million
Digital Equipment Corp	$12.6 million
R. J. Reynolds	$12.6 million
Gulf Oil	$11.5 million
3M	$11.3 million

Source: Guide to Corporate Giving (1983), as reprinted in the San Francisco Chronicle, April 13, 1983.

Brahmin clients into IBM. But that broker understood his client's need for growth in her portfolio.

Growth seekers come in so many types that constructing one profile is impossible. However, all growth-oriented investors share one characteristic: patience. They do not sell at the first sign of a profit so long as there is still a good reason to continue to buy the stock. They stick with an investment for the long haul, selling only when the vehicle's growth stalls. For instance, they might have sold Scholastic, Inc. (learning aids for elementary and high school students) when the population of school-aged children dropped, and are perhaps buying it again. Now, let's look at two categories of growth seekers.

The Younger Growth Seekers

George and Julie are in their early thirties. They've been married for four years and have two children. Like the typical young growth seeker, they have 25 to 40 years of earnings ahead. They live on their salaries but can afford to put some money into stocks, mutual funds, and perhaps real estate. In their planning they anticipate a day when their investments will have to have grown exponentially in order to pay first for their children's education and then their own retirement. Why exponentially? Think of it this way: money doubles every six years in a savings account compounding at 12%. If inflation is also at 12%, they need investments that can significantly outpace a safe investment in the bank. For instance, many projections indicate tuition costs, now running $10,000 and more, will double in the next ten years.

Growth stocks offer George and Julie the best opportunity to equal or exceed the inflation rate. Growth stocks by definition beat the inflation rate; otherwise they're not really growing. Compared with investments which conserve capital but continually lose buying power regardless of the income they produce, the choice is clear. By investing in the stocks of companies which are growing quickly, George and Julie give themselves an opportunity to meet their future cash needs more easily. They don't need any more income now, so the low dividends won't hurt them. And the capital gains they should realize will put their children through college.

The Older Growth Seekers

Older growth seekers I define as those over 45. I urge — dragoon where necessary — my clients to begin retirement preparation not later than age 45. Health statistics indicate that the chances of developing a chronic disease increase geometrically after age 50. For that reason, no one age 45 should count on being able to work past 60. So now is the time to build up the portfolio you'll live off later.

Typically, however, the older growth seeker is a person in a high tax bracket. She has all the income she needs for daily living, but she wants her assets to continue to outpace inflation. By investing in the stocks of companies which are growing, and perhaps paying small dividends, the older growth seeker benefits from an increasingly valuable portfolio while avoiding the tax liability which significant dividends on top of an already large income would produce.

Recently a woman in her early fifties came to see me. The beneficiary of a trust fund, she put much of her income into a savings account from which she made large donations to charities — mainly a home for battered women. Because her health is poor, she had become concerned about providing the home with an endowment. We developed a plan. She now puts part of her income into growth stocks — primarily in companies with good records on labor relations, minority hiring, women in management, and product safety. Her hope is that the portfolio she has arranged to leave the home will secure its future.

FIGURE 6-4   A Portfolio of Alternative Energy Stocks

Name	Social Screen Ratings							
	AF	LA	EN	NE	DE	AE	CO	AG
AFG Industries	2	2	3	1	2	1	1	2
ALCOA	2	0	0	2	2	2	2	2
Amer. Solar King	2	2	1	2	2	1	1	2
Ametek, Inc.	2	0	0	2	2	1	3	2
Appl. Solar En. Corp.	2	2	1	2	5	1	1	3
At. Richfield	2	4	2	2	3	2	3	3
Besicorp Group	3	3	3	2	2	1	1	2
Boeing Co.	2	2	0	2	5	2	3	5
Browning-Ferris	2	3	2	2	2	2	2	2
Butler Mfg.	2	3	3	2	2	3	1	2
Fafco	2	3	1	2	2	1	1	2
Hawaiian Elect.	2	0	0	2	2	2	2	2
Honeywell, Inc.	4	4	0	2	4	2	2	4
Johnson Controls	5	0	0	2	2	3	3	4
Magma Power	2	0	0	2	2	1	0	2
Mor-flo	2	2	0	2	2	1	1	2
Novan Energy	2	0	1	2	2	1	1	2
Opt. Coat. Lab	2	3	0	2	5	1	3	3
Pac. Gas & El.	2	0	2	1	2	1	1	2
Peabody Intl.	2	0	1	2	2	0	1	2
Reynolds Metals	2	2	0	0	0	1	3	1
Robertshaw Cont.	2	0	0	2	2	3	2	2
Scient.-Atlanta	2	0	0	2	3	3	3	3
Signal Cos.	2	0	0	2	2	3	3	3
Thermo Electron	2	3	1	2	2	1	1	2
Wind Baron	2	3	1	2	2	1	1	2
Zurn Ind. Inc.	2	0	0	2	2	2	1	2

Explanation of Symbols

Social Screen Rankings:
1,2 = above average
3   = average
4,5 = below average
0   = no information

Social Screen Key:
AF = South Africa.   LA = Labor.   EN = Environment.   NE = Nuclear Energy.   DE = Defense.   AE = Alternate Energy.   CO = Conservation of Energy.   AG = Aggregate Ranking.

Source: Franklin Research & Development Corp., 222 Lewis Wharf, Boston, MA 02110, August 1983, pp. 18–19. Reprinted by permission.

LOOKING FOR GROWTH

Where do you look for growth among traditional investments? Common stocks. Only there will you find the range of choices which will allow you to satisfy your ethical guidelines. The alternatives will not produce the growth you are looking for. Bonds give you your money back with interest, but they do not grow in value unless you buy when their price has fallen considerably. Collectibles like antiques may fill the bill, but you have to be able to find a buyer, and their market is not nearly so simple as the stock market. Although all investors should have savings programs, over time bank accounts can never equal the strong growth of common stocks.

The best play for growth is to find fast-growing industries and identify the best companies in them, to buy their stocks, and to hold them until the moment comes to sell.

The simplest approaches to investing work best. I have a client who is a librarian. By nature she is very precise and direct. At the nadir of the 1980–82 bear market she bought Dreyfus Corporation, explaining, "Well, everyone seems to have their money in money market funds, and it has a large money fund." In just over six months Dreyfus doubled. Another client told me, "I was at a small party where four of us were building passive solar features into our houses. Who makes solar glass?" That question led me to AFG Industries. It went from 8½ to 24 in 1982.

Among the industries popular among my clients as of this writing are geothermal energy developers, nonmilitary service industries, health food processors, manufacturers with good labor records, environment- and energy-conscious shelter manufacturers, and ethical drug companies with good records. How to identify these stocks, and how to know when to sell them, is what the rest of this chapter is about.

Analyzing Marketplace Trends

Rule number one: don't get carried away by what everyone else is doing. Be a scout, not a member of the wagon train. If everyone is buying solar stocks, consider whether the price of those stocks exceeds what you can reasonably expect to realize from them over time. Let's assume that you decide a field is overbought and you must look elsewhere. How do you go about it?

What's Happening Where? Consider carefully the state of the world, the state of the economy, and the state of the consumer marketplace. Your goal is to find an industry which is growing faster than the economy, and to find a company within that industry which promises to grow faster than the industry. Jim Lowell of Lowell & Blake Associates uses a similar indicator. "We prefer putting our money into industries which keep lowering prices for their goods. Take the high tech area. Those companies are growing so fast that they have to keep promoting everyone. I don't think their managements are naturally more responsive. They just feel they have to keep what skilled labor they have happy."

A *Sampling of Trends.* A careful analysis of contemporary trends and life style changes will help you locate a fast-growing company. "Trends" and "life style changes" are much-abused terms. Some have reduced them to synonyms for "fads," like hula hoops, mood rings, and pet rocks. However, the steady increase in the number of mothers in the work force since the early 1950s represents both a trend and a change in life style.

FIGURE 6-5   The Savvy 24
The Best Places for Women to Work.

In 1982 and again in 1983, *Savvy* magazine analyzed companies where women had the greatest opportunities. The two lists are *not* mutually exclusive, and omission of those in the first group from the second does not reflect their performance.

1982	*1983*
American Express Company	CBS, Inc.
Atlantic Richfield Company	Citicorp
AT&T	General Electric
Chemical New York Corp.	Levi Strauss
Connecticut General Corp.	Pacific Gas & Electric
Continental Illinois Corp.	Procter & Gamble
Control Data Corp.	Texas Instruments
Digital Equipment Corp.	3M Company
The Equitable Life Assurance Society of the United States	
General Mills	
Hewlett-Packard Co.	
Honeywell	
IBM	
Johnson & Johnson	
Quaker Oats Co.	
Security Pacific Corp.	

Source: "The Savvy 16," *Savvy,* May 1982, pp. 39–44; Scholl, "Savvy Corporations of the Year," *Savvy,* June 1983, pp. 30–37.

The distinction between fads and trends may seem unimportant, but by definition a growth investment goes up for more than one year. Spotting incipient fads and selling at their peak requires considerably more luck and inside information than skill and study.

Here are a dozen trends which have become pronounced over the last five years.

- Women having first babies later in life
- Increase in the birth rate (the baby boomlet)
- An aging population
- Alternative energy development
- Passive solar housing
- Accelerating need to clean up air and water
- All-pervasive computerization
- Home entertainment — the electronic house
- Lower per capita alcohol consumption
- Mortality shift from acute to chronic diseases
- Greater concern for healthful life styles
- Increasing crime in the suburbs

You can amplify this list with dozens more. The ethical investor must examine the range of trends for those which will accelerate and lead to the development of companies fitting his or her social criteria.

Identifying Demands Arising from Trends

Once you identify trends, consider what demands each of the trends will create. Let's look at five of the trends I mentioned and see what kinds of demands they create.

The Baby Boomlet. Creates a demand for children's apparel, educational materials, toys, baby products, foods children will eat, children's entertainment.

An Aging Population. Creates a demand for aspirin and over-the-counter remedies, medical technology, hospitals, elderly housing, home entertainment.

Passive Solar Housing. Creates a demand for solar glass, solar hot water panels, thin film photovoltaics, lenders willing to finance solar projects.

FIGURE 6-6   National Gay Task Force Survey: Sexual Orientation Hiring Policies

Allied	2	Celanese	I
American Airlines	5	Chase Manhattan	I
American Brands	I	Chemical New York	I
ABC	I	Citicorp	I
American Can	2	Colgate-Palmolive	I
American Cyanamid	2	Continental Group	5
American Express	I	Control Data	I
American Motors	I	CPC International	I
AT&T	I	Crown Zellerbach	I
Anheuser-Busch	I	Dana	3
ARA Services	I	Deere & Co.	5
Avon Products	I	Dow Chemical	2
BankAmerica	I	Du Pont	3
Bendix	I	Eastern Air Lines	4
Bethlehem Steel	I	Eastman Kodak	2
Boeing	4	Eaton	3
Boise Cascade	I	Engelhard	6
Borg-Warner	3	Exxon	3
Bristol-Myers	I	Firestone	I
CBS	I	First Chicago	3
Carnation	I	Ford Motor	3

Categories of Response

I. Company has stated specifically that it does not discriminate on the basis of sexual orientation.
2. Company has stated that it does not discriminate on the basis of sexual orientation unless it interferes with job performances, disrupts other employees or adversely affects the company.
3. Company has stated that it hires and promotes employees solely on the basis of their ability to do the job. No specific mention of sexual orientation.
4. Company has stated that it is not aware of or does not inquire about employees' sexual orientations. No specific discussion of what response would be if an employee's sexual orientation should come to management's attention.
5. Company has stated that it obeys all laws that apply in employment and personnel matters. No expression of willingness to establish a policy against discrimination in localities where there is no legal protection for gay employees.
6. Company did not address issue directly or did not provide enough information for categorization.

Source: Reprinted in *News for Investors,* published by the Investor Responsibility Research Center in Washington, DC; October 1982, p. 187. Reprinted by permission.

Changes in Mortality Characteristics. Create a demand for drugs and technology related to heart disease and cancer treatment, diagnostic equipment, extended care facilities, hospitals, health maintenance organizations.

Lower per Capita Alcohol Consumption. Creates a demand for sparkling waters, white wine, beer, fruit juices.

Allow your mind to wander over the many demands a trend inevitably creates. Be both rational and irrational. For instance, when you think of the baby boomlet, remember that children find Ronald McDonald almost irresistible. A company that could produce a healthful snack food dressed

FIGURE 6-6   *(continued)*

General Electric	I	Pfizer	I
General Foods	2	Philip Morris	2
General Mills	2	Pillsbury	2
General Motors	2	PPG Industries	2
Georgia-Pacific	4	Procter & Gamble	3
Gillette	6	Quaker Oats	5
Goodyear Tire	3	Republic Steel	3
Greyhound	2	Revlon	I
Gulf Oil	3	R. J. Reynolds	I
Gulf & Western	2	Rockwell Intl.	I
Honeywell	I	Scott Paper	I
Inland Steel	I	Sears, Roebuck	I
IBM	2	Sperry	5
InterNorth	6	Standard Oil (CA)	I
Johnson & Johnson	I	Standard Oil (IN)	3
Kellogg	2	Stop & Shop	I
Kimberly-Clark	2	Sun	2
Levi Strauss	5	Supermarkets Gen.	6
Eli Lilly	I	Tesoro Petroleum	5
Lockheed	5	Texaco	2
R. H. Macy	I	Texas Utilities	3
McDonald's	3	Time	2
McDonnell Douglas	2	TransAmerica	5
Mead	5	Trans World	3
Merck	I	TRW	3
Merrill Lynch	I	UAL	I
3M	3	Union Carbide	I
Mobil Oil	3	Union Oil of CA	I
Monsanto	4	Union Pacific	5
Motorola	5	Warner Communica.	I
Norton Simon	I	Wells Fargo	I
Ogden	I	Weyerhaeuser	I
Pacific Gas & Elec.	I	Whirlpool	5
Pan Am	3	F. W. Woolworth	5
Panhandle Eastern	3	Xerox	3
J. C. Penney	I		

up like something no rational mother would let her child touch would make a fortune. McDonald's, incidentally, illustrates a problem ethical investors often have. While its menu may be objectionable on nutritional grounds, it is hard to fault a company that pledges part-time summer employment to about thirty thousand youths in its company-owned stores.[3]

THE FINANCIAL CLUES

After identifying companies which will benefit from developing trends and also satisfy your ethical screen, the next step is to determine whether investing in a particular company makes sense financially.

What Does the Market Tell You?

Getting a quick read on the market's view of a stock is as easy as buying a newspaper that prints full stock reports. There, listed beside the company's name, you'll find its dividend yield and price/earnings (p/e) ratio. (You'll find the same information in Moody's, S&P, and Value Line.)

Dividend Yield. The dividend yield for a growth company (the price of the stock divided by its annual dividend) will be quite low. In 1982 Ametek (solar hot water panels and thin film photovoltaics) paid a dividend of $1.20. When the stock was selling at $30 a share, its dividend yield was 4%, or about the average yield of stocks on the *Standard & Poor's* 500.

$$\frac{1.20}{30} = 0.04 \text{ or } 4\%$$

Big dividend yields do not entice growth seekers to invest in companies.

Price/Earnings (p/e) Ratio. To calculate the p/e, divide the price of the stock by the latest 12-month earnings. Remember, a dividend is not the same as earnings. A high p/e is not necessarily bad. The p/e is nothing more than a popularity index, and growth stocks will have relatively high p/e's. But watch out. High p/e's mean that if the company stumbles, the price of the stock will drop a lot. In 1976 Eastman Kodak (a company with a strong commitment to its workers) sold at $120/share — over 25 times earnings. Over the next two years the price dropped to under $50/share. Earnings had risen only 6%, not enough to justify such a high p/e.

In any industry, the fastest-growing corporations command the highest p/e's. Many analysts and brokers recommend buying only stocks with low p/e's, since they are undervalued; others recommend only high p/e stocks, since they are clearly growth leaders. From time to time each group is right.

There's a real difference between buying a stock at eight times earnings and one at 20 times earnings when their earnings are growing at the same rate. Suppose Company A is a regional bank growing at 15% a year and selling for eight times earnings, and Company B is a microcomputer company growing at 15% a year and selling at 20 times earnings. I'd rather buy Company A. Why should I pay $20 for $1 worth of earnings when I could pay $8 for the same earnings in a company growing at the same rate?

These are the basic quick financial tests. Any general stock market guide will give you the whole range of ratios you can apply, and there are dozens.

What Does the Company Tell You?

If you're still interested in a company after considering the market's view of it, look at what the company's performance tells you about its growth prospects.

Dividend Payout Ratio. The annual report's financials contain a statement of the *dividend payout ratio*, the percentage of earnings paid out each year in dividends to shareholders. Under either this heading or "common dividends as a percent of income available for common," you will find a tabulation of this ratio for the preceding ten years. In 1983 Sysco Corporation (a supplier of food whose company motto is: "don't sell food, sell peace of mind") paid a dividend of 32¢ a share on earnings of $1.94. This is a dividend payout ratio of 17%:

$$\frac{.32}{1.94} = 17\%$$

This important ratio indicates that management has retained sufficient reserves for research and development, advertising, sales promotion, expansion, and the other costs of growing. Many of the fastest-growing companies pay no dividend at all.

Ten-Year Financial Summary. The ten-year financial summary, found in the company's annual report, and the three services provide key information. What does the company's revenue growth look like? How steadily and how quickly is it growing? How did the company fare during the last two recessions? Are expenses growing faster than revenues? What about the return on the common shareholders' equity? Is it steady or growing? This reveals how profitable the company is when compared to the money the shareholders have invested plus the retained earnings from previous years. If the company would be better off closing its operations and buying Treasury bills, you haven't found a fast-growing corporation.

Now look at the ten-year history of the per share information. How have the earnings kept up? Has the company raised its dividend every year? If so, management has given the public a strong indication of its confidence in its ability to keep the company prosperous. Frequent stock splits give the same sign.

What Do the Analysts Tell You?

The annual report gives you the company's history and the most optimistic view of its future. But what you need is a realistic view of the company's growth potential. The most important data are earnings projections. These projections can have a drastic effect on a company's stock. No fabulous track record will make up for a drop in earnings the next year.

If a company issues earnings projections, you can get them from the company. Most don't. Your local library may carry *Standard & Poor's Earnings Digest* or *Value Line*, which lists their projections of many companies' earnings. If these publications do not provide the information you want, check with your broker. An analyst with a brokerage firm may project the earnings for the company you're tracking. However, Joan Bavaria of Franklin Research & Development points out that analysts can fall in love with the companies they follow. Some even end up working for them. She always seeks a number of analysts' views.

At this point you have all the information you need to make a decision. You have identified trends; identified products for which these trends will produce demands; identified companies which make these products; screened out companies not meeting your ethical criteria; analyzed what the market thinks of these companies; studied what the company says; and analyzed what the experts say the future holds for the company. Armed with this information, you are ready to place an order.

7   INVESTING FOR NOW

WHAT WOULD YOU THINK of a broker who, over two years, reduced the value of a client's portfolio by 30%? What would you think then if his client, an elderly widow, continued to recommend him to all her friends?

I learned of just such a case when I first entered the business. I thought the broker deserved a firing squad and the client required a guardian. But the broker knew his client, and she knew what she needed. Her husband had died four years before, leaving an estate consisting of $100,000 in life insurance, their house in the suburbs, and a very small savings account. She sold the house for $150,000, bought a co-op in New York, and put her remaining funds in the hands of a financial adviser. He bought a portfolio of growth stocks, and her net worth rose. "But," she complained to me, "I didn't have enough cash to buy birthday presents for my grandchildren." She found a new broker who understood her problem. Few of her stocks were paying even nominal dividends. He cashed in her growth stocks and bought her a mixture of blue chips, utilities, and bonds. Her asset value declined quite a bit when Wall Street entered a bear market, but during her nine remaining years she lived comfortably on the ever-increasing income her new portfolio produced.

WHAT IS INVESTING
FOR INCOME?

Investing for income means just what it says. Concerned investors looking
for income want the money their investments produce now. They care
more about having a steady flow of income than about increasing their net
worth or their estate.

Growth seekers may not include any income vehicles in their portfolios, but unless an income seeker is completely unwilling to take a risk,
all income portfolios should have some growth investments as a hedge
against inflation.

Types of Income

Income falls into two categories: *fixed* and *variable*. Fixed-income vehicles
never vary the amount of income they pay. These include bonds, annuities,
and commercial paper. Figure 7-1 tabulates the available fixed-income
vehicles. Variable-income vehicles, as their name implies, do not produce
a steady flow of income. Rather, as with high-quality common stocks, the
income can vary from year to year, though the amount of dividends usually
increases.

Obviously one limitation on the amount of income one can expect is
the amount of capital one has to invest. A $10,000 nest egg cannot bring
you $1,000 a month in income. To gain high current income, you must
invest mainly in debt instruments such as bonds, certificates of deposit
(CDs), or money market funds. But not entirely.

The Rewards and Risks of Income

The chief reward of investing for now is that you secure the money you
need every month. You don't have to rely for living expenses on the stock
market's vagaries. Traditionally, investors have associated a lower risk with
investing for income. However, the inability of income vehicles to keep
pace with the galloping inflation of the 1970s and early 1980s challenged
that assumption.

Because the income seeker's portfolio is weighted toward debt, only
the most severe corporate crisis will result in a loss of income. When
corporations find themselves in financial straits, they skip dividends on

common stock, then the dividends on the preferred, and as a last resort interest on debt.

Income Security. The income portfolio usually contains less risky vehicles than the growth portfolio. That is, you stand less chance of losing your capital. Part of the lower risk factor lies in the nature of the income investment. Federal and municipal bonds, of course, have very low risk factors. (The recent default on Washington Public Power Supply System bonds is the exception that proves the rule.)

More stable, mature corporations pay higher interest and dividends, so they rarely disappoint the income seeker in hard times. AT&T (a defense contractor with a good equal employment record) has paid dividends every year since 1881. Potomac Electric Power (a nonnuclear utility) has had an average dividend growth rate of 7.4% a year for the last five years and has paid dividends since 1904. And the Bank of Boston (featured on Franklin Research & Development's buy list several times) has paid dividends since 1784!

A number of large corporations offer excellent possibilities for income-seeking investors. They provide security not to be found in other entities, as well as the prospect of sufficient growth to maintain dividend yields. For the ethical investor they offer some extraordinary instances of social commitment. Quaker Oats, Cummins Engine, and Aetna Life and Casualty spring to mind.

Price Stability and Risk. Investing for income is not risk free. It is just less risky than investing for growth. Look at what used to be the bluest of the blue chip stocks, U.S. Steel. It dropped from 30 to 15 in 1982. To some extent you protect yourself — at least when buying blue chips — if you wait for very high returns before buying. That means buying low. But what looks low may be just the beginning of a precipitous decline. Take International Harvester. From 1972 through 1979 it traded between $20 and $40 a share. In 1982 it was at $3. You might have considered $20 a bargain in 1979 only to feel a fool in 1982.

WHO INVESTS FOR INCOME

Ethical investors seek high income either because of their circumstances or their nature. They need to produce high current income from their investments. The majority of income seekers are elderly or retired, but not

FIGURE 7-1 Selected Fixed-Income Securities, Short Term

Type of security	Restrictions on size of purchase	Original maturity range	Quality spectrum	Liquidity and marketability	Tax status	How interest is earned
U.S. Treasury bills	$10,000 minimum	90 days to 1 year	Highest possible	Excellent	Fed: taxable; State: exempt; Local: exempt	Discounted; 360-day year
Federal Financing Bank bills	$10,000 minimum	90 days to 1 year	Extremely high	Excellent	Fed: taxable; State: exempt; Local: exempt	Discounted; 360-day year
Project notes of local authorities and local public agencies	$1,000 minimum	90 days to 1 year	Extremely high	Average	Fed: exempt; state and local: possibly exempt	Interest-bearing; 360-day year
Export-Import Bank discount notes	$100,000 minimum	30 days to 1 year	Extremely high	No secondary market; investor selects maturity	Federal, state, and local: taxable	Discounted; 360-day year
Federal National Mortgage Association discount notes	$50,000 minimum	30 to 270 days	Very high	Good; four dealer firms; investor selects maturity	Federal, state, and local: taxable	Discounted; 360-day year
Banks for Cooperatives bonds	$5,000 minimum	Usually 180 days	Very high	Good	Fed: taxable; State: exempt; Local: exempt	Interest-bearing; 360-day year
Farm Credit Banks discount notes	$50,000 minimum	5 to 150 days	Very high	Good; three dealer firms; investor selects maturity	Fed: taxable; State: exempt; Local: exempt	Discounted; 360-day year
Federal Home Loan consolidated discount notes	$100,000 minimum	30 to 360 days	Very high	Good; five dealer firms; investor selects maturity	Fed: taxable; State: exempt; Local: exempt	Discounted; 360-day year
Federal Intermediate Credit Bank bonds	$5,000 minimum	Usually 270 days	Very high	Good	Fed: taxable; State: exempt; Local: exempt	Interest-bearing; 360-day year

	Minimum	Maturity	Safety	Marketability	Tax status	Interest
State and local government notes	$5,000 minimum	30 days to 1 year	Ranges from very high to intermediate	Average	Fed: exempt; state and local: possibly exempt	Interest-bearing; 360-day year
Bankers' acceptances	No minimum; can find amounts as small as $5,000	1 to 270 days	High; depends on strength of endorsing bank or banks	Average	Federal, state, and local: taxable	Discounted; 360-day year
Negotiable certificates of deposit	$100,000 minimum; sometimes smaller	30 days to 1 year, possibly longer	High to intermediate; depends on strength of issuing bank	Average to good	Federal, state, and local: taxable	Interest-bearing; 360-day year
Commercial paper	$100,000 minimum; sometimes smaller	1 to 270 days	High to intermediate; depends on strength of company	No secondary market; investor selects maturity	Federal, state, and local: taxable	Discounted; 360-day year
Repurchase agreements and reverse repurchase agreements	$1 million minimum; sometimes smaller	Generally 1 day; can be up to 30 days or indefinitely	High	No secondary market; investor selects maturity	Federal, state, and local: taxable	Interest-bearing; 360-day year

Source: Adapted from D. M. Darst, *The Complete Bond Book,* pp. 274–283, © 1975 by McGraw-Hill, Inc. Reprinted with permission.

all. Consider Allison, for example, a 28-year-old social worker, whose field is notorious for its low salaries. She inherits $30,000. By nature a cautious person, splurging on a BMW does not appeal to Allison. Instead she wants to preserve her capital for the right condominium. Until then, she wants to generate enough income so she can go to Venice. Or consider Rosemary, a 38-year-old sociology professor. She cannot see investing in something which she hopes will return 25% when she knows she can get 12% without risk. And then there is Mike, a 45-year-old dentist. He tried investing for growth once and nearly wiped out his savings. Now he just wants safety and a steady return. Investing for income is the answer for all these people.

WHERE TO FIND
FIXED INCOME

Few areas of investing delineate the differences between the types of ethical investor better than the income field. If you count yourself a "new wave" investor, you may wish to avoid U.S. Treasury obligations, multinational corporations' debt, or defense contractors' stock. But if your focus is on worker issues, the quality of American material life, or inner-city revitalization efforts, then you may find these vehicles of interest. A person adopting either approach will find ideas in this chapter, but not all fit both approaches.

Corporate Bonds

A *corporate bond* is a long-term debt the corporation promises to repay on a certain date. In the meantime, it pays a specified rate of interest.

Risk. Corporates are the riskiest fixed-income vehicles. Many people buy them thinking only of their high income, forgetting their potential for capital risk. Bond prices fall when interest rates rise, and bond prices rise when interest rates fall. Let's take a look at a quality bond and compare it to the prime rate. Figure 7-2 shows what happened to the H. J. Heinz (food processing) 7½% bond issued in 1972 at par ($1000) and due in 1997. *Moody's* rates this issue A+.

In hyperinflationary times the income seeker's risks may be greater than those of the growth seeker, because it becomes impossible to maintain

FIGURE 7-2   Performance of H. J. Heinz Corporate Bond, 1972–1982

Year	High	Low	Prime Rate (Range)
1972	104	99½	4¾ to 6
1973	102¾	99¼	6 to 10
1974	95	77	8¾ to 12
1975	84⅝	80	7 to 10¼
1976	88⅝	84	6¼ to 7¼
1977	90⅝	88	6¼ to 7¾
1978	87½	87⅛	8 to 11¾
1979	86½	80	11½ to 15¾
1980	85¼	75	11 to 21⅛
1981	76	59	15¾ to 20½
1982	78	66⅞	11½ to 17

a return greater than the level of inflation. Several years ago when inflation was in the high teens, even money market funds paying 16% could not keep up. Of course, looking back we can see now that it was an extraordinarily opportune time to buy good-quality long-term bonds, then yielding 15%. For example, A-rated Continental Telephone of California offers some at 7⅝% due in 1997. They sold at 51 in 1982 for a current yield of over 15%, not to mention the $490 in capital gains in 15 years or when they're called. On the risk side, if you had bought that bond at par and had had to sell it to cover medical expenses in 1982, you would have suffered a $490 capital loss.

Convertible Bonds. Convertible bonds offer the income investor a solid opportunity to inject some growth into a portfolio. Convertible bonds are debt which investors can turn in for an established number of shares of common stock when the price of the common stock has risen sufficiently to make it worthwhile. I noted in Chapter 2 how an investor can calculate that amount at the time of purchasing the bond. The price the investor pays for the conversion feature is a lower rate of interest on the bond. For example, in March 1983 Hospital Corporation of America (the largest hospital chain in the United States) sold $200 million of debt due in 2008 at 8½%. That issue is convertible into stock at a 25½% premium over its market price at the time of the bonds' issue (or the price of the stock that day times 1.255). Among the corporations recently issuing large amounts of convertible debt are Allied Stores, MCI Communications, John Deere, American General, Teradyne, Macmillan, and Wang Laboratories.

Some corporations dispose of their holdings in other corporations by issuing debt that is convertible into the stock of another corporation.

These issuers include General Cinema bonds for R. J. Reynolds stock; Corning Glass for Owens-Corning Fiberglas; CIGNA for Paine, Webber, Jackson & Curtis; and Sun Co. for Becton, Dickinson & Co.[1]

Finding Appropriate Vehicles. Thoughtful investors, of course, are concerned about the corporations to which they lend money. Therefore, you should apply the same ethical considerations you use to buy common stock. A good way to identify appropriate stocks or bonds is to check what the ethical mutual and money funds have their money in. (See Appendix C.)

Preferred Stock

Preferred stock usually pays a fixed dividend. Depending on the type of preferred you hold, the company's fortunes — short of bankruptcy — don't matter to you. Preferred stock prices fluctuate like a bond's; they go up when interest rates fall and down when interest rates rise. Preferred stock is a good bet only when interest rates are about to fall and the particular issue promises a good capital gain. Unlike a bond, most preferred never matures. The company never has to return your principal and terminate the obligation. Some preferred stocks are convertible into common stock at a specified price. This means that if a company which meets your criteria has a convertible preferred, you can gain higher income now by buying the preferred and converting it later into common.

Municipal Bonds

Because municipal bonds often support social services, they are of special appeal to an ethical investor. As we saw in Chapter 2, when you buy municipals you buy debt issued by a state, town, municipality, or agency, often for a specific purpose. Municipal bonds are not for everyone. For one thing, the interest rate risks match those for corporate bonds. Also, because the income from munis is tax free, issuers offer a lower rate of interest than corporations. Check the charts in Chapter 9 to determine whether your tax bracket justifies buying municipals over corporates.

Municipal bonds may not always meet ethical or financial criteria. For instance, one of the more controversial issuers of muni bonds was the Washington Public Power Supply System (WPPSS). It issued more than $8 billion in *revenue anticipation* (that is, repayable by the income generated by the project) bonds to construct five nuclear power plants and then in May 1982 offered another $590 million due in 2017. *Moody's* rated the bonds Aaa and *Standard & Poor's* AA. But even with those ratings, the legal, political, economic, and financial snare, which had already led WPPSS to scrap two of the five plants, meant it had to offer an astounding 14¾% yield. And remember, this was tax-free income to the buyer. When these were issued, bonds of the same grade were yielding 13%. In July 1983 WPPSS became the largest municipal defaulter in history, proving that even munis carry a risk and justifying their nickname, "Whoops." For more discussion of municipal bonds, see Chapter 9.

U.S. Treasury Obligations

U.S. Treasury obligations provide the investor with the safest, highest-quality income vehicles available. The issue posed by Treasury obligations is whether they meet the individual's ethical guidelines. Most professionals feel they cannot. Because their proceeds go into the general fund of the United States, the investor cannot determine whether his funds are being spent for defense or housing.

Federal Agency Obligations

Federal agency obligations include over one hundred types of notes, bonds, and certificates. They do not present the same problem for ethical investors as Treasury issues because they go to an identifiable agency, often for an identifiable purpose. They usually are backed by the issuing agency, and are slightly more risky than Treasuries.

The ethical investor must scrutinize government agencies as closely

FIGURE 7-3   Top Players in the Tobacco Industry

The AAV Companies	Lowes Corporation
American Brands, Inc.	Opelika Manufacturing Corp.
American Maize Products Co.	Philip Morris, Inc.
Conwood Corp.	R. J. Reynolds Industries, Inc.
Dibrell Brothers, Inc.	Standard Commercial Tobacco Co.
Farm House Foods Corp.	U.S. Tobacco Co.
Gulf & Western Industries, Inc.	Universal Cigar Corp.
Imperial Group, ADR	Universal Leaf Tobacco Co., Inc.

as corporations. Apparently attractive issues may conceal problems for some ethical investors. For example, the Tennessee Valley Authority (TVA) and the Export-Import Bank (EX-IM) have close ties to the nuclear power industry. The following are examples of some relatively safe issuers. Figure 7-4 suggests others.

Student Loan Marketing Association. "Sallie Mae" buys student loans insured by state student loan agencies or by the U.S. government. The securities it issues finance loans to college and trade-school students. While Sallie Maes are not secured by the government, the agency invests only in student loans insured by state agencies or the government.

Small Business Administration. The SBA guarantees a portion of loans made by lenders to qualified small businesses. The lender may sell the guaranteed portion of the loan.

The Farm Credit System. Established over 65 years ago, the Farm Credit System makes loans through three sets of institutions. These include the 12 Federal Land Banks, which provide mortgage credit of up to 40 years through 520 Federal Land Bank Association offices; the 12 Federal Intermediate Credit Banks, which provide short- and intermediate-term loan funds to farmers and ranchers through 427 local Production Credit Associations; and the 13 Banks for Cooperatives, which make loans to agricultural marketing, supply, and business service cooperatives. These loans are fully collateralized.

Farm Credit securities go under the title Federal Farm Credit Banks Consolidated Systemwide Securities. They come in the form of short-term discount notes, six- and nine-month bonds, as well as longer-term bonds. They are sold through both banks and securities dealers. These issues may pose some problems for ethical investors, since it is impossible to determine to whom the underlying loans have been made. For instance, it is quite possible that some loans were made to agribusiness concerns with less than stellar labor records.

Federal National Mortgage Association. FNMA, or "Fannie Mae," is a corporation chartered by the U.S. government but owned by its stockholders. Fannie Mae helps finance housing, which in turn fosters employment in the building trades.

Federal Home Loan Banks. These institutions issue securities to raise money which is then loaned to member savings and loan associations. The thrift

FIGURE 7-4   Selected Fixed Income Securities, Long-Term

Type of security	Restrictions on size of purchase	Original maturity range	Quality spectrum	Liquidity and marketability	Tax status	How interest is earned
U.S. Treasury notes and bonds	$1,000 minimum; some are $10,000 minimum	1 to 20 years or more	Highest possible	Excellent to good	Fed: taxable; State: exempt; Local: exempt	Semiannual interest payments
Federal Financing Bank notes and bonds	$1,000 minimum; some are $10,000 minimum	1 to 20 years or more	Extremely high	Good	Fed: taxable; State: exempt; Local: exempt	Semiannual interest payments
Local housing authority bonds	$5,000 minimum	1 to 40 years	Extremely high	Good	Fed: exempt; state and local: possibly exempt	Semiannual interest payments
Federal Home Loan Mortgage Corporation guaranteed mortgage certificates	$100,000 minimum	Up to 30 years; 15-year repayment condition	Extremely high	Average	Federal, state, and local: taxable	Semiannual interest payments; a part of principal is returned annually
Federal Home Loan Mortgage Corporation mortgage-backed bonds	$25,000 minimum	12 to 25 years	Extremely high	Average	Federal, state, and local: taxable	Semiannual interest payments
Federal Home Loan Mortgage Corporation participation certificates	$100,000 minimum	15 to 30 years	Very high	Average	Federal, state, and local: taxable	Monthly interest payments
Export-Import Bank debentures and participation certificates	$5,000 minimum	3 to 7 years	Extremely high	Average to good	Federal, state, and local: taxable	Semiannual interest payments
Farmers Home Administration insured notes and certificates of beneficial ownership	$25,000 minimum	1 to 25 years	Extremely high	Average	Federal, state, and local: taxable	Annual interest payments

FIGURE 7-4 *(continued)*

Type of security	Restrictions on size of purchase	Original maturity range	Quality spectrum	Liquidity and marketability	Tax status	How interest is earned
Federal Housing Administration debentures	$50 minimum	1 to 40 years	Extremely high	Below average in small amounts	Federal, state, and local: taxable	Semiannual interest payments
Government National Mortgage Association mortgage-backed securities and participation certificates	$5,000 minimum. PC's; $25,000 minimum, mortgage-backed securities	1 to 25 years	Extremely high	Average	Federal, state, and local: taxable	Semiannual interest payments
Government National Mortgage Association modified pass-through certificates	$25,000 minimum	1 to 25 years; average life is 12 years	Extremely high	Average to good	Federal, state, and local: taxable	Monthly interest payments
Federal National Mortgage Association mortgage-backed bonds	$25,000 minimum	2 to 25 years	Extremely high	Average to below average	Federal, state, and local: taxable	Semiannual interest payments
Federal Home Loan Banks Bonds and notes	$10,000 minimum	1 to 20 years	Very high	Good	Federal, state, and local: taxable	Semiannual interest payments
Federal National Mortgage Association secondary-market notes and debentures, and capital debentures	$10,000 minimum	3 to 25 years	Very high	Average to good	Federal, state, and local: taxable	Semiannual interest payments
Federal Land Banks bonds	$1,000 minimum	1 to 10 years	Very high	Good	Fed: taxable; State: exempt; Local: exempt	Semiannual interest payments
Tennessee Valley Authority notes and bonds	$1,000 minimum	3 to 25 years	Very high	Average	Fed: taxable; State: exempt; Local: exempt	Semiannual interest payments

International Bank for Reconstruction and Development, Asian Development Bank, and Inter-American Development Bank notes and bonds	$1,000 minimum in dollar-denominated issues; amounts vary in other currencies	3 to 25 years	High	Average to below average	Federal, state, and local: taxable; on foreign currency issues withholding taxes possible	Semiannual interest payments
State and local government notes and bonds	$5,000 minimum	1 to 50 years	Very high to low, depending on rating	Average to good	Fed: exempt; state and local: possibly exempt	Semiannual interest payments
Corporate variable rate notes	$5,000 minimum on initial offering; $1,000 minimum in secondary market	15 to 20 years, or 6 months if "put" is exercised	Very high to low, depending on rating	Good to very good	Federal, state, and local: taxable	Semiannual interest payments
Corporate notes and bonds	$1,000 minimum, sometimes higher	1 to 50 years	Very high to low, depending on rating	Good	Federal, state, and local: taxable	Semiannual interest payments
Corporate preferred stocks	$100 minimum or less, depending on par value of the stock	Usually no maturity	Very high to low, depending on rating	Average to below average	State and local: taxable for all investors; federal: for corporate investors only, 85% or 60% exempt	Quarterly dividend payments

Source: Adapted from D. M. Darst, *The Complete Bond Book,* pp. 274–283, © 1975 by McGraw-Hill, Inc. Reprinted with permission.

institutions use the proceeds to make home loans, thereby creating jobs in the building industry.

Certificates of Deposit

Bank issues, certificates of deposit (CDs), and money market certificates offer a high degree of safety. The federal government insures them through the Federal Deposit Insurance Corporation for up to $100,000.

In choosing a bank, the ethical investor should follow the guidelines in Chapter 12. In general, smaller local banks will not have a loan portfolio including loans to foreign governments. Primarily they loan to local businesses and homeowners. Some banks, like South Shore Bank of Chicago, have particularly strong social records.

WHERE TO FIND
VARIABLE INCOME

Apart from money market funds (discussed in Chapter 12), all variable-income vehicles demand significantly more of the income investor's attention than fixed-income vehicles. The investor must monitor the yields, selling issues when necessary to maintain the value of the portfolio. Since virtually all of these vehicles are common stocks, variable yields have the additional advantage of the possibility of significant capital appreciation. In short, they may be worth the greater risk.

For ethical investors seeking high income, common stocks offer a tremendous opportunity. The size of a company's dividend will limit your choice of stocks, but many publicly traded corporations offer big dividends and have the potential to meet your ethical criteria. Not all companies can afford to pay large dividends. Younger, faster-growing companies must retain a significant portion of their earnings to finance research and development, new plants and equipment, and an expanded sales force, among other things. Therefore, the ethical investor seeking high income must look to utilities, regional banks, and more mature large companies.

Utilities

Unlike other companies, utilities receive a monopoly or partial monopoly on electric, gas, water, or telephone service in their area. The state monitors their performance and guarantees them a fair rate of return. This makes them particularly safe investments.

One of the principal advantages of larger companies, and especially utilities, is their long record of dividend payments. An investor can easily check these records in *Moody's* or other services. They show which have paid dividends even in their most difficult years. For example, Hawaiian Electric Company, a holding company, is a favorite among income-seeking ethical investors. Its dividends per share have increased 89% since 1974 from $1.54 to $3. It is currently building geothermal plants and wind turbines in an effort to replace its oil-burning capacity.

Electric. Electric utilities pose some obvious ethical problems relating to the type of fuels they use to generate power. A recent study by Ritchie P. Lowry, publisher of *Good Money*,[2] divided 25 major electric utilities into three groups: those with a substantial dependence on nuclear power, those with a growing dependence on nuclear power, and those with no dependence on nuclear power. Between 1974 and 1982 stock issued by the utilities which relied on nuclear power appreciated 24%. Those with nuclear power coming on line grew at a rate of 52%. However, the nonnuclear group grew 184%. Obviously, nonnuclear utilities make both social and financial sense.

The problems with electric utilities are not limited to those relying on nuclear energy. Another fuel — coal — leads to a multitude of land use and pollution problems, not the least of which is acid rain. Ethical investors often avoid Detroit Edison and the Cleveland Electric Illuminat-

FIGURE 7-5   The Cost of Power Plants

These figures reflect the estimated *average* cost (per installed kilowatt) of electric generating plants that are *in operation today*. General Electric, which provided the estimates, emphasizes that the cost of individual plants may have varied considerably. Also, the cost of building *new* generating capacity in today's economy would be considerably higher for all types of plants. The cost of a new nuclear plant, for example, would fall between $3000 and $4000 per installed kilowatt of capacity.

Gas Turbine	$ 400
Oil	$ 765
Hydro	$1100
Coal	$1150
Nuclear	$1285

Source: Don Best, "Solar Business Review," *Solar Age*, August 1983, p. 55. This article first appeared in the August issue of *Solar Age* © 1983 SolarVision, Inc., Harrisville, NH 03450 USA. All rights reserved. Reprinted and published by permission.

ing Company because of their resistance to air pollution regulation. Hydropower is not trouble-free either. Usually it relies on dams and reservoirs which often flood productive farmland and displace long-time residents. Jim Lowell adds another objection: "I never touch utilities. In order for the shareholder to get anything, the consumer has to get screwed."

Still, the electric utilities offer society a clear benefit which few are willing to forgo. Most ethical investors try to find those electric utilities with the best environmental track records while scrupulously avoiding nuclear utilities. Figure 7-6 contains a list of selected electric utilities and the types of fuel they burn. It also indicates their five-year dividend growth rate.

A company that often receives high marks as a socially responsible investment is Citizens' Utilities, an AAA-rated holding company with interests in electric (nonnuclear), telephone, gas, and water utilities in 20 states. It has a deserved reputation for experimenting with new ideas, like generating electricity from sugar cane waste in Hawaii. Another prime candidate, Southwestern Public Service, boasts state-of-the-art pollution controls on its coal-fired power plants. A third candidate, Idaho Power, serves southern Idaho and a small part of eastern Oregon. Its fuel mix is currently estimated at 63% hydro and 37% coal.

Water. Water utilities also offer investments with big dividends. Among those you should consider: American Water Works Company; California Water Service Company; Connecticut Water Service; Consumers Water Company; Elizabethtown Water Company; Hackensack Water Company; Indianapolis Water Company; and San Jose Water Works. One of my favorites is Southern California Water. Although it supplies a very small part of its service area with electricity purchased from Southern California Edison, a nuclear generator, it is otherwise strictly a water utility. In 1982 Southern California Water sold for $12 a share — 7.2 times earnings — and yielded 12.7% ($1.48) per share. It has raised its dividend in each of the last ten years for a total increase of 48%. However, it also illustrates a problem investors face with utilities. Quite often lists such as Figure 7-6 do not pick up companies' sidelines, like Southern California Water's electric business. Even *Standard & Poor's Stock Guide* does not reflect sidelines. For that reason, the ethical investor must carefully study a utility's annual report before investing.

Telephone. Telephone utilities offer good possibilities. My favorite is Southern New England Telephone, perhaps because I grew up in their territory.

FIGURE 7-6   Some Electric Utilities Without Nuclear Involvement

Company	Fuel Mix %	Dividend	3/12/84 Yield	5-Year Div. Growth Rate 1978–83
Allegheny Power	99C-1H	$2.60	10.00%	8.6%
Black Hills Pwr. & Lt.	99C-1G	1.68	7.80	15.7%
Central Illinois Light	98C-1G-1O	2.14	10.97	5.2%
Central Illinois Pub. Serv.	99C	1.52	10.13	4.8%
Central Louisiana Electric	80G-20C	1.84	10.14	N.A.
Hawaiian Electric	98O	3.12	9.20	6.9%
Idaho Power	65H-35C	3.08	9.00	6.2%
Interstate Power	97C-2G-1O	1.82	10.79	3.9%
Iowa Public Service	100C	2.68	10.67	5.9%
Ipalco Enterprises	99C-1O	2.76	10.03	6.7%
Kansas Power & Light	98C-2G	2.76	9.36	6.6%
Kentucky Utilities	100C	2.36	10.31	3.1%
Louisville Gas & Electric	95C-5H	2.36	9.93	3.4%
Minnesota Power & Light	90C-10H	2.40	9.32	5.5%
Montana Dakota Utilities	99C-1G	2.44	8.48	10.2%
Montana Power	53C-46H-1G	2.80	9.91	6.9%
Nevada Power	95C-5G	2.72	9.84	6.3%
No. Indiana Pub. Service	96C-2O-2G	1.50	10.71	0.0%
Oklahoma Gas & Electric	54G-46C	1.92	9.60	3.7%
Orange & Rockland Utilities	43O-43G-10C	1.92	9.72	5.9%
Potomac Electric	90C-10O	1.94	9.76	5.8%
So. Indiana Gas & Electric	98C-2G	2.48	9.20	10.2%
Southwestern Public Service	52C-47G-1P	1.74	8.80	6.3%
Teco Energy	91C-9O	2.04	8.00	9.1%
Tucson Electric Power	90C-10G	2.60	7.03	10.7%
Utah Power & Light	95C-3H-2G	2.32	10.85	5.7%

C = Coal
G = Gas
H = Hydro
N = Nuclear
O = Oil
P = Purchased

Source: John D. Rooney, Jr., Moseley, Hallgarten, Estabrook & Weeden, Inc., copyright © 1983, used by permission.

A better reason is that they have raised their dividends in eight of the last ten years and increased them from $2.63 in 1972 to $4.56 in 1982. That's a jump of 73.38%. Some other solid telephone utilities are AllTel; North-West Telephone; Rochester Telephone; Telephone & Data Systems; and United Telecommunications. There should be more as a result of AT&T's break-up — both "Baby Bells" and new competitors.

Regional Banks

Regional banks are smaller banks serving a limited region, not ones with loans all over the country. You can expect that on the whole they will concentrate on loans to homeowners and local businesses.

Smaller banks' stocks offer the income-seeking investor high dividends, although not as high as those of the electric utilities. Also, their record for raising dividends is good. Among the regional banks' stocks, one leading ethical money manager gives high marks to First Penn Corp., Citi-South Georgia, Ameritrust, and Tri-State. Another likes the State Street Bank of Boston. First Virginia Bank often appears on socially responsible buy lists.

By contrast, the money center banks, like New York's Citicorp or San Francisco's Bank of America are really national and international operations. Their international loan portfolios are heavily weighted toward such countries as Poland, South Africa, Brazil, and Argentina.

Beware: deregulation and the competition it brought to banking have led some smaller banks into risky ventures. Oklahoma's Penn Square Bank and Tennessee's United American Bank come to mind. The Federal Deposit Insurance Corporation (FDIC) handled 48 bank failures in 1983 — the highest number since 1941. It projects a larger number for 1984.[3] The FDIC (for banks) and the Federal Home Loan Bank Board (for savings and loans) publish lists of banks with high percentages of nonperforming loans. These tabulations — they don't list individual loans — may be valuable if you're considering a bank whose performance you can't follow easily in your daily reading.

Still, the ethical investor will find many opportunities among regional and smaller banks. The guidelines for locating a bank in Chapter 12 will help you identify the good small ones.

Blue Chips

While utilities and regional banks are the best place for the income-seeking ethical investor to look, the blue chips are next in line. These are successful, mature companies like Minnesota Mining & Manufacturing (3M) and Merck. Because of their maturity and success, they do not need to retain earnings to the degree a less mature company does, so they can pay out a good portion of their profits in the form of dividends.

Blue chip companies participate in virtually every sector of American business. They also offer the benefit of diversification. These stocks meet many investors' ethical criteria and often pay high dividends. But beware. Dividends can be cut. In 1982, for instance, AMAX, Inc. (mining) cut its dividend from $2.40 to $.80. High dividends may reveal coming cuts. If a company's dividend approaches its earnings per share, the dividend coverage may be in danger. For example, Avon Products (beauty care) in 1982 earned $2.75 per share and paid $2.50. In 1983 the numbers were $2.85 and $2. Its average payout was 81%.

Many shrewd investors keep an eye on blue chips in a down market and buy them whenever a strong company's stock falls to where the dividend is effectively greater than 9%. For instance, F. W. Woolworth, a consistent dividend payer since 1912, hit many people's buy lists in July 1982 when it fell to $18 a share and paid a dividend of $1.80 for a 10% yield. Just three years earlier the stock had sold for $32, paid a $1.60 dividend, and yielded 5%.

For the investor primarily concerned with work-place issues rather than defense or environmental issues, the large international oil companies consistently offer high dividends. Exxon (considered one of the firms where blacks are most likely to succeed) dropped to $27 a share in 1982 while paying $3 a share for an 11% yield. An oil company often singled out as

FIGURE 7-7   Industries That Create the Most Hazardous Waste

	Volume of waste (millions of metric tons)[a]	% of total waste produced
Organic chemicals, pesticides, explosives	11.73	34%
Primary metals, smelting, refining	8.97	26
Electroplating	4.14	12
Inorganic chemicals	3.97	11.5
Textiles, dyeing, finishing	1.90	5.5
Petroleum refining	1.73	5
Rubber, plastics	1.03	3
Other	1.03	3

a. Figures are for 1977.

Source: Council on Environmental Quality as quoted in the New York Times, March 13, 1983, p. F1. Copyright © 1983 by the New York Times Company. Reprinted by permission.

having a strong commitment to pollution control is Arco (Atlantic Rich-field Company). Early on, Arco supported diverting highway trust funds for mass transit. From 1973 to 1982 their dividends jumped nearly 400% from $.50 to $2.40.

The greater security of investments in mature corporations comes from their financial stability, their consistently high dividend performance, their high public profile, and their more stable stock market action. They usually have a stable base to help them weather economic storms. Notable excep-tions like Chrysler and International Harvester sometimes give blue chips a bad name. But many alert investors saw their problems coming well ahead of time.

Cyclicals

This term is used to describe companies that pass through regular boom-bust-boom cycles. They tend to be companies dealing in natural resources, commodities, large consumer durables (i.e., refrigerators), housing, or transportation. Companies such as Asamera (precious metals), Chrysler, and Delta Air Lines are typical cyclicals. In this category the Pax World Fund favors Burlington Northern, Inc., a railroad company.

As with the blue chips, the secret to success with cyclicals lies in hitting their price lows. By buying when they are down, the ethical investor has a chance for both a large dividend and a capital gain as the company moves back into profitability. Watch cyclicals closely. You should sell when their dividends fall to between 4.5% and 5% of their current price. At that point the stock has appreciated considerably, and soon the company will enter the "bust" stage.

Eight Rules for Income Seekers

By way of a summary, here are my eight do's and don'ts for income seekers.

1. Do set a minimum yield you will buy. On bonds use a minimum current yield. On stocks, it's O.K. to use a different minimum yield than the one for bonds.
2. Do set a minimum quality you will buy.
3. Do check a stock's ten-year dividend record before buying.
4. Do review your portfolio three or four times a year, taking capital gains, reinvesting in higher yielding, and selling off dogs.

5. Don't be afraid to be completely out of the market. In 1981–82 many people wisely kept their assets primarily in money funds while they waited to see what would come of Reaganomics.
6. Don't let new ideas scare you. But if someone invents a better mouse trap, ask some mice before you buy.
7. Do ask yourself every time you invest, "How easily can I get my money out? Is that easily enough for me?"
8. Don't break your rules once you make them.

8 MUTUAL FUNDS

NOT EVERY ETHICAL INVESTOR should buy stocks and bonds. Among those who shouldn't are parents who have $1000 to start an education fund for their child; persons whose only assets are $2000 IRA accounts; and investors who have neither the time nor the interest to monitor a portfolio. Mutual funds are ideal for these investors. Steven Moody at U.S. Trust Co. in Boston says, "The small investor really should consider mutual funds. Many of the investors in the Calvert Fund [for Social Investment, an ethical mutual fund advised by U.S. Trust] are smaller investors who would be at a distinct disadvantage trying to invest for themselves. A mutual fund gives them diversification and professional management."

I cannot attempt in one chapter to cover the full range of mutual funds. Instead, after describing what mutual funds are, I will focus on those that operate along some sort of ethical guidelines. The Dreyfus Third Century and the Pax World Fund are the best known of these, while the Calvert Fund for Social Investment and Working Assets are exciting new entries in the field.

WHAT IS A MUTUAL FUND?

A mutual fund pools its shareholders' resources under professional management for a specific purpose. The fund managers define the purpose when they start the fund and describe it in the fund's prospectus. The purpose may be nebulous, like providing high income. Or it may be as specific as investing in companies returning from the brink of bankruptcy or in particular government securities.

Look for a fund with an investment objective similar to your own. Since each fund must register with the SEC a statement of its goals and a definition of what it intends to buy, the investor can be certain that the fund will remain committed to its ends. For example, Pax World Fund characterizes its objective as investing in companies that are not defense related. No matter how great an opportunity Grumman may present, this leading manufacturer of fighter planes will not qualify for Pax. A mutual fund cannot change its investment objective or any other major policy without the consent of its shareholders.

Everything you need to know about a mutual fund is listed in its prospectus. By law, you must receive a copy before you invest. Read it closely. It's the best consumer protection you have.

Types of Mutual Funds

Open-End and Closed-End Funds. An *open-end* mutual fund can issue an unlimited number of shares. The price is based on the *net asset value* (NAV) per share. NAV is the total value of the fund's portfolio divided by the number of shares outstanding, minus a management fee. The NAV changes daily as the market value of the portfolio and the total assets in the fund fluctuate. When people buy into the fund, it creates new shares and uses their money to buy more securities meeting its guidelines. The fund will also *redeem* shares, allowing investors to withdraw their money, at any time.

A *closed-end* mutual fund has a fixed number of shares outstanding. Closed-end funds offer their shares for a limited time and then "close" the portfolio, allowing no more money to be invested. Once the fund closes, the only source of shares is another investor. Closed-end funds trade using the same auction system as stocks. They usually sell at a substantial discount to net asset value. As of this writing, no closed-end mutual funds invest along socially responsible guidelines.

Load and No-Load Funds. Open-end mutual funds are divided into two categories, depending on whether a share purchaser pays a sales charge (*load*). Ethical funds fall into both categories.

FIGURE 8-1   Employer-Sponsored Child Care Programs: A Selected List of
Companies

Cardiac Pacemaker, Inc., St. Paul, MN	Maui Pineapple Company, Kahului, HI
Connecticut General Life Insurance Co., Bloomfield, CT (CIGNA Corp.)	Merck & Company, Rahway, NJ
	Missouri Pacific Railroad, St. Louis, MO
Corning Glass, Corning, NY	National Semiconductor, Santa Clara, CA
Disney World, Lake Buena Vista, FL	Polaroid Corp., Cambridge, MA
Hartford Steam Boiler, Hartford, CT	Stride-Rite, Boston, MA
Intermedics, Freeport, TX	Wang Laboratories, Lowell, MA

Source: U.S. Department of Labor, Employers and Child Care: Establishing Services Through the Workplace (1982).

When you see a newspaper quoting an asking price higher than the bid price, you know that a load is built in. The bid price, or what you could sell your shares for, is the net asset value per share. The asking price is the NAV plus the load. Brokers sell traditional load funds, such as Merrill Lynch's funds, with about an 8½% commission tacked onto the NAV. In theory, the broker advises you on which fund to select and is therefore due a commission.

Many funds sell their shares directly to the public without a broker's intervention. Most of them do not charge a load and therefore are called no-load funds. You buy their shares at the NAV.

The Advantages of Mutual Funds

Most people say they invest in mutual funds because they involve less risk than individual stocks or bonds. I agree.

Professional Portfolio Management.   Professional money managers run mutual funds. These people have track records of managing money successfully. Their previous day's performance is listed in most newspapers. But the best performance indicator is not what happened yesterday but over the long haul. You should study performance in both bull and bear markets. After all, anybody can look good in a red-hot market. Two handy places to start this research are *Forbes's* annual mutual fund assessment in its August issue and *Barron's* quarterly, *Barron's*/Lipper Gauge. A variety of services also monitor the funds.

Diversification. Small investors always have trouble diversifying and balancing their portfolios. If all their eggs are in one basket, the chances of having them scrambled increase dramatically. No matter how carefully small investors do their research, they remain vulnerable to factors no one can anticipate, such as the hotel fire that killed most of Arrow Electronics' top management a few years ago.

Mutual fund managers must view each purchase as part of a portfolio. This means balancing risks and opportunities, and diversifying. By law, no more than 5% of a fund portfolio can be invested in one company, and no more than 25% can be in companies in the same industry. In September 1982, for instance, the Dreyfus Third Century Fund held 64 different investments in 24 industry groups.

Research Capacity. The research effort a mutual fund can put into each purchase is also far beyond the capabilities of most individuals. Many portfolio managers have analysts who prepare private reports on industries and specific companies. Their size gives them the clout to get their questions answered. Two socially responsible funds, Pax and Dreyfus Third Century, submit lengthy questionnaires to the management of any corporation in which they are considering investing, and they get responses.

The Disadvantages of Mutual Funds

Mutual funds are investment products sold at a profit to investors. There is no guarantee that any fund will meet its investment objective, perform as it has in the past, or keep you from losing money. Funds as a group have seen very good and very bad years. There are other drawbacks to consider.

FIGURE 8-2   Top Ten Sponsors of Violence on TV

Prudential	Nissan Motors
I. C. Industries	Coleco Industries
Pabst Brewing Co.	Mattel, Inc.
Bic Pen Corp.	Beecham
Mazda Motors of America	Denny's, Inc.

Source: Report of the Spring 1983 Television Monitoring Program of the Coalition for Better Television, Prime-Time Viewing, January 30–June 15, 1983. Reprinted by permission.

Overdiversification. If a fund buys stocks across a broad range of industries, investors find it difficult to sort out the news that affects their investment. If housing starts are up, is that good? If the price of natural gas drops, will the value of their holdings fall? Some funds have 60 stocks in their portfolios; that's a lot of diversification. Other funds have as many as seven hundred. That's more than anyone needs. This problem becomes acute where socially responsible funds are involved, because these funds buy companies, not industries.

The Load Factor. A load virtually guarantees that your price will be considerably higher than it would be if you were to buy the same dollar values of stocks, including the broker's commission on your purchases. Loads run about 8½% and are paid off the top when you buy fund shares. Brokerage commissions usually range between 1½% and 2½%, and are paid when you buy and when you sell. A $1000 investment in an 8½% load fund leaves only $915 to invest after the sales charge. The fund must go up 8½% before you break even.

THE ETHICAL MUTUAL FUNDS

All of the ethical mutual funds are open-end funds with broad diversification by company rather than by industry. They differ widely in their philosophies.

Calvert Social Investment Fund

Established in October 1982, the Calvert Social Investment Fund (CSIF) is part of the Calvert Group of funds. It is a no-load open-end fund. CSIF offers investors a choice of two portfolios: the Money Market Portfolio (discussed in Chapter 12) and the Managed Growth Portfolio. The Managed Growth Portfolio requires a $1000 minimum initial investment.

Overall, says Calvert's D. Wayne Silby, the fund "seeks to provide an economic return to its investors and an economic and social return to society that will contribute to the quality of life for all."[1] In order to implement its goals, the fund applies four social criteria to any company. It must:

1. Deliver safe products and services in ways that sustain the natural environment.

2. Manage itself with participation throughout the organization in defining and achieving objectives.
3. Negotiate fairly with its workers and provide opportunities for women, the disadvantaged, and others for whom equal opportunities have often been denied.
4. Foster awareness of a commitment to human goals, such as creativity, productivity, self-respect, and responsibility.

CSIF's subadviser is the United States Trust Company of Boston, which I've mentioned several times. It screens prospective investments for both their financial and their social performance under the fund's criteria. CSIF Managed Growth has total assets of more than $6.1 million.[2]

Dreyfus Third Century Fund

The Dreyfus Third Century Fund initially offered its shares to the public in March 1972. A no-load, open-end mutual fund, Third Century normally invests in common stocks or securities convertible into common stocks. The fund emphasizes capital growth. A unique member of the Dreyfus Group of mutual funds, Third Century is the largest of ethical funds, with $136.3 million in assets on September 30, 1983.[3] Its minimum initial investment is $2500. Between 1974 and 1982 an investment in Dreyfus Third Century would have returned 373%, as compared with only 110% if an investor had invested in the Dow Jones Industrial index. And in 1983 the fund was up 20.1%. This is an impressive performance for any fund, ethical or not.

Third Century grew out of the environmental movement. It evaluates companies' performance in the areas of environmental protection and improvement, proper use of natural resources, occupational health and safety standards, consumer protection (including product purity), and equal opportunity employment. The fund evaluates its corporate questionnaires, Occupational Safety and Health Administration (OSHA) records, and other public records. It compiles statistics on equal employment opportunity, occupational health, product safety, and environmental protection performance, and then ranks companies against their competitors. Using this ranking, Dreyfus creates a group of eligible companies in each industry group. Finally, Dreyfus looks at the eligible companies' balance sheets before putting them on its buy list.

Third Century's goal is investment to encourage social progress and change. Because it compares companies' policies within their industry group and not on an absolute scale, Third Century's standards are the most lenient of all ethical mutual funds. The fund does not exclude defense contractors or liquor producers. Jeffrey F. Friedman, Third Century's president, recently gave the *Wall Street Journal* a concise statement of its philosophy: "We found that when we went to foundations, they would ask, 'Do your companies have a South African connection?' That's a bizarre definition of social responsibility when you look at the problems of the world. Why South Africa and not the Soviet Union or Iran?" Third Century has a pragmatic approach which appeals to a great many investors, though it also has strong critics. The same article quoted Timothy Smith, executive director of the Interfaith Center on Corporate Responsibility, as describing Dreyfus's social criteria as "big enough to drive a nuclear weapon through."[4]

New Alternatives Fund

While not founded as an ethical fund, this energy-oriented fund is attractive to some ethical investors. The prospectus describes it as open-ended with an emphasis on long-term capital gains on equities issued by companies with interests in solar and alternative energy development. Within these guidelines, which could encompass many highly speculative vehicles, the fund's approach is conservative, leaning toward more established companies. At least 80% of the companies in which the fund has invested are listed on the American or New York Stock Exchanges. The fund's interpretation of "alternative energy" is broad. It includes coal. New Alternatives has launched an unwritten policy of screening companies on ethical standards and is beginning to take its place among ethical funds.

New Alternatives charges a 6% load, and its minimum initial investment is $2650.[5] New Alternatives opened its doors in September 1982 and reported net assets of $200,000 as of September 30, 1983.

Pax World Fund

Pax World Fund is a no-load, open-end diversified fund. According to its prospectus Pax endeavors "through its investment objectives to make a contribution to world peace through investment in companies producing

FIGURE 8-3   Agent Orange Defendants

Defendants in a federal class-action law suit filed by Vietnam veterans.

Dow Chemical Co.	Thompson Chemical Corp.
Monsanto Co.	Hercules, Inc.
Diamond Shamrock Corp.	T. H. Agriculture and Nutrition Co.
Uniroyal, Inc.	

Source: R. Blumenthal, "Test Cases Chosen in Herbicide Trial," the *New York Times,* December 12, 1983, p. B28.

life-supportive goods and services." It is committed to investing in "nonwar-related industries, firms with fair employment practices, companies exercising pollution control, and some international development." Pax does not invest in liquor, tobacco, or gambling.

In 1971 a group of Methodist clergy discovered that their church regularly received letters from individuals asking how to invest in companies not manufacturing weaponry. After finding no organization that specialized in this type of investment, the ministers went to Wall Street firms asking for assistance in setting up a fund. The firms said it could not be done. They then formed Pax, which proved the experts wrong. Pax was the first fund to adopt a broad range of issues for its screens. It pioneered much of the territory ethical investors explore today. It demonstrated that defense companies are not a necessary part of a successful investment portfolio.

Luther E. Tyson, president of Pax World Fund, told me that whenever a violation of Pax's social criteria obligates it to sell its shares in a corporation, he contacts management and tells it of Pax's decision and the reasons behind it.

"Whenever you say 'social responsibility,'" he continued, "there's a question in institutions' minds as to whether that means less income." However, Pax's primary investment objective is to provide income, which may explain why 22½% of Pax's shareholders bought its shares for their IRA accounts. The fund now manages approximately $10.8 million.

Between 1975 and 1980, a bad period for both the economy and mutual funds, Pax's net asset value per share rose approximately 61%. In 1983 Pax provided its investors with a total return (capital gains plus income) of 22.9%. Its minimum initial investment is $250.

FIGURE 8-4   Top 50 Publicly Traded Research, Development, Test, and Evaluation
Contractors for the Department of Defense (1982)

1. Rockwell International Corp.
2. Boeing Co.
3. Martin Marietta Corp.
4. McDonnell Douglas Corp.
5. TRW, Inc.
6. General Electric Co.
7. General Dynamics Corp.
8. Lockheed Corp.
9. Westinghouse Electric Corp.
10. Honeywell, Inc.
11. Northrop Corp.
12. International Business Machines Co.
13. Raytheon Co.
14. United Technologies Corp.
15. Sperry Corp.
16. Vought Corp., subsidiary of LTV Corp.
17. Avco Corp.
18. Aerojet General Corp., subsidiary of General Tire & Rubber Co.
19. GTE Products Corp.
20. RCA Corp.
21. Morton Thiokol Corp.
22. International Telephone & Telegraph Corp.
23. Grumman Aerospace Corp., subsidiary of Grumman Corp.
24. Texas Instruments, Inc.
25. Textron, Inc.
26. Harris Corp.
27. Litton Systems, Inc.
28. Singer Co.
29. Hercules, Inc.
30. Science Applications Inc., subsidiary of Science Applications International Corp.
31. Calspan Corp., subsidiary of Arvin Industries, Inc.
32. Ford Aerospace and Communications, subsidiary of Ford Motor Co.
33. Teledyne Industries, Inc.
34. Motorola, Inc.
35. FMC Corp.
36. Global Associates, subsidiary of Atlas Corp.
37. BDM Corp.
38. Western Electric Co., Inc., subsidiary of American Telephone & Telegraph Co.
39. Computer Sciences Corp.
40. Hazeltine Corp.
41. Eaton Corp.
42. Emerson Electric Co.
43. Magnavox Government & Industrial Electronics Co., subsidiary of North American Philips Corp.
44. R & D Associates, subsidiary of Logicon, Inc.
45. General Motors Corp.
46. Bendix Corp.
47. AAI Corp., subsidiary of United Industrial Corp.
48. Kentron International, Inc.
49. E-Systems, Inc.
50. Tracor, Inc.

Source: Adapted with permission from information supplied by N.A.R.M.I.C., a research program of the American Friends Service Committee, 1501 Cherry St., Philadelphia, PA 19102.

The Pioneer Fund

Founded in 1928, the Pioneer Fund is the oldest mutual group managing money along ethical guidelines. The Pioneer group of mutual funds includes Pioneer, Pioneer II, and Pioneer Three. It has received very little credit for its efforts. Pioneer has shunned investments in alcohol, tobacco, and, in two of its three funds, drugs. The only drug stock, Syntex, is in Pioneer. Here is an example of the avoidance approach which has worked for years. Because of its investment policy Pioneer has managed funds for a number of church organizations. However, Pioneer does not commit itself to broadly defined social criteria. In fact, its prospectuses don't mention the criteria at all. Still, the fact of its long-standing commitment earns it a special place among ethical funds.

Small investors are pleased by Pioneer's low ($25) minimum initial investment. However, Pioneer does charge an 8.5% load. Pioneer Three has been in operation less than a year. Pioneer, as of December 31, 1983, would have returned $20,643 on a $10,000 investment made five years earlier. In 1983 it was up 23.7%. Pioneer II would have returned $26,886 on a similar investment over the same period and was up 29.7% in 1983.

Renaissance Asset Management

Now in registration with the Securities Exchange Commission, the Renaissance Fund will be available to the investing public in early 1985. President and founder is Jerome L. Dodson, formerly president of Working Assets Money Fund. The Renaissance Fund is not a social responsibility fund in the normal sense of the term.

The Fund will seek high performance through both "contrarian" and "renaissance" aspects. The contrarian strategy involves buying good stocks when they are out of favor. The renaissance strategy involves selecting an out-of-favor stock only when the company is financially strong and exhibits most of five "renaissance" factors: high-quality products and services; a marketing-oriented management; innovative and responsive to change; treats its employees well; and sensitive to the communities where it operates. The Renaissance Fund uses these criteria because it feels that a company with these characteristics will have an enlightened and progressive management, which is a good indicator of business success.

For ethical investors who do not have the time to manage their own portfolios, mutual funds are ideal. For parents or grandparents who wish to start investing on a child's behalf, few vehicles could be more appropriate than a mutual fund to which they can contribute throughout the years. And mutual funds make ideal vehicles for individual retirement accounts (IRAs) and other retirement savings. Thus the ethical mutual funds in the 1980s offer good investment opportunities and every prospect for continued health.

9 TAX-ADVANTAGED INVESTMENTS

M
ANY ETHICAL INVESTORS are concerned about the ultimate use of their tax dollars. If you share these concerns you should know about ways to find investments with tax benefits. The government offers tax benefits for a particular type of investment when it wants to encourage one of three things:

1. Private investment in public projects. Without private financing, public construction projects such as sewers, nuclear power plants, schools, or housing for the elderly would require immediate allocations of tax monies.
2. Savings. Societal safety nets always have more holes than netting. Savings also produce economic growth by making money available for loans to businesses.
3. Private investment in private enterprise. The government might want to channel private investment into certain areas, like energy exploration or heavy equipment manufacturing, to stimulate the economy.

When you benefit from a tax-advantaged investment, you are doing nothing more than what the government wants you to do. But beware: some government projects the government encourages may pose insurmountable ethical problems.

Only our legislators' imaginations limit the range of tax benefits. In this chapter and the next, I'll discuss the most common forms and techniques. This chapter deals primarily with the means governments have chosen to encourage investment in public projects and to stimulate savings. It also describes a miscellany of investment-related tax advantages which don't fall neatly into any single category.

TAX-FREE INVESTMENTS

Tax-free investments, like municipal bonds, are investments offering income (interest or dividends) that is not taxed. Some government obligations are partially tax free. Interest on U.S. Treasury obligations, for example, is not taxed by the states but is by the federal government. By buying tax-free investments ethical investors can decide for themselves how to spend money that would otherwise go to pay taxes. But keep in mind that the tax-free aspect applies only to the interest. You pay capital gains taxes on any profit if you sell.

Safety-oriented ethical investors like the fact that money placed in tax-free investments can grow quite fast, assuming reinvestment of the interest in tax-free vehicles. Figure 9-1 shows two examples. In one column is the return on a Massachusetts 10% bond rated A-1 due in 1999. In the other is the return on an Illinois 9% bond rated AAA due in 1997.

FIGURE 9-1   Return on State-Issued Bonds Assuming Reinvestment of Interest Earned on $10,000 Face Value

	Return on Massachusetts 10% bond	Return on Illinois 9% bond
1984	$1,000.00	$900.00
1985	1,100.00	981.00
1986	1,210.00	1,069.29
1987	1,331.00	1,165.53
1988	1,464.10	1,270.42
1989	1,610.51	1,384.76
1990	1,771.00	1,509.39
1991	1,948.10	1,645.24
1992	2,142.91	1,793.31
1993	2,357.20	1,954.70
1994	2,592.92	2,130.63
1995	2,852.21	2,322.38
1996	3,137.43	2,531.40
1997	3,451.17	2,759.22
1998	3,796.30	$23,417.27
1999	4,175.92	
	$35,940.77	

Municipal Bonds

Municipal bonds include all debt issued by states, countries, municipalities, or quasigovernmental authorities. The issuer may back its bonds either by its taxing power or by the revenue generated from a particular activity. For example, Seattle issues bonds to fund its transit system. The revenues it generates pay off the bonds.

The Internal Revenue Code exempts interest on municipal bonds from federal taxation. But it is exempt from state taxation only in the state in which the bond was issued. The Montgomery, Alabama, Medical Clinic Board issues bonds to help meet its needs for capital. The federal government does not tax the interest these bonds pay, nor does Alabama. If the buyer lived in any other state, the interest received would be subject to its income tax. The only exceptions to this rule are bonds issued by Puerto Rico and the American Virgin Islands, whose interest is exempt from all state taxation.

Who Should Buy Munis? Issuers of tax-free bonds borrow at a lower rate than corporate issuers. For that reason, they make sense only for those whose total after-tax income is higher in municipals than in corporates. Figure 9-2 will help you decide whether municipals are right for you. Municipal bonds have a distinct disadvantage for smaller investors. They

FIGURE 9-2   Taxable Income Versus Tax-Free Income Charts

Use this chart to determine whether, given the prevailing rate of interest on municipal bonds in your state, they will yield more than taxable issues. If, for example, you are in the 25% bracket and munis in your state yield 6%, an 8% taxable bond would provide the same yield.

Tax bracket	Muni Interest								
	5.5%	6%	6.5%	7%	7.5%	8%	8.5%	9%	10%
25%	7.3%	8.0%	8.7%	9.3%	10.0%	10.7%	11.3%	12.0%	13.3%
30%	7.9	8.6	9.3	10.0	10.7	11.4	12.1	12.9	14.3
35%	8.5	9.2	10.0	10.8	11.5	12.3	13.1	13.9	15.4
40%	9.2	10.0	10.8	11.7	12.5	13.3	14.2	15.0	16.7
45%	10.0	10.9	11.8	12.7	13.6	14.6	15.5	16.4	18.2
50%	11.0	12.0	13.0	14.0	15.0	16.0	17.0	18.0	20.0

Formula

$$\frac{\text{Municipal bond yield}}{100\% - \%\text{ tax bracket}} = \text{taxable security's yield for the same return}$$

usually trade in lots of five. Each certificate has a $5000 face value, and you cannot purchase $1000 or $2000 worth of most issues. But for the ethical investor in a higher tax bracket, their advantages are great.

Municipal Bond Funds and Unit Trusts. Municipal bond funds and unit trusts give investors the tax advantages of municipal bonds. However, at this writing, none is run on ethical guidelines. In structure, muni bond funds and unit trusts resemble a mutual fund, including the fact that they are under continuous professional management or supervision. However, they are different in that the sponsors generally assemble a set portfolio before they offer a fixed number of units to the public. Ethical investors can examine the portfolio before they invest.

Municipal bond funds and unit trusts offer diversified portfolios in terms of issuers, purposes, maturity, and sometimes geographical location. Many funds purchase only munis issued in a particular state, such as New York (the Empire State Fund) or California (the California Insured Municipals Income Trust). If you reside in a state which has such a fund, the income is exempt from both state and federal taxes. Income from other bond funds, like the Kemper Tax Exempt Insured Income Trust, is not exempt from state taxation beyond the small percentage of the portfolio made up of bonds from your state.

These vehicles ordinarily trade in units of $1000. Although they are closed-end funds, units trade at net asset value. Shares are liquid and trade as easily as municipal bonds. An investor can choose whether to receive income monthly or semiannually or have it reinvested.

U.S. Obligations

The interest on U.S. Treasury and most U.S. agency obligations issues is not subject to state income taxes, although it is taxed by the federal government. Thus they may provide a slight tax advantage. However, as noted earlier, many ethical investors choose to avoid U.S. Treasury obligations because it is impossible to determine where the proceeds go.

Flower bonds are U.S. government obligations which investors may purchase at prices substantially below their face or maturity value. A few of these deep discount bonds may be used at face value in payment of estate taxes. However, because the laws governing flower bonds have undergone some recent changes, your financial adviser or lawyer should study the situation carefully before you make a purchase. For the ethical

investor, flower bonds pose the same problem as any general obligation of
the U.S. government.

LONG- AND SHORT-TERM
CAPITAL GAINS

The Internal Revenue Code treats short- and long-term capital gains
differently. As of this writing, you realize a *short-term capital gain* when you
hold an asset for a year or less and sell it for a profit. However, Congress
was considering reducing the holding period from one year to six months.
The government taxes your profit on short-term gains as if it were ordinary
income (e.g., salary). If you sell an asset — your house or a security —
for a gain at least a year and a day after you purchased it, you realize a
long-term capital gain. Long-term gains are taxed much more favorably than
short-term gains.

Assume in 1981 you bought a hundred shares of Pic & Save (close-
out merchandise stores) at $15 per share. In 1983 you sold them at $45
per share. Your gross long-term capital gain is $3000. Your net gain is what
you sold the asset for less what you paid for it and the broker's fees on
both the purchase and the sale. We'll assume broker's fees of 1½% on
both ends.

$$(\$1500 \times .015) + (\$4500 \times .015) = \$90 \text{ total commissions}$$
$$\$4500 - (\$1500 + \$90) = \$2910 \text{ net capital gain.}$$

Now to determine the amount taxed, multiply your net gain times 40%:

$$\$2910 \times .40 = \$1164 \text{ capital gains taxed}$$

You add that figure (40% of your net capital gain) to your ordinary income
and pay taxes on the total. Thus, if you are in the maximum federal tax
bracket (50%), your long-term capital gains cannot be taxed at more than
20% (.4 × .5 = .20). In this case your taxes would be

$$\$1164 \times .50 = \$582 \text{ taxes}$$

Your after-tax net capital gain would be

$$\$2910 - \$582 = \$2328 \text{ after-tax net}$$

Now let's apply these figures to someone in the 35% bracket:

$$\$1164 \times .35 = \$407.40 \text{ tax on gain}$$
$$\$2910 - \$407.40 = \$2502.60 \text{ after-tax net}$$

For people with high current income, investing money in stocks that should appreciate significantly makes considerable sense when the long-term capital gains tax benefits are considered.

By giving favored treatment to long-term capital gains, the government encourages investment, not speculation. This appeals to ethical investors who generally realize that speculation runs counter to the concept of ethical investing. They take advantage of the long-term capital gains provisions whether or not they need a tax break. But don't fall into the trap of letting tax considerations override investment decisions. Some investors foolishly develop a phobia about taking capital gains. Others hang on to an asset hoping to hold it just long enough to qualify for long-term capital gains, regardless of the economic sense it makes.

The ethical investor should never forget that the moment to sell sometimes comes before a year and a day pass. Long-term capital gains status may not be worth passing up a favorable selling price, especially if what you are holding has run up very quickly. A World-War II refugee and self-made millionaire once told me, "I never worry about long-term versus short-term. Let me make a million dollars. I'll give Uncle Sam half of it — he made me rich."

Treatment of Dividends

The Internal Revenue Code grants investors favorable treatment of taxable dividend income. As of this writing, individuals may exclude the first $100 of taxable dividends from the income they report. Husbands and wives filing jointly may each exclude up to $200 on their joint return so long as each received $100 in taxable dividends during the year. For the ethical investor this is yet another advantage to owning carefully selected common stocks. Two hundred dollars may seem insignificant, but it means you can buy 100 shares of Quaker Oats, which pays approximately $2 per share per year, and incur no tax liabilities until you sell the stock.

On occasion the Internal Revenue Code classifies dividends as a return of capital. Such dividends either partially or entirely escape taxation. Tax-favored dividends are not a reason to buy a particular stock. For one thing, it is difficult to determine what the tax treatment will be ahead of time. If a tax-favored dividend comes along, treat it as a "freebie." Figure 9-3 is a partial list of the companies whose dividends received this treatment in 1982. I eliminated nuclear utilities and weapons manufacturers, two groups often qualifying for this treatment. For instance, Grumman Corp. (military

FIGURE 9-3   Selected Utilities with Return of Capital Dividends

---

Some portion of the dividends paid by the following companies was nontaxable in 1982.

Arizona Public Service	Niagara Mohawk Power
Bangor-Hydro Electric Co.	Northern Indiana Public Service
El Paso Co.	Pacific Power & Light
Kansas Gas & Electric	Union Electric Co.

---

planes) paid $1.45 in 1982. Those who received the dividend paid no tax on it.

Utilities' Dividend Reinvestment Plans

The Economic Recovery Tax Act of 1981 exempts from taxable income up to $750 of some utilities' dividends on an individual return and up to $1500 on a joint return, provided that the shareholders receive those dividends in the form of stock before January 1, 1986. Whether you seek income or growth, this provision can provide you a real benefit. Here's how it works. Suppose you owned 200 shares of Kentucky Utilities, a coal-based, nonnuclear electric utility that has not missed a dividend since 1939. It paid $2.20 per share in 1982. If you had asked the company to reinvest your 1982 dividends ($440), you'd have received 24.3681 shares on account with the utility. The stock dividends would compound tax free until December 31, 1985, when the program ends.

To take advantage of the dividend reinvestment plans, invest in a utility that meets your ethical and financial criteria and that has a dividend reinvestment plan approved by the IRS. Virtually all electric utilities have qualified plans. Notable exceptions include General Public Utilities (Three Mile Island), which has suspended all dividends, and Pennsylvania Power & Light, which chose not to qualify its plan because for the near term most of its dividends will be nontaxable as a return of capital. Once you buy into a qualifying utility, make sure you register the shares in your name. *Street name stock* (stock held for you in your brokerage firm's name) will not qualify. Then notify the company that you wish to participate in its dividend reinvestment program.

Almost all dividend reinvestment plans operate on a commission-free basis, and many offer discounts of from 3% to 5% off the current market price. Under this plan, the stock received purchased through a reinvest-

FIGURE 9-4   Some Corporate Participants in Ohio's 1983 Tax Limitation Referenda

In 1983 Ohio Citizens to Stop Excessive Taxation placed two propositions on the ballot: one to repeal a 90% increase in the state income tax enacted that year and the other to require a three-fifths majority of the state legislature to enact future increases. Both issues failed. The following publicly traded corporations contributed $10,000 or more.

For Tax Limit Measures
(Total Contributions: $728,000)

Rubbermaid, Inc. ($10,000)
Superior Savings Association (52,000)

The Timken Co. (10,000)
Worthington Industries (15,000)

Against Tax Limit Measures
(Total Contributions: $2,651,000)

Ashland Oil, Inc. ($10,000)
Anchor Hocking Corp. (22,000)
Armco, Inc. (20,000)
Brown & Williamson Tobacco Co. (15,000)
Cincinnati Gas & Electric Co. (13,200)
Cleveland Electric Illuminating Co. (18,500)
Columbia Gas Transmission Co. (25,000)
Columbus & Southern Ohio Electric Co. (12,100)
Conoco, Inc. (20,000)
CSX Corp. (25,000)
Dayton Power & Light (20,000)
First National Supermarkets (10,000)
General Mills, Inc. (10,000)

Health Care and Retirement Corp. of America (25,000)
E. F. Hutton Co. (10,000)
Kroger Co. (50,000)
McDonald & Co. (brokerage) (15,000)
Merrill, Lynch, Pierce, Fenner & Smith (10,000)
Norfolk Southern Co. (25,000)
Ohio Edison Co. (22,000)
Ohio Power Co. (15,000)
Philip Morris (10,000)
R. J. Reynolds Industries (22,000)
Sears, Roebuck & Co. (30,000)
Standard Oil Co. (Ohio) (50,000)
United States Steel Corp. (25,000)

Data courtesy of Carl Olson, Chairman, Stockholders Against the Government Burden, P.O. Box 7273, Alexandria, VA 22307.

ment program has a *zero cost basis*. That means when you sell the stock, it will be treated as if you had paid nothing for it. You will pay a capital gains tax on the shares' sale price less the commission on the sale. The ordinary rules on capital gains holding periods apply to stock dividends.

SOME TECHNIQUES FOR SAVING TAX DOLLARS

One Saturday morning I received a call from a client who devotes much of her leisure time to bird watching. She had just seen a newspaper report of Scott Paper's plan to use dioxin to kill hardwoods in its forests. She had a few hundred Scott shares.

"I don't want the money," she told me. "And I feel I really ought to fight them on this. But what can I do? I thought you might be able to tell me what environmental groups are fighting the use of dioxin. I want to give them the stock. They'll know what to do with it." One of the groups I suggested ultimately received the stock. My client got considerable satisfaction out of her gift. But she got something else she didn't expect: a tax break.

The way in which you dispose of investments can have quite beneficial tax consequences. This section looks at a few of the more common techniques.

Gifts to Charitable Organizations

As my client discovered, giving stock to a charitable organization provides the donor with a tax benefit. Investors often choose to give away shares whose sale would result in larger capital gains. The investors do not realize the gains on the gift, and the charity gets the stock's full value. For donors it's as advantageous as if they had given checks for the full value. They get the same deduction. However, the organization must have qualified as a charity under the IRS guidelines. Only gifts to IRS-recognized charities earn the tax benefit.

Gifts to Children

Under the Internal Revenue Code, you can give up to $10,000 to each of your minor children or grandchildren without incurring a gift tax. If you plan to pass securities to your children eventually, you can do it now and shift the tax burden of the income to your children. In theory, the children will be in a lower tax bracket than you are for many years.

But suppose you're worried that instead of spending the money on college tuition, they may spend it on BMWs and Club Med. You can protect yourself by placing these assets in trust for a specific purpose. Your lawyer is the best person to advise you on this.

Swaps

If you find yourself with a large capital gain, you can offset it by selling something in which you have a loss. A somewhat more sophisticated way of accomplishing the same thing is called a *swap*.

FIGURE 9-5   Ten Companies with the Largest Number of Common Stockholders of
              Record

American Telephone & Telegraph	3,148,000
General Motors	1,035,000
Exxon Corp.	865,000
International Business Machines	726,000
General Electric	481,000
GTE Corp.	467,000
Sears, Roebuck	434,000
Texaco, Inc.	373,000
Southern Co.	347,000
American Electric Power	346,000

Source: New York Stock Exchange Fact Book, 1983, p. 37. Reprinted with permission.

For ethical investors, swapping bonds or stocks in order to establish a loss has the dual benefits of saving taxes while providing an opportunity to reevaluate holdings. Suppose you have a capital gain of $30,000. By selling some of your municipal bond holdings at a loss, you could *offset* (balance) the gain. But if you don't want to give up the high, tax-free income, you can work with your broker to realize both advantages. In a swap, capital gains and losses offset one another dollar for dollar. However, you don't have to offset long-term gains with long-term losses. In fact, the rule of thumb is long-term gains against short-term losses. If your capital losses exceed your gains, the IRS will allow you to use them to offset your income, but only up to $3000 per year. Any amount above that is carried forward to the next year's return.

To figure out which bonds to swap in order to get the loss you need, select the bonds that have declined in price or quality, or whose issuers now don't pass your ethical screens. Then calculate their market value, their average maturity, their quality, and their interest rates. Next, make up a replacement portfolio that mirrors as closely as possible the bonds you are going to sell. Usually this can be accomplished by sticking to the quality, price, and annual income of the old portfolio but adding a few years to the average maturity.

The proceeds from the sale of the bonds you now hold finance the purchase of the new bonds. The later maturity is the price of the swap. Of course, you can keep the old maturity dates by putting in some extra money or by sacrificing income. I find most people prefer to stretch the maturity a bit.

The same technique works with stocks. In order to maintain balance in your portfolio, however, you should stick to companies within the same industry or which are affected by the same economic factors.

A woman I spoke with recently was concerned about the ethics of tax avoidance. Tax-advantaged investments involve nothing more than taking what the government asks us to take. The government encourages people to purchase municipal obligations and to give to charities. And it permits devices like bond swaps, which the investor may use to reduce taxable income. By taking advantage of tax laws, ethical investors are simply redirecting their tax dollars into still more worthwhile projects.

10 TAX INVESTMENTS

I'VE CALLED THIS CHAPTER "Tax Investments"[1] because if I titled it "Tax Shelters," a lot of ethical investors wouldn't read it. That would be a big mistake — both ethically and financially — for people whose income lands them in a 40% to 50% federal tax bracket.

The negative reaction to the idea of shelters comes from Americans' abhorrence of devices which seem to let the rich — even if they happen to be rich themselves — evade taxes. Let's dispose of this nonsense quickly. Legitimate tax investments only defer tax payments while, hopefully, leading to large returns. Although tax shelters are much riskier vehicles, they work on the same principles as IRAs and Keogh Plans, discussed in Chapter 11. They are tax deferral devices. Congress created them to promote specific types of economic development, such as energy exploration and experimentation, housing and office construction, and investments in capital assets, particularly equipment.

WHO BUYS TAX SHELTERS?

For sheltering income to make sense, an investor must be in at least the 40% federal tax bracket. If you're married and filing jointly, you would need an income of $59,000, after adjustments. Even if you fall into this bracket, however, you should not consider tax investments until you have taken full advantage of vehicles like IRA accounts, utility reinvestment plans, and the simpler tax-advantaged investments discussed in the last chapter. Tax shelters tie up your money much more than any of these vehicles and at considerably greater risk.

THE THEORY BEHIND
TAX INVESTMENTS

In order to understand how tax investments work, you need to appreciate a bit of the theory behind our system of business entities and tax incentives.

Business Entities

Let's look at the different ways a business can be structured.

Sole Proprietorship. Al wants to start a business leasing computers to small businesses. All he needs is a phone and a Yellow Pages ad, and he has just become a *sole proprietor.* All the profits are his, and if one of his machines eats all of a customer's records, so are all the liabilities.

Partnership. Suppose Al does well and wants to expand, but he lacks sufficient capital. He persuades his friend Alix to become his *partner.* The two agree to share the profits and the liabilities. If disaster strikes, they could seek refuge in bankruptcy. In both sole proprietorships and partnerships, the owners are personally liable for losses regardless of the amount they invested in the business.

Corporation. Time passes, and Al and Alix's business grows. They decide they want to *incorporate.* Unlike becoming a sole proprietor or forming a partnership, forming a corporation is a privilege granted by the state. Al and Alix must fulfill a number of statutory requirements in order to incorporate.

One of the main reasons for incorporating is that it limits an investor's liability to the amount of the investment. This is the concept of limited liability, and it is why the names of British corporations end with Ltd. Corporations also differ from sole proprietorships and partnerships in that they pay income taxes as an entity. The dividends they pay are taxed again as income to the shareholders.

FIGURE 10-1   The Biggest Air Polluters

(Ranked by Pounds of Toxic Pollutants Spewed into the Air per Year)

1.	Monsanto	11,088,385	27.	Phillips	989,270
2.	Du Pont	10,963,406	28.	B. F. Goodrich	938,100
3.	Dow	10,353,047	29.	Perstorp	731,000
4.	Amoco	6,633,400	30.	Hercor	690,800
5.	Celanese	5,451,760	31.	St. Croix	690,800
6.	Mobay	5,355,392	32.	Tenneco	634.590
7.	Hercules	4,775,400	33.	GAF	562,000
8.	Borg-Warner	4,768,300	34.	IMC	552,200
9.	Union Carbide	3,135,361	35.	Standard Oil of California	552,020
10.	FMC	2,334,000	36.	Rubicon	510,435
11.	Shell	2,330,508	37.	Commonwealth	476,924
12.	Allied Chemical	2,284,260	38.	Standard Chlorine	462,010
13.	BASF Wyandotte	1,862,930	39.	Hercofina	437,130
14.	Stauffer	1,772,208	40.	Gulf	400,010
15.	Eastman Kodak	1,708,875	41.	Diamond Shamrock	394,390
16.	Georgia-Pacific	1,694,700	42.	Corco	390,150
17.	Olin	1,624,682	43.	Goodyear	373,000
18.	American Cyanamid	1,599,290	44.	Jefferson	280,634
19.	ARCO	1,586,789	45.	ABTEC	275,400
20.	PPG	1,586,520	46.	Ashland Oil	246,075
21.	Borden	1,571,800	47.	Kalama	242,940
22.	Exxon	1,217,262	48.	Hannah Mining	225,180
23.	Sun	1,150,732	49.	Occidental Petroleum	
24.	Vulcan Materials	1,098,330		(Hooker)	224,925
25.	Reichold	1,055,260	50.	AMAX	215,460
26.	U.S. Steel	1,029,434			

Source: National Clean Air Coalition and U.S. Environmental Protection Agency, as reprinted in *Everybody's Business Scorecard,* p. 58.

Tax Benefits

Tax investments, as I said earlier, are Congress's way of encouraging certain kinds of business activity. Congress wants to stimulate new capital invest-ment, so it grants generous *tax credits* and *depreciation allowances.* A tax credit means your investment in, say, a new plant becomes a credit against the taxes you owe. Depreciation allows you to spread the cost of, say, a new truck over its useful life. When Al and Alix's new computer leasing business was a sole proprietorship or a partnership, those tax benefits reduced their personal income taxes. But a corporation pays taxes as an entity, so the benefits reduce the corporation's tax bills, and only indirectly its shareholders'. Their dividends may increase, but they do not get the benefits of the tax breaks directly.

Limited Partnerships

Limited partnerships provide just the vehicle to encourage investments in low-income housing, energy exploration, and other areas Congress wishes to encourage.

A limited partnership is a hybrid. As in a partnership, general partners with unlimited liability manage the business. (Often the general partners are not individuals but corporations.) But as in a corporation there are investors, called *limited partners,* whose liability is limited to the amount of their investment. What makes limited partnerships ideal as tax investment vehicles is that the IRS treats them like partnerships. The investment credits and depreciation go toward reducing the individual investor's personal income taxes rather than the entity's.

Virtually all tax shelters today are limited partnerships. However, as a result of the 1982 Tax Act, many high-priced shelters can become corporations in the future. The new law will not affect the broad-based public vehicles with hundreds of investors. Rather, the Tax Act changed the rules on what are called *Subchapter S* corporations. These corporations, which have 35 or fewer shareholders, may elect to have their shareholders treated as partners for tax purposes. However, the shareholders may claim losses in any one year only up to their stock's adjusted basis. They may take the remaining losses in following years.

TAX SHELTERS AND HOW THEY WORK

Tax shelters in the end are not as complicated as they seem. For liability purposes you are treated like a stockholder; for tax purposes you are treated like a partner. You defer paying taxes on the income you invest while receiving the tax credits and deductions which come with the investment. In exchange, you're putting your money at risk. Of course, the government hopes to receive substantial tax payments from you eventually.

I regard tax shelters as splendid opportunities for the ethical investor seeking growth. The return on these investments — aside from the tax benefits — can be spectacular.

What Is a Shelter?

Buying a shelter means buying a program of acquisitions of some type of asset which you hope will return capital gains and income as well as tax

FIGURE 10-2   Investments in Tax Shelters
January–July 1983

Type	Total Invested (in millions)
Oil and gas	$1,415
Real estate	2,217
Equipment leasing	145
Other	180

Source: Robert A. Stanger & Company, as quoted in the *New York Times*, 19 July 1983, p. D1. Copyright © 1983 by The New York Times Company. Reprinted by permission.

benefits. In this context *shelter* means current expense — paying cash for some project — which you deduct from your gross income.

How Shelters Work. Suppose you're in the 50% tax bracket and you put $15,000 into a housing rehabilitation project. This sort of project has a lot of appeal for most concerned investors. The project provides you with $35,000 in deductions over the first five years the limited partnership owns the building. (Typically these deductions come from the costs of upgrading the buildings and their depreciation after rehabilitation.) A $35,000 deduction in the 50% tax bracket saves $17,500 in taxes. Looking only at the taxes, after a few years you have no money in the deal. And the rents are bringing you income. That's how Congress has structured these vehicles. But if the general partner hires Moe, Larry, & Curly, Inc., to do the renovations and the Stan & Ollie Corp. to manage the building, you'll be looking at a capital loss, not at a stream of deductions and income.

Private Partnerships. A limited partnership may be private or public. A private partnership involves 30 or fewer limited partners who contribute substantial sums — usually $35,000 or more. They tend to be unique opportunities for the ethical investor to benefit from anything from oyster farming to small-scale hydroelectric dams. But there is a difficulty in evaluating private limited partnerships since the general partner's last venture probably didn't involve the same location or precisely the same project.

Public Partnerships. Public partnerships often have more than one hundred limited partners. These must file prospectuses with the Securities Exchange

FIGURE 10-3   *Money* Magazine's Top 14 Tax Shelters

Oil and Gas

Callon (300 Franklin St., P.O. Box 1287, Natchez, MS 39120)
Columbian Energy (First National Bank Building, One Townside Plaza, Topeka, KS 66603)
Dyco (1100 Shelard Tower, Wayzata Blvd. at Hwy. 18, Minneapolis, MN 55426)
Hawkins Exploration (320 S. Boston Bldg., Tulsa, OK 74103)
HCW (Church Green; 101 Summer Street, Boston, MA 02110)
Samson Properties (2700 First National Tower, Tulsa, OK 74103)
Woods (National Foundation West Bldg., 3555 N.W. 58th St., Oklahoma City, OK 73112)

Real Estate

Consolidated Capital Properties (1900 Powell St., Emeryville, CA 94608)
Equitec (7677 Oakport St., P.O. Box 2470, Oakland, CA 94618)
JMB/Carlyle (875 N. Michigan Ave., Chicago, IL 60611)
Landsing Diversified Properties (800 El Camino Real, Menlo Park, CA 94025)
Public Storage Properties (990 S. Fair Oaks Ave., P.O. Box 6000, Pasadena, CA 91109)

Equipment Leasing

Equitec (7677 Oakport St., P.O. Box 2470, Oakland, CA 94618)
Phoenix Leasing (P.O. Box 1179, Mill Valley, CA 94942)

Commission (SEC). In public offerings the general partner must have substantial net worth, usually $250,000, or 15% of the money raised. Public programs are a better choice for a new tax shelter investor because their management tends to have a track record with similar projects which investors can examine.

Financial Criteria

The guiding principle for investing in tax shelters is that the investment — leaving aside any tax benefits — must fit your financial and ethical criteria. The financial criteria for deciding whether to invest are simple enough.

1. You should be in a 40% to 50% tax bracket, earning at least $50,000 a year.
2. You should invest only money you will not need any return on for at least three years.
3. You should not invest money you can't afford to lose. You "pay" for the tax advantages by taking a sizable risk.

FIGURE 10-4   Tax Shelter Comparison Chart

	REAL ESTATE				
Type of Investment	Residential	Commercial	Raw Land	New Construction	Government Subsidized Housing
Minimum Investor Net Worth*	20–75K	20–150K	50–100K	75–150K	100–150K
Tax Bracket	35%	35%	50%	50%	50%
Minimum Investment Contribution	2,500–50K	2,500–50K	5–100K	10–150K	50–150K
Cash Flow	0 to Moderate	Moderate to Good	None	0 to Good	0 to Very Low
Sheltered Income	Yes	Partial	No	Yes	Yes
Liquidity	Low	Low	Low	Low	Very Low
Appreciation Potential	Moderate to Good	Moderate to Good	Moderate to Good	Moderate to Good	Very Low
Type of Shelter	Moderate	Moderate	None	Varies	Deep Shelter
Large First Year Deduction	Limited	Limited	None	Limited	Yes
Investment Tax Credit Opportunity	None	None (Rehab. Credit Possible)	None	Possible on Personal Property Only	None
Capital Gains Potential	Yes	Yes	Yes	Yes	Yes, But Gain Unlikely
Economic Risks	Moderate to Low	Low	High	Moderate to High	Moderate to High
IRS Audit Risk	Low	Low	Low	Moderate	Moderate to Low
Tax Preference Items	Excess Depreciation Over SL	Excess Depreciation Over SL	None	Excess Depreciation Over SL	Excess Depreciation Over SL
Investment Interest	Possible	Possible	Likely	Possible	Possible
Recapture Or Ordinary Income On Sale	Depends Upon Depreciation Method	Depends Upon Depreciation Method	No	Depends Upon Depreciation Method	Limited
Crossover to Phantom Income	Possible	Possible	No	Possible	Possible

ITC — Investment Tax Credit   **IDC** — Investment Drilling Credit   **SL** — Straight Line Depreciation

* Minimum Investor Net Worth is in addition to home, furnishings and automobiles.

FIGURE 10-4 *(continued)*

Type of Investment	OIL & GAS				
	Development	Balanced	Exploratory	Income	Feeding
Minimum Investor	50–250K	50–250K	100–250K	50–100K	100K
Tax Bracket	50%	50%	50%	50%	50%
Minimum Investment Contribution	5–150K	5–150K	5–150K	5–50K	5–10K
Cash Flow	0 to Moderate	0 to Moderate	0 to Good	Moderate to Good	0
Sheltered Income	Partial	Partial	Partial	Partial	No
Liquidity	Low to Moderate	Low to Moderate	Low to Moderate	Moderate	Good
Appreciation Potential	Low	Moderate	Uncertain	Moderate	Uncertain
Type of Shelter	Good	Good	Excellent	Low	Excellent Deferral
Large First Year Deduction	Yes	Yes	Yes	No	Yes
Investment Tax Credit Opportunity	Personal Property (Limited)	Personal Property (Limited)	Personal Property (Limited)	Unlikely	None
Capital Gains Potential	Low	Low	Low	Low	No
Economic Risks	Moderate	High	Moderate	Moderate	High
IRS Audit Risk	Low	Low	Low to Moderate	Low	Moderate to High
Tax Preference Items	IDC On Productive Well, Excess % Depletion	IDC On Productive Well, Excess % Depletion	IDC On Productive Well, Excess % Depletion	Limited	None
Investment Interest	Unlikely	Unlikely	Unlikely	Unlikely	Unlikely
Recapture Or Ordinary Income On Sale	Productive Well, IDC, ITC	Productive Well, IDC, ITC	Productive Well, IDC, ITC	ITC	All Ordinary
Crossover to Phantom Income	Unlikely	Unlikely	Unlikely	Unlikely	Unlikely

You may write Spectrum Financial Group for an updated version of the comparison chart.

AGRICULTURE			OTHER		
Breeding	Ranching	Farming	Movies	Equipment Leasing	R & D
100K	100K	100K	150K	50–100K	100K
50%	50%	50%	50%	50%	50%
10–25K	5–25K	10–25K	10–25K	25–50K	10–60K
Low	Low	0 to Moderate	Unknown	0 to Good	Unknown
Yes	Some	Varies	Yes, Until Crossover	Yes Until Crossover	Could Be At Capital Gains Rates
Low	Low	Low	Low	Low	Low
Uncertain	Uncertain	Moderate	Uncertain	Limited & Uncertain	Good
Good	Good	Moderate	Moderate Front End	Varies	Excellent
Yes	Varies	Varies	Moderate	Varies	Excellent
Animals	Equipment, Trees, Animals	Equipment & Trees	Limited	Available If Limits Are Met	None
Yes	Yes	Yes	Possible	Yes, Limited	Yes
High	Moderate to High	High	High	Varies	High
Moderate to High	Moderate to High	Moderate	High	Moderate	Moderate
Excess Depreciation Over SL	Excess Depreciation Over SL	Excess Depreciation Over SL	Unlikely	Excess Depreciation Over SL	No
Unlikely	Unlikely	Unlikely	Possible	Possible	Not likely
Yes ITC	Yes ITC	Yes	Yes	Yes	Not If Properly Structured
Possible	Possible	Possible	Likely	Yes	Unlikely

Source: © 1981 Prologue Press, Box 1146, Menlo Park, CA 94205. Reprinted with permission.

Nature of the Investment

Limited partners are generally attracted to these ventures by the quality of the management and its track record in providing satisfactory tax consequences (i.e., ones the IRS did not question). Limited partners contribute only money. By law, limited partners may not become involved in the partnership's management. If they do become involved, then they lose their limited liability. Of course, they have a right to share in the distribution of profits. And they receive an annual accounting of the partnership's performance.

If you're accustomed to buying and selling stocks and bonds, limited partnership interests will come as quite a shock. While you can buy 100 shares of IBM from any broker, you cannot go to a single broker and select from all the partnerships currently offered. Brokerage houses tend to sell only certain programs, so if you don't like what your broker is offering, you will have to shop elsewhere.

Limited partnership interests are not readily transferable because there is no marketplace (like the New York Stock Exchange) for trading them. Quite often the general partner will offer to try to match buyers and sellers of existing interests, but at a significant fee. Usually the general partner must approve the transfer of a limited partnership interest.

WHAT'S AVAILABLE IN TAX INVESTMENTS

Let's take a closer look at the different investment areas, their advantages, and their disadvantages.

Real Estate Partnerships

The most common tax investments are real estate limited partnerships. Dozens of public real estate partnerships have long histories of good returns for their investors. Often the minimum investment is as low as $2500. Generally the investors' contributions are *leveraged* by means of a mortgage which gives the partners a write-off for interest in addition to other deductions. Leveraging means that considerably more money is going into the project than would be possible if it relied solely on investor contributions.

Real estate tax shelters provide deductions for depreciation as well as for the cost of improvements to existing buildings. In the first few years of your investment, you will receive deductions of up to 70% of your investment. Rentals generally repay 5% of your investment annually and are partially tax free. Each program usually lasts between five and 20 years. After that, the sponsor sells the properties, and the partners split the proceeds. The gain on sale, not the tax benefits, provides the economic rationale for the investment.

For example, Carlyle, a public partnership, buys apartment buildings, office buildings, and shopping centers, which it rehabilitates and sells. Carlyle's minimum investment is $5000, with $1000 increments. Its properties provide investors with deductions of up to 85% of their investment over the first five years and some tax-free income (about 4% per annum). After approximately five years, Carlyle begins to sell off the partnership's real estate and distribute the capital gains. Capital gains for their partnerships have averaged 32% annually after the fifth year. Other real estate tax shelters invest in industrial parks, subsidized housing, and even rental warehouses. In some instances the cash flow is higher initially than in Carlyle's shelters. Also, it is important to note that capital appreciation is highly variable and depends on a project's specific circumstances.

If you are concerned about environmental issues or displacement of certain types of residents, real estate tax shelters can prove unpalatable. Often you can learn what types of investments the general partner will make. But it is unusual with public partnerships to be able to determine in advance what particular parcels will become partnership property. (Private partnerships are usually assembled for a particular project.) It is worth finding out what developers the general partner has worked with in the past and what their records are.

Real estate limited partnerships can have a strong appeal to the ethical investor. And more opportunities are arising every day. For instance, Jim Lowell of Lowell & Blake Associates told me that "the big opportunity in tax shelters is coming from the fact that more and more colleges and charitable institutions are financing building through limited partnerships. The colleges get the money they need, and the investor gets a more than legitimate deduction."

Energy Exploration and Development

Most energy and exploration tax investments involve oil and gas. While an increasing number of alternative energy investments are coming onto the market, they are still not common.

A typical oil and gas program is the Samson Properties' Drilling Program. It requires a minimum investment of $50,000, so it obviously targets the high-income investor. Many oil and gas partnerships require minimum investments of $2500. The reason I've chosen Samson as an example is that it has a relatively long record, which appears in Figure 10-5.

Samson's record is good, but the figures for the 1978 partnership should remind you that tax shelters offer no guarantees. The distributions listed are actual payments to investors. While an investor writes off an investment in Samson during its first two years, the chart does not include the value of the tax benefits.

Recently I've begun to see a few *private placements* (not registered with the SEC) such as Hillsborough Hydroelectric, which develop alternative sources of energy. They range from quite conservative, high-income-producing programs to extremely risky investments which offer the possibility of enormous capital gains.

The appropriateness of an energy partnership for your portfolio will depend largely on your view of the industry and the company involved. Most oil and gas shelters specify the region in which the drilling will take place. Since many of the drillers offering limited partnerships also are publicly traded companies — Callon, Dyco, and Petro Lewis, among others — you have the advantage of being able to obtain considerably more information about the corporate general partner than would be available in most other types of shelters.

Equipment Leasing

Equipment leasing deals offer the same low minimum investments — generally from $2500 up — as other public programs. They feature deductions for depreciation as well as investment tax credits ranging from 90% to 100% of the initial investment over their first four years.

Equipment leasing programs generally last between five and fifteen years. You receive a stream of taxable income from the rental of the equipment during the life of the program and, with luck, a capital gain on the residual value of the equipment when it is sold at the program's end. In any event, you should have generated enough income at the end of the program to make it worthwhile even if the equipment is unsalable.

Equipment leasing offerings are the most difficult shelters for ethical investors to appraise. The offerings rarely specify the equipment to be

FIGURE 10-5   Samson Properties' Performance

Partnership	Years Since Formation	Distributions Through 10/1/82	Estimated Annualized Return*
1973	10.1	551%	62%
1974	9.0	169%	19%
1975	7.4	162%	39%
1977	5.2	118%	33%
Natural Gas	4.7	181%	85%
1978	4.5	27%	4%
1978 Y/E	4.2	79%	29%
1979	3.8	74%	17%
1979 Summer	3.5	34%	19%
1979 Investors	3.4	33%	17%
1979 Drilling	3.2	36%	23%

* These percentages have been estimated by *Brennan Reports* from data supplied by the general partner through October 1, 1982.

Source: Brennan Reports, Inc., P.O. Box 882, Valley Forge, PA 19480, January 1983, p. 4. Reprinted with permission.

purchased. They speak in general terms of computer equipment, construction equipment, and so on. Also, investors do not know who makes the equipment the partnerships will purchase. And the investor rarely knows to whom the equipment will be leased. Once you find out who the lessee is, you may not feel comfortable with the partnership's choice.

SOURCES OF INFORMATION

Even aside from equipment leasing, the ethical investor faces problems in getting information about tax investments. Most shelters are not offered by publicly traded companies. So determining an offerer's civic-mindedness, its minority hiring record, its concern for the environment, and the like can prove difficult. Still, offering memoranda, prospectuses, and specialized newsletters can help. Periodicals sometimes cover particular shelter offerers, too.

Offering Memoranda and Prospectuses

If the shelter is a private placement, then the *offering memorandum* (a document describing the general partner, the investment, its objectives,

FIGURE 10-6   Corporations Opposing California's 1978 Tax Limitation Referendum,
Proposition 13

In 1978 taxpayer activist Howard Jarvis solicited enough signatures to place a property tax limitation measure on the California ballot. Only one sizable, publicly traded corporation, Host International, Inc., contributed more than $250 in favor of the tax-cut initiative. The companies listed below contributed $10,000 or more to the campaign against Proposition 13, which passed 65% to 35%.

Atlantic Richfield Co.	Occidental Petroleum
ARA Transportation Group	Pacific Lighting Corp.
BankAmerica Corp.	Pacific Mutual Life
California Federal Savings & Loan	Rockwell International
Carter, Hawley, Hale Stores	Southern California Edison
Dart & Kraft Industries	Southern Pacific Co.
Federated Department Stores	Standard Oil of California
The Irvine Co.	TICOR

Source: Data courtesy of Carl Olson, Chairman, Stockholders Against the Government Burden, P.O. Box 7273, Alexandria, VA 22307.

and its risks) is usually the size of a hefty dictionary and makes equally uninteresting reading. While it spells out the facts, it gives most readers no feel for the intangibles. For instance, is management smart and reliable? Is the team exploring for oil any good at finding it? These considerations take logic and experience to appraise.

If the offering is public, the investor will receive a prospectus filed with the SEC. Usually the offerer also sends a brochure explaining the investment in simple language and charting the performance of the industry and of the particular general partner. As with the private offering memorandum, it will tell you how much money is being raised, what it will be spent on, the risks involved, and the tax benefits.

Tax Shelter Letters

Some private newsletters cover tax shelter offerings in detail. These letters are designed for people who plan to put considerable sums into a diversified program of shelters. These letters are expensive, but their good advice makes them worthwhile. The cost of subscribing is tax deductible. Here are the ones I prefer. Their addresses are in the bibliography.

Brennan Reports. This fine newsletter offers descriptions of various offerings and analyzes the rewards and risks of each. It also spotlights developments

FIGURE 10-7   Top Ten Trade/Membership/Health Contributors to Federal
Candidates, 1981–82

Realtors Political Action Committee	$2,115,135
American Medical Association Political Action Committee	$1,737,090
Build Political Action Committee of the National Association of Home Builders	$1,005,628
American Bankers Association BANKPAC	$ 947,460
Automobile and Truck Dealers Election Action Committee	$ 917,295
NRA Political Victory Fund (National Rifle Association of America)	$ 710,902
Associated General Contractors Political Action Committee	$ 683,766
American Dental Political Action Committee	$ 609,450
National Association of Life Underwriters Political Action Committee	$ 563,573
National Association of Retired Federal Employees	$ 562,725

Source: Federal Election Commission (1983).

in tax laws which apply to tax shelter vehicles. Brennan will send you a
sample letter on request.

Investor's Tax Shelter Reports. This 16-page monthly contains a wealth of
information on public tax shelters. It compares current oil and gas partnerships on 19 factors, such as technical staff expertise, borrowing provisions, and the financial strength of the sponsor. It also compares performances on past partnership programs.

The Stanger Report. Geared mainly to investment professionals, this letter
offers comprehensive, useful general information. It provides comparisons
of the various structures of different deals in a single industry. The *New
York Times* and the *Wall Street Journal* often quote its publisher, Robert
Stanger.

Tax investments are not for every ethical investor. No one in less
than a 40% tax bracket should consider them. And even those individuals
shouldn't until they take advantage of other sheltering devices like Individual Retirement Accounts (IRAs), discussed in the next chapter. But
for those whose finances qualify them for tax shelters, these programs can
offer solid investments in worthwhile enterprises.

11 RETIREMENT PLANNING

I N 1952 Ed was 60 and Edna, his wife, was 54. For 35 years he had taught at a small college and his wife had worked in its development office. Their life centered on the school, and they wanted to live nearby when they retired. They bought a lot next to it and with their own hands built a small house. From their modest salaries they had amassed a small portfolio of quality stocks. Both were eligible for nominal pension benefits and for Social Security. Their future seemed secure. But in 1967 Ed suffered the first in a series of strokes from which he died in 1971. His medical expenses emptied their portfolio.

By 1973 Edna faced some cruel choices. The house required substantial repairs which she could no longer make herself, and inflation had eroded her retirement benefits. An active woman, she spent much of her time doing volunteer work. So she rejected the idea of a retirement home. After months of solitary anguish over her choices, she mentioned her problem to the college's development director.

The solution was obvious, he said. The college was expanding and needed her house for faculty housing. If she would sell it at a price below its market value, the college would guarantee she could live in it until she died, and would assume responsibility for its upkeep. The purchase money would replenish her savings. Today Edna still lives in the home she and Ed built.

THE RULES OF
RETIREMENT PLANNING

Edna's experiences illustrate some key rules of retirement planning.

1. Begin planning and saving for your retirement today.
2. Assume you will live into your eighties and will suffer from the health problems which accompany old age.
3. Don't count on your pension plan or Social Security to pull you through.
4. Seek professional assistance in developing your plan.
5. Consider your assets not just in terms of their worth to you but also in terms of their value to others.

Don't Procrastinate!

My toughest meetings with clients always involve people facing imminent retirement without the resources they need to live comfortably. Most people seem to become aware of retirement at about 50 but don't begin seriously planning until 55 or 60. By that time it's too late to make the easy adjustments in life style and savings programs which can make retirement comfortable. Every year you let go by without setting something aside for retirement limits your options significantly.

Retirement planning should begin no later than 35. By then you are probably no less than halfway to retirement. At that age many think $2000 put annually into an Independent Retirement Account (IRA) or a Keogh Plan is so small as to be meaningless, but compounding interest combined with steady contributions makes retirement funds grow rapidly. And you gain some immediate tax benefits from your contributions.

Inflation

You must assume inflation will erode your savings. During Ed and Edna's working years, and for a decade and a half after they retired, inflation was almost nil. When Ed died in 1971, it was running about 3%. But as this is being written, the Reagan Administration is citing an inflation rate twice the 1971 rate as its major economic success.

Let's assume the inflation rate stabilizes at 8% per year. In nine years you would need twice as much income as you now generate just to keep pace with the cost of living. Are you prepared to live on half as much as you do now? Are you prepared to watch your income lose half its value every nine years?

Almost all guides to retirement planning assume you will be able to live quite comfortably on considerably less than you currently do. The income chart in Figure 11-1 illustrates how these assumptions work. Retirees generally need approximately 80% of their pre-retirement income to maintain a similar life style. Of course some expenses decline, like those related to going to work every day. But if inflation is at 8%, that 20% decline in expenses will be eaten up in two and a half years. Still worse for retirees, medical costs have outpaced inflation for at least 15 years.

Starting the Planning Process

Ensuring that you don't have to face a serious decline in your life style is a main goal of retirement planning. I have found most ethical investors to be thoughtful planners by nature. However, even they tend to have a blind spot about retirement planning. They should bring the same deliberateness they apply to the routine investment decisions to these areas.

How do you get started? Your first step should be an analysis of your financial picture. The inventory in Appendix A will get you started. Then look at the resources you'll have when you retire. In particular, investigate your company's pension plan, if it has one. You should then set about deciding what you'll need when you retire. Explore an Individual Retirement Account (IRA) or a Keogh Plan. If these vehicles alone will not meet your needs, then you should plan a retirement portfolio. In any case, when you've accumulated this information, you should discuss your situation with a specialist in retirement planning.

PENSIONS

The first step in retirement planning is to carefully examine your company retirement plan.

Daniel was a truck driver in the Chicago area and a member of the Teamsters. In 1976 he reached 65 and retired. When he applied to the union's pension fund for retirement benefits, he discovered that despite 23

FIGURE 11-1   Equivalent Retirement Income

Gross preretirement income	Taxes[1]	Work-related expenses[2]	Savings and investments[3]	Net pre-retirement income[4]	Post-retirement income taxes[5]	Equivalent retirement income[6]
Single people						
$10,000	$ 2008	$ 480	$ 240 (3%)	$ 7272	—	$ 7272 (73%)
15,000	3703	678	678 (6%)	9941	—	9941 (66%)
20,000	5783	853	1280 (9%)	12,084	$ 198	12,282 (61%)
30,000	10,355	1179	2357 (12%)	16,109	1282	17,391 (58%)
50,000	22,249	1665	4163 (15%)	21,923	3752	25,675 (51%)
Married couples						
$10,000	$ 1444	$ 513	$ 257 (3%)	$ 7786	—	$ 7786 (78%)
15,000	2860	728	728 (6%)	10,684	—	10,684 (71%)
20,000	4488	931	1396 (9%)	13,185	—	13,185 (66%)
30,000	8047	1317	2634 (12%)	17,999	$ 63	18,062 (60%)
50,000	17,824	1931	4826 (15%)	25,419	1965	27,384 (55%)

[1]Includes Federal income tax, Social Security taxes, state and local income taxes (calculated at 19% of Federal income taxes). Does not include property taxes.

[2]Estimated at 6% of income after taxes.

[3]Estimated at a percentage (shown) of income after taxes.

[4]Gross preretirement income less taxes, work-related expenses, and savings and investments.

[5]Post-retirement taxes are on income in excess of Social Security benefits, which are not taxable. Retirees without Social Security benefits would need higher retirement income.

[6]Equivalent retirement income as a percentage of preretirement gross income shown in parentheses.

The last column of the table below shows the income required after retirement to maintain preretirement living standards. These figures were calculated by the President's Commission on Pension Policy in 1980 for people at various income levels.

Source: Copyright © 1982 by Consumers Union of United States, Inc., Mt. Vernon, NY 10553. Reprinted by permission from *Consumer Reports,* March 1982, p. 125.

years in the union, he did not qualify. The reason: in 1960–61 his employer had laid him off for nine months. Under the pension plan's rules, contributions to the plan had to be continuous. While he was unemployed, the U.S. Supreme Court later held, he had had the *right* to make contributions and maintain his eligibility. However, Daniel had not done so — even if he could have made the payments out of his unemployment checks — since no one had told him he would lose his eligibility if he didn't. So, he lost his retirement benefits. The number of retirees who have found to their horror that they would receive no pension benefits has decreased since Congress passed the Employment Retirement Income Security Act in 1974. But it still happens. I've outlined your ERISA rights in Box 11-1.

Like health insurance plans, pension plans work on the idea that only a few contributors will benefit. For that reason, you should read the fine print of your plan and take the time to find out how your pension works.

BOX 11-1   Your ERISA Rights

The Employment Retirement Income Security Act (ERISA) guarantees certain legal rights and protections, specified in the "bill of rights" section of your Pension Plan's Summary Plan Description. Every SPD must give this information.
  You have the right to:

- Examine without charge all plan documents at the plan administrator's office and other locations, such as union halls.
- Obtain copies of all plan documents upon written request.
- Receive a summary of the plan's annual financial report.
- Obtain a statement defining your status in terms of receiving benefits.

You also have:

- Protection against imprudent operation of your plan. The people who operate your plan must do so prudently and in the interests of plan participants and beneficiaries.
- Protection against discrimination. You may not be fired in order to prevent you from receiving your pension.
- The right to a written explanation if your claim is denied in whole or in part.

You may take these steps to enforce your claim:

- File suit in a federal court if you request materials from the plan administrator and do not receive them within 30 days.
- File suit in a federal or state court if your claim for benefits is denied or ignored.
- Seek assistance from the U.S. Department of Labor or file suit in a federal court if plan fiduciaries misuse the plan's money, or if you are discriminated against.

Source: Adapted from *Consumers Digest* magazine, January/February 1982, p. 23.

ERISA guarantees you access to all necessary documents. This can be an important right if your employer, like the publishing giant Harcourt Brace Jovanovich, Inc., decides to use 40% of its employee pension fund to build a new corporate headquarters, leaving the pension fund with a mortgage on the edifice and a lease.

INDIVIDUAL RETIREMENT ACCOUNTS AND KEOGH PLANS

In addition to its Bill of Rights for pension holders, ERISA also created Individual Retirement Accounts (IRAs) and Keogh Plans. These retirement savings programs designed for the individual are extraordinarily useful devices for both retirement planning and sheltering income from current taxes.

IRAs and Keogh Plans have the obvious benefits of encouraging individuals to save for their own retirement. They also funnel billions into lending institutions, thus encouraging capital formation. Depending on your view of the ways in which the depositories use the funds, this may be good or bad. Ethical investors should maintain the same close supervision over the holders of their retirement funds that they do over funds they manage themselves.

For best results, you should begin your IRA or Keogh program early. Still, starting even at 40 or 45 can result in a substantial fund. Only those now in a very low tax bracket who will be in a much higher tax bracket when they retire do not benefit from IRAs. If you are an intern headed for private practice, an IRA is probably not for you, except perhaps as a long-term savings plan.

The Basic Rules

Eligibility. Only those who are self-employed may set up a Keogh Plan. Anyone with income can establish an IRA. If you or your spouse is under the age of 70½ and currently earns income, you may establish an IRA, even if you have another retirement plan or a Keogh Plan.

Contributions. You may contribute up to 100% of your gross earnings, up to an annual maximum of $2000 to your IRA. (The contribution rules for Keogh Plans, which are different, are discussed below.) Your contributions must be in cash — not stocks, bonds, or other property. If both you and your spouse have earned income, you may set up separate IRAs and contribute up to $2000 to each. If your spouse does not work, you may set up a spousal IRA, which permits you to contribute up to 100% of your gross earnings to an annual maximum of $2250. You may divide the amount as you wish between your account and the spousal account, so long as you contribute no more than $2000 to either account. At this writing, Congress was considering increasing the contribution limit to spousal IRAs.

Tax Shelter. IRAs shelter income. Your contribution reduces your gross taxable income by an equal amount. If you are in a 40% bracket, each contribution of $1000 to your IRA effectively costs you only $600. You would have paid the other $400 in taxes had you not put it into the IRA. Even if you take a standard deduction, you may deduct the IRA contribution from your gross income.

After age 59½, the money you withdraw from your IRA is taxed as ordinary income in the year in which you withdraw it. Presumably then you will be in a lower bracket than when you contributed the money. As long as your money remains in the IRA, you pay no taxes on the dividends, interest, and capital gains which accrue.

Taking Money Out. Let's suppose you're 25. You begin making the maximum contribution to your IRA this year and continue making a $2000

FIGURE 11-2   The Ten Worst Air-Polluting Plants

Company	City	Pounds Per Year*
Monsanto	Decatur, Alabama	6,601,770
Dow	Freeport, Texas	5,486,022
Amoco	Decatur, Alabama	3,896,400
Borg-Warner	Washington, West Virginia	3,892,000
Celanese	Bishop, Texas	3,588,000
Du Pont	Laplace, Louisiana	3,220,972
Hercules	Hopewell, Virginia	2,263,125
Dow	Plaquemine, Louisiana	2,254,465
FMC	South Charleston, West Virginia	2,184,000
Shell	Deer Park, Texas	1,901,388

*Pounds per year of one or more of 33 chemicals considered by the Environmental Protection Agency as potential "hazardous air pollutants."

Source: National Clean Air Coalition and U.S. Environmental Protection Agency, as quoted in *Everybody's Business Scorecard*, p. 59.

FIGURE 11-3   Growth of an Individual Retirement Account

The table shows how well an IRA can provide for your retirement. The interest rates chosen provide an estimated range that might be received by your IRA. but the rates could change greatly. To calculate the maximum for a married couple, simply double all the figures.

Age Begun	Total deposit at age 65 (at $2000 per year)	Compounded Daily at Assumed Interest Rates					
		8%		11%		14%	
		Value at age 65	Monthly payment*	Value at age 65	Monthly payment*	Value at age 65	Monthly payment
25	$80,000	$632,554	$5099	$1,621,049	$16,327	$4,398,527	$53,833
30	70,000	413,125	3330	920,124	9267	2,155,727	26,383
35	60,000	266,845	2151	518,769	5225	1,052,610	12,882
40	50,000	169,330	1365	288,950	2910	510,043	6242
45	40,000	104,323	841	157,354	1584	243,182	2976
50	30,000	60,986	491	82,001	' 825	111,927	1369
55	20,000	32,097	258	38,853	391	47,369	579
60	10,000	12,838	103	14,147	142	15,617	191

*Based on a 22-year life expectancy after 65, including survivor benefits. All figures are approximate, based on the unlikely event that such interest rates could be sustained for 40 years.

Source: Reprinted with permission from Consumers Digest magazine, May/June 1982, p. 16.

deposit annually for 40 years. If your IRA pays 12% compounded annually, when you reach 65 your IRA will be worth $1,718,000. (Of course if inflation is running at 12%, you are just maintaining your contribution's buying power.) Figures 11-3 and 11-4 provide information on IRA growth.

Numbers like that make withdrawals seem very attractive. However, contributions and earnings on them must remain in your IRA until you reach 59½. After that, you may withdraw part or all of the funds. At age 70½ you *must* begin withdrawing funds from your account. The government does not want to give up the taxes on your funds forever. If you wait until you are 70½ to begin withdrawing funds from your IRA, the IRS will require you to make withdrawals in nearly equal installments over a fixed period, not to exceed either your life expectancy or the combined life expectancy of you and your spouse.

If you withdraw money from an IRA before you are 59½, unless you die or become disabled, you must pay taxes on it at your current rate *plus* a 10% penalty. This makes IRAs an unappealing vehicle for short-term savings. After 59½, the 10% penalty disappears. So for those between 59½ and 70½ an IRA acts much like a tax sheltered savings account. You can continue making contributions to it up to 70½, as long as you continue to earn income.

FIGURE 11-4   How Fast Can Your IRA Money Grow?

Time	Amount Deposited Each Year in a 12% IRA*			
	$ 500	$ 1,000	$ 2,000	$ 4,000**
After 5 years	$ 3,460	$ 6,900	$ 13,800	$ 27,600
10 years	9,800	19,600	39,200	78,500
15 years	21,500	43,000	86,000	172,000
20 years	43,000	86,000	172,000	345,000
25 years	82,300	165,000	330,000	660,000
30 years	155,000	310,000	620,000	1,250,000

*Figures are approximate and are based on 12% interest rate.
**For two-income married couples.

Source: B. G. Quint, "IRA: Is It Right For You?" Reprinted from the June 8, 1982 issue of Family Circle Magazine, p. 61. © 1982 The Family Circle Inc.

Lump-Sum Pension Distributions. Suppose your employer terminates either you or its pension plan. In either event, you receive a lump-sum distribution of your interest in the pension plan. The IRS offers you two options. First, you could put the entire sum into your IRA. This option has no tax consequences. You will not include the lump-sum distribution in your income for tax purposes. But beware! You have only 60 days from the day you receive your distribution to get the money into your IRA. Missing the deadline means that you will pay some taxes on the distribution, regardless of what you do with it.

Your second option is to keep some of the distribution for your own purposes. The Internal Revenue Code assesses a special advantageous tax rate — called ten-year-forward averaging — on the amount you keep. Ten-year-forward averaging means that the government taxes the distribution as if it were your only income and 'as if it were spread over a ten-year period. In order to qualify for this treatment you must have participated in the plan for more than five 'years. Also, only your employer's contribution, the income on that contribution, and the income from your contribution (not the principal) are eligible for the rollover. (See Figure 11-5.)

Keogh Plans

Essentially the same rules apply to a Keogh as to an IRA, with two significant exceptions.

FIGURE 11-5   Lump-Sum Distribution Rollover Tax Rate

The ten-year-forward averaging tax is a special rate applied to the lump sum distribution alone, regardless of your income from other sources. It is not affected by whether you file a joint or a separate return. Typical ten-year-forward averaging tax rates for various sizes of distributions are shown in the following table.

Example of Ten-Year-Forward Averaging Taxes (1982 Rates)

Lump Sum	Ten-Year-Forward Averaging Tax	Tax as a % of Lump Sum Distribution
$ 25,000	$ 2,020	8%
40,000	4,800	12
50,000	6,760	14
100,000	17,150	17
150,000	29,510	20
300,000	80,920	27
400,000	124,680	31
500,000	174,680	35
600,000	224,680	37

Source: Lump Sum Distributions: What Are They and How Do I Make the Most of Them, E. F. Hutton & Co., Inc., 1983, p. 5. Reprinted with permission.

Contributions. Because they are not beneficiaries of other pension plans, those eligible for a Keogh Plan may make annual contributions — until 1986 — of up to $30,000 or 20% of their gross income, whichever is less. Starting in 1986, the contribution ceilings will be adjusted for increases in the cost of living. Those who establish a Keogh Plan may also set up an IRA. IRA contributions are not deducted from Keogh contributions.

Borrowing. Keogh Plan participants may borrow up to $50,000 or 50% of their vested benefits — but not less than $10,000 — from their plans. They must repay these loans within five years. If they use the loan to buy a home, repayment may be extended.

Setting Up an IRA or Keogh Plan

You have a number of choices in setting up an IRA or a Keogh Plan, and each has an ethical dimension. See Figure 11-6 for a summary of your options in setting up a retirement account.

FIGURE 11-6   IRA/Keogh Options

Where Should You Keep Your IRA Money?

Kind of Investment	Fees	Insured?	Current Earnings rate	Comments
Banks, Savings & Loans, and Credit Unions	Fixed Rate Time Deposit — 18 months or more Variable Rate Time Deposit — 18 months or more	Yes Yes	12%–15% 13%–15%	Rate stays same for entire period of deposit Rate will change periodically, say, every week or every month
U.S. Individual Retirement Bonds	Special issue of U.S. Treasury bonds	Guaranteed by U.S. Govt.	9%	Rate low now as compared with other investments
Growth Mutual Funds	Usually a package of common stocks	No	Varies widely	Risky investment — opportunity for big growth or loss
Income Oriented Bond or Stock Mutual Fund	A package of bonds and/or common stocks emphasizing income	No	Varies widely	Objective: high current income, plus some long-term growth
Insurance Company Plans	Stocks, bonds, money funds, etc.	No	Varies widely	At retirement, offers an annuity that provides a stated annual income for rest of your life
Self-Administered Brokerage Account	Whatever you wish, including stocks, bonds, money funds	No	Varies widely	Degree of risk and/or income, depends on the investments you choose.

Source: B. G. Quint, "IRA: Is It Right for You?" Reprinted from the June 8, 1982 issue of *Family Circle Magazine,* p. 58. © 1982 The Family Circle Inc.

Banks. Virtually all banks have plans for IRAs which provide you with a fixed rate of interest for a period of years. The bank, of course, must meet your ethical criteria, for it will lend your contributions to its customers. A bank IRA is federally insured up to $100,000.

Mutual Funds. As people have become increasingly aware of IRAs and Keoghs, mutual funds have boomed. In early 1983, as the tax deadline approached, mutual funds had to press every available body into answering phone calls from investors anxious to open these accounts. IRAs and Keoghs are largely responsible for the $40 billion increase in mutual fund shares between October 1, 1982, and September 30, 1983. Pax World Fund estimates that 22½% of their investors buy shares for retirement accounts.

   If you set up a retirement account with a mutual fund, you take more of a chance than with a bank in exchange for an opportunity for large capital gains. Until your retirement account exceeds $10,000, put your assets into either bank CDs, ethical money market funds, or ethical stock funds, depending on the level of risk you wish to take. The Calvert Fund for Social Investment allows you to shift your money from its stock portfolio to its money fund without penalty, so you can easily sit out a bear market.

Stock Brokerages. A self-directed IRA permits you to run it as you see fit. Your brokerage can set one up for you. Self-directed IRAs are ideal vehicles for ethical investors because they can buy mutual fund shares, stocks, bonds, or any other vehicle through that brokerage for their account. If you find that you're doing better in your regular portfolio than in your IRA, you should roll over the assets into a self-directed account. Generally, I do not think holders of small IRA accounts should try stocks, since they lack sufficient funds to diversify.

BEYOND IRAS AND KEOGHS

Pensions, IRAs, or Keoghs cover some people's retirement needs. But for many others these vehicles meet only a fraction of their needs. They must look to their portfolios for the additional cash. When you're younger, investing for the long term is reasonable, but as you approach retirement, especially as you need more cash, your portfolio should begin to stress income. Increasingly, you ought to consider your investment portfolio outside of your IRA with safety and income in mind.

While retirees should not plan to use up all the capital they have accumulated over the years, they should plan to spend some of it. Also, while their portfolios ought to be reoriented toward income, a significant portion of it should go toward investments which provide a hedge against inflation. At the very least, portfolio income should rise 8% each year during retirement.

Income-Producing Assets

Often I see retirees in a cash bind just because they've forgotten potential sources of investment income. During retirement you will not be concerned about asset growth so much as with maintaining asset value while generating enough cash to live on. Before you retire, you should review all of your assets in terms of the income they can produce. For instance, does your life insurance policy have cash value? Presumably your children are grown and on their own, so cashing it in may make sense. Or, can it be converted into an annuity with a right of survivorship for your spouse? You and your spouse need the assurance of continued income. Your spouse won't need a lump sum on your death.

Approaching retirement also signals the need for a reappraisal of your portfolio. Have you checked the value of your stocks recently? Just because they don't pay much in dividends doesn't mean they aren't worth a great deal. Perhaps you should sell them and buy higher-yielding securities. I recently persuaded a 75-year-old client to sell his Wang Laboratories common stock. It is a favorite of mine and passed all his ethical screens, but its dividend is very small. High-quality income vehicles to increase his cash flow substantially were what he needed.

I opened this chapter with a problem whose solution benefited both a retiree and a worthy institution. The lesson here is to be open to retirement financing ideas which may sound a little offbeat. A bit of honest creative financing can make the difference between a comfortable retirement and struggling.

Some financial advisers have developed approaches of great appeal to ethical investors. For example, in an interview with *U.S. News & World Report*, financial adviser Fred Nauheim recommended a charitable remainder trust as a good way to fund the retirement years. He noted, "Property such as a home or securities — anything that has given the owner a large, unrealized capital gain — can be donated to a charity, which in turn sets up an annuity for the former owners based on the market value of the property donated. The owners also enjoy substantial tax deductions. The charity sells the home or securities and pays no capital gains tax. Neither do the former owners."[1]

Safety and Risk

Watch your tax bracket. If it has dropped since retirement, you may have investments which are not working hard enough for you. You may not need to pay a premium for sheltered income any more. I've known widows who held municipals their husbands had bought years earlier, not realizing that in their current tax bracket they would have more to spend if they sold the municipals and bought corporates.

Also, don't play with risky investments. The basic portfolio strategy for retirement is to generate income, minimize risk, diversify, and look for investments that provide a hedge against inflation. I've had people say to me, "It's so little, and I want to try to make it grow fast so I can get more income from it." That's a bad attitude for any investor to have, whether retired or not. All growth vehicles involve risk. That little amount won't feel so small if you lose it.

Tax-Deferred Annuities

Investors often use tax-deferred annuities as a vehicle to supplement retirement income. The Internal Revenue Code permits investors to delay paying full taxes on the money invested in annuities until they begin to receive income from them. At retirement the investor's income and tax bracket presumably will be lower than when the money was earned. The principal on an annuity is tax free since it is a return of capital.

An annuity offers a rate of interest that is guaranteed by a legally required reserve maintained by a life insurance company. The safety of the principal is also guaranteed. Those who might put their money into pass-book savings accounts or other equally safe investments will find annuities particularly attractive. However, as the recent failures of Baldwin United and Charter Insurance prove, annuities are not as safe as an insured bank account. You can lose at least some of the yield you're promised.

For the ethical investor annuities are also a dubious opportunity. The insurance company's portfolio probably will not conform to most ethical investors' guidelines. At present no annuity is run along ethical guidelines.

Retirement planning is nothing more than a variation on good financial planning. The principles remain the same; only your circumstances have changed. Where once you may have needed tremendous growth from your investments, now you need less growth and more income. Your planning for retirement should evolve as a natural part of your lifelong money management efforts.

12 MANAGING YOUR MONEY EVERY DAY

WHEN I WAS GROWING UP, my parents ran an Italian-language newspaper which served the industrial cities along Connecticut's coast. The paper survived on the ads placed by local savings and loans, insurance agencies, and groceries. Italians ran these businesses, and they sought business from others who spoke Italian. Not until much later did I realize that every ethnic group adopts the same pattern as it enters American society. Today blacks, Hispanics, women, and other groups, recognizing the success of these tactics, have organized financial institutions and insurance companies that foster their goals by seeking support from those with similar commitments. This chapter describes how, through managing your daily money affairs, you can support such institutions.

BANKS

As Poland tottered toward bankruptcy and its military junta scoured the countryside for Solidarity members, a spokesman for one of New York's leading banks indicated his institution's approval of the new regime. "We don't care what kind of government a country has," he said in effect, "so long as they pay their loans on time." This lack of moral sensitivity should not have surprised anyone, but no one has to support it. Alternatives exist, though they are not easy to find, particularly outside major metropolitan areas.

FIGURE 12-1   Hispanic-Owned Banks by Asset Size

| | | Federal Reserve System (Dollar Amounts in 000s) As of March 31, 1983 | |
	Date Established	Total Assets	Total Deposits
International Bank of Commerce Laredo, TX	Sept. 2, 1966	318,772	290,831
Bank of Miami Miami, FL	April 30, 1956	318,200	270,664
Banco de Ponce New York, NY	Dec. 12, 1972	177,889	177,276
Banco Popular de PR New York, NY	Dec. 2, 1964	120,295	112,593
Continental NB of Miami Miami, FL	May 10, 1974	77,238	70,392
Continental NB El Paso, TX	Sept. 16, 1974	66,555	62,460
Pan American NB Dallas, TX	May 2, 1974	43,121	37,064
Brownsville NB Brownsville, TX	Aug. 23, 1974	40,556	35,420
Zapata National Bank Zapata, TX	Nov. 16, 1961	38,906	35,481
Capital Bank Nat'l Assn Washington, DC	June 18, 1974	33,302	25,635
Santa Ana State Bank Santa Ana, CA	July 1, 1971	32,434	28,360

Source: Reprinted with permission from *Hispanic Business* magazine, September 1983, p. 13. P.O. Box 6757, Santa Barbara, CA 93160. (805) 964-9041.

Types of Banks

Until very recently you could easily distinguish one type of bank from another and evaluate their commitment to their community just based on their names. *Savings banks* (also called *mutual banks*) and *savings and loans* were owned by their depositors. Both were originally organized as membership groups where members pooled their money. Credit unions also operate on this concept.

Savings banks are usually state chartered. Savings and loans can have either federal or state charters. Typically these banks serve the middle and lower classes. Often members of particular ethnic or religious groups would establish savings and loans or thrift institutions to provide small loans or mortgage money to their community.

FIGURE 12-1   *(continued)*

El Pueblo State Bank Espanola, NM	March 20, 1973	32,307	29,386
South Texas NB Laredo, TX	Dec. 5, 1977	31,425	29,842
Bank of Albuquerque Albuquerque, NM	July 9, 1974	29,151	26,924
Centinel Bank Taos, NM	March 1, 1969	29,053	25,815
Capital National Bank New York, NY	July 7, 1975	28,821	25,791
Los Angeles NB Los Angeles, CA	Dec. 18, 1973	27,518	23,827
Hemisphere National Bank Miami, FL	April 17, 1979	27,130	24,937
Metropolitan NB McAllen, TX	Nov. 17, 1972	23,850	21,584
Plaza NB Albuquerque, NM	Aug. 5, 1975	22,276	20,790
United SW NB Santa Fe, NM	Dec. 17, 1973	21,017	17,252
California Security Bank San Jose, CA	Nov. 8, 1973	17,751	16,055
New York National Bank Bronx, NY	Feb. 22, 1982	15,926	14,264
Plaza Bank NA San Antonio, TX	May 10, 1976	15,333	14,079
Nueces National Bank Corpus Christi, TX	Jan. 2, 1973	15,079	13,252
Washington National Bank Chicago, IL	Dec. 2, 1977	12,967	11,796
Industrial National Bank E. Chicago, IL	Dec. 18, 1978	5,808	5,386
TOTALS		1,622,680	1,467,156

By contrast, *commercial banks* have always looked toward larger businesses and the accounts of the people who run and benefit from those businesses. These have been the banks with the large trust departments which handled institutional as well as individual trust funds.

In recent years the lines between these various banks have begun to blur. Banking is being deregulated. Commercial banks have gotten into the savings business, and savings banks have gotten into commercial loans. And depositor-owned institutions have begun to disappear.

The appearance of the full-service bank — offering everything from life insurance to brokerage services — may not be a blessing. The experience of the Great Depression of the 1930s suggests that many smaller financial institutions which are closely tied to a particular city or region better serve the nation than large, multiservice institutions, whose managements' miscalculations can have disproportionate effects on society.

The logic of deregulation — at least to the larger banks who have encouraged it — is that there are now sufficient institutional structures to prevent the abuses which contributed to the economic collapse in the thirties. The establishment of government insurance programs, such as the Federal Deposit Insurance Corporation (FDIC) for national banks and the Federal Savings and Loan Insurance Corporation (FSLIC) for federally chartered savings and loans, have stabilized the system, they argue, so the safeguard provided by diversification is no longer needed. However, the evidence is virtually all to the contrary. Since the advent of deregulation, bank lending policies have been blind not only to the quality of foreign governments but also to the quality of credit risks. It is only necessary to cite the collapse of the Penn Square Bank in Oklahoma, the bankruptcy of the Butcher banks in Tennessee, and the near collapse of Continental Illinois. The current and prospective debacles in the banking industry should convince even the skeptic that where banks and bankers are concerned, small is beautiful. Banks should know their markets and stick to them.

Choosing a Bank

For ethical investors, a bank's ties to its community and its lending policies should be the crucial factors. However, ethical investors can never be 100% sure that any institution's loan policy will fully accord with their own ethical standards. Banks do not give out information on their loans that would allow an ethical investor to make an informed judgment. Here are my guidelines for finding a satisfactory bank.

Smaller Is Usually Better. The smaller the bank, the closer to home its borrowers are likely to be. A typical savings bank does not make international loans. Even the smaller regional banks avoid them, leaving them to the big money center banks (see Figure 12-2) such as Citicorp of New

FIGURE 12-2   Top Ten Money Center Banks

Citicorp	Chemical N.Y.
BankAmerica	Continental Illinois
Chase Manhattan	First Interstate
Manufacturers Hanover	Bankers Trust
J. P. Morgan	Security Pacific

York or Bank of America in San Francisco. (However, as this was being written, the government and the money center banks were dragooning the regional banks into bailing out Brazil.[1])

Lending Philosophy. Finding out about a publicly traded bank's foreign loans is easy. Just look at either its annual report or its 10K report to the SEC, which usually list overseas loan exposure country by country. It is virtually impossible, however, to find out whether those same banks are, for example, loaning to corporations with suspect minority hiring practices. No bank I know of opens its loan portfolio to public scrutiny. Even if it did, the portfolio would require constant monitoring because of daily additions and deletions. For that reason, the best guide to a bank's character is its lending philosophy. This I find best reflected in a bank's annual reports, and sometimes its promotional materials. Without a statement of lending philosophy, the best guide is the nature of the bank. If it is a small savings bank, you may assume that most of its deposits go into personal loans, consumer purchase loans, auto loans, and mortgages.

Some Interesting Banks

Over the last two or three years I have learned of one extraordinary bank and two exceptional banks. These are not the only banks I recommend.

FIGURE 12-3   Black-Owned Banks

Freedom National Bank of New York	Liberty Bank & Trust Company, New Orleans
Independence Bank of Chicago	Consolidated Bank & Trust Company, Richmond, Va.
Seaway National Bank of Chicago	
First Bank National Association, Cleveland	Highland Community Bank, Chicago
Industrial Bank of Washington, Washington, D.C.	Citizens Savings Bank & Trust Company, Nashville
United National Bank of Washington, Washington, D.C.	Tri-State Bank of Memphis
Citizens Trust Bank, Atlanta	The Douglass State Bank, Kansas City
Mechanics and Farmers Bank, Durham, N.C.	City National Bank of New Jersey, Newark
Midwest National Bank, Indianapolis	Union National Bank of Chicago
First Enterprise Bank, Oakland	Century National Bank, Jacksonville, Fla.
First Independence National Bank of Deposit, Detroit	Gateway National Bank, St. Louis
First Texas Bank, Dallas	Tri-State Bank, Markham, Ill.

Source: Black Enterprise, June 1982, p. 145.

Rather they are examples of what banks can and should do for those they serve.

South Shore Bank of Chicago. South Shore Bank is an extraordinary example of what a bank can accomplish. Between 1958 and 1973 the racial composition of Chicago's South Shore had changed from all white to 90% black. In 1973 a small group of investors bought a failing bank in that neighborhood and set out to demonstrate that a bank could revitalize a neighborhood and make a profit. Contrary to banking wisdom, the new investors committed themselves to lending the majority of the bank's resources to help the people of the South Shore, not to seeking out "safer" loans in other neighborhoods. Since 1973 the bank has made money by operating community development subsidiaries and by loaning to businesses and property owners in an inner-city neighborhood that remains 90% black.

South Shore Bank, however, depends on deposits raised outside its

FIGURE 12-4   Banks Founded and Operated by Women

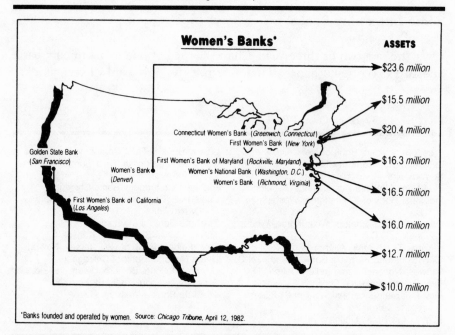

Source: *Chicago Tribune*, 12 April 1982, as reprinted in *Everybody's Business Scorecard*, p. 54.

primary market. A savings account or a long-term deposit there helps offset the extraordinary cost of its development loans. These loans require follow-up by someone who teaches the borrower how to run a business or a rental property; they cost the bank a great deal to handle.

Depositors incur no additional cost or risk when they place funds in South Shore Bank. The bank offers a full range of competitive investment opportunities, and every depositor is insured up to FDIC's $100,000 limit. The bank has a total of about $22 million in outside deposits. Church groups and religious orders own about half these deposits. The concerned investing public, both institutional and private, holds the balance.

Norwest Bank Bloomington. Norwest Bank Bloomington, in Minnesota, is a medium-sized bank with a strong commitment to corporate responsibility. The bank defines its commitment in terms of its *stakeholders'* (employees, suppliers, customers, and shareholders) needs. Its Social Policy Task Force Program, made up of employees representing all levels and divisions, makes recommendations to top management on subjects ranging from community development to privacy, work schedules, and decision making. The bank involves its employees in policy making so they will perceive social and ethical concerns as a part of their jobs. Norwest Bank Bloomington has demonstrated how a business can show responsibility toward and responsiveness to its shareholders.

Chemical Bank of New York. Chemical Bank is a money center bank and certainly will not fit every ethical investor's criteria. However, it has pioneered in some areas of social commitment. Chemical has a strong record in small business and community loans. In 1969 Chemical began its urban affairs department, which introduced the concept of "street bankers" — lending officers assigned to specific communities. These bank officers specialized in developing programs to meet the needs of community-based, nonprofit organizations, in particular those seeking to foster improved housing. Also, since 1970 Chemical has sought small business clients. Through its Urban Service Group, Chemical specializes in lending programs tailored to particular needs of small and minority-owned businesses.

Chemical recognizes that the political and commercial future of large banks depends on the soundness and well-being of the small enterprises on which the economy rests.[2] The bank makes no loans to South Africa and is considered an outstanding contributor to a host of social causes. *Savvy* magazine called it one of the best places for women to work.

FIGURE 12-5   Black-Owned Savings and Loans

Family Savings & Loan Association, Los Angeles

Illinois/Service Federal Savings & Loan Association of Chicago

Carver Federal Savings & Loan Association, New York

Independence Federal Savings & Loan Association of Washington, Washington, D.C.

Founders Savings & Loan Association, Los Angeles

Broadway Federal Savings & Loan Association, Los Angeles

First Federal Savings & Loan Association of Scotlandville, Baton Rouge

Citizens Federal Savings & Loan Association, Birmingham, Al.

United Federal Savings & Loan Association, New Orleans

Advance Federal Savings & Loan Association, Baltimore

Mutual Federal Savings & Loan Association of Atlanta

Home Federal Savings & Loan Association, Detroit

Allied Federal Savings & Loan Association, Jamaica, N.Y.

Mutual Savings & Loan Association, Durham, N.C.

Berean Savings Association, Philadelphia

Cleveland Community Savings Company

Tuskegee Federal Savings & Loan Association, Tuskegee Institute, Al.

People's Savings & Loan Association, Hampton, Va.

Enterprise Savings & Loan Association, Long Beach, Ca.

Standard Savings Association, Houston

Source: *Black Enterprise*, June 1982, p. 159.

Influencing Banks' Ethical Choices

Banks don't like their customers to think of them as powerful financial institutions. Pittsburgh's Mellon Bank, the nation's fourteenth largest, with $25 billion in assets, claims it's "a neighbor you can count on." But on February 8, 1983, Mellon and two other Pittsburgh banks foreclosed on loans to Mesta Machine Company. Mesta filed for bankruptcy the next day. As a result Mellon froze $1.1 million in Mesta's account, which kept its workers from being paid. The United Steel Workers asked Mellon to release the funds. Mellon refused, saying it needed permission from the bankruptcy court.

Mellon did nothing until late May. Then the Denominational Mission Strategy, a church group organized to explore remedies for unemployment in the steel areas, began raising questions about Mellon's substantial loans to foreign steel companies. Very shortly thereafter, United Steel Workers president Lloyd McBride sent letters to union locals, members, and retirees urging them to transfer their Mellon accounts to other banks. As support for the boycott grew, Mellon leaped into action. The Mesta workers got paid.[3]

Mellon's experience reveals the large banks' vulnerability. Unlike Chemical Bank, most resist admitting the extent to which they rely on support in their communities. However, they will respond when faced with the threat of losing the good will of the small depositors on whom their strength rests.

CREDIT UNIONS

Credit unions are cooperatively owned financial institutions organized to meet the financial needs of their members. They offer savings and investment plans, consumer loans, IRAs, and sometimes checking services and credit cards. They provide loans to members only, and only members may open savings accounts. For those eligible to join one, a credit union offers the ethical investor an excellent alternative to a bank. Over 46.5 million Americans belong to 21,402 credit unions.

Credit unions are never organized for profit. Their emphasis is on service to their members. Members may receive somewhat higher rates on their savings than local banks can offer, and they may borrow at a somewhat lower rate. Deposits in many state and all federally chartered credit unions are insured by the National Credit Union Administration, a federal agency which, like the FDIC and FSLIC, insures deposits up to $100,000.

In the past only large companies, unions, and government entities could offer credit union services. However, deregulation has opened these advantages to small companies as well. Also, until 1982 only persons with a "tight common bond" could form a credit union. This usually meant employment by a single company or membership in a union. Now small employee groups may form credit unions even though they work for different entities. See Figure 12-6 for sources of information on joining and forming credit unions.

ETHICAL MONEY MARKET FUNDS

When I began writing this book, interest rates were at an all-time high, and investors were throwing money at money market funds. Two years later, interest rates had declined and money market funds had fallen somewhat out of favor. Nonetheless, they offer excellent places to keep your savings, especially if you think you may have to tap them in a hurry.

Besides the money market accounts offered by your local bank, ethical investors should be aware of two money market funds geared to specific social criteria. The Working Assets Money Fund, as its name indicates, is

FIGURE 12-6   Where to Obtain Information on Credit Unions

National Credit Union Administration Regional Offices	
Address	*Area served*
Region I (Boston) 441 Stuart St. Sixth Floor Boston, MA 02116 (617) 223-6807	Connecticut, Maine, Massachusetts, New Hampshire, New Jersey, New York, Puerto Rico, Rhode Island, Vermont, Virgin Islands
Region 2 (Capital) 1776 G St. NW Suite 700 Washington, DC 20006 (202) 682-1900	Delaware, District of Columbia, Maryland, Pennsylvania, Virginia, West Virginia
Region 3 (Atlanta) 1365 Peachtree St. NE Suite 500 Atlanta, GA 30367 (404) 881-3127	Alabama, Arkansas, Florida, Georgia, Kentucky, Louisiana, Mississippi, North Carolina, South Carolina, Tennessee
Region 4 (Chicago) 230 South Dearborn Suite 3364 Chicago, IL 60604 (312) 886-9697	Illinois, Indiana, Iowa, Michigan, Minnesota, Missouri, North Dakota, Ohio, South Dakota, Wisconsin
Region 5 (Austin) 611 East Sixth St. Suite 407 Austin, TX 78701 (512) 482-5131	Arizona, New Mexico, Oklahoma, Texas
Region 5 (suboffice) LEA Complex 10455 E. 25th Ave. Aurora, CO 80010 (303) 837-3795	Colorado, Idaho, Kansas, Montana, Nebraska, Nevada, Utah, Wyoming
Region 6 (San Francisco) 77 Geary St. Second Floor San Francisco, CA 94108 (415) 556-6277	Alaska, American Samoa, California, Guam, Hawaii, Oregon, Washington

CUNA's public relations department (P.O. Box 431, Madison, Wisconsin, 53701) will send you a brochure entitled "Credit Unions: What They Are, How to Join, and How to Organize One."

Source: D. Sammons, "Giving Credit," *INC.,* June 1983, pp. 166, 170.

most concerned about job creation and work issues. The fund managers put it this way:[4]

> We seek instruments that create jobs and develop the American economy.
> . . . We will attempt to avoid investments in those firms that pollute the
> environment, manufacture weapons . . . or generate nuclear power . . . [or]
> investments that tend to drain capital from the United States or that finance
> repressive regimes. We will not knowingly invest in the obligations of cor-
> porations that . . . consistently violate regulations of the National Labor
> Relations Board or the Equal Employment Opportunity Commission or that
> appear on the AFL-CIO Union Label Department's "Do Not Patronize" list.[4]

You can open an account in this fund with as little as $1000. Subsequent investments must exceed $100. You may request checking privileges on your account.

The Calvert Social Investment Fund Money Market Portfolio runs its money fund along the same guidelines it uses for its mutual funds. I described their standards in Chapter 8. Calvert's minimum initial invest-ment is $1000, and subsequent investments must exceed $250. Checking privileges are available.

INSURANCE

Everyone needs insurance of one form or another, whether homeowner's insurance, life insurance, casualty insurance, or key person insurance. Insurance companies make money by selling their policies and then loaning the receipts in much the same way large banks loan deposits. Also as with banks, concerned investors have no idea whether a company's loan policy is consistent with their standards.

Insurance is a very difficult subject for ethical investors to sort out. On the one hand, the proceeds raised from selling insurance are invested largely without regard to ethical considerations. On the other, the insur-ance industry has shown a commitment to public involvement in social issues which no other industry approaches. Many major insurance com-panies make low-interest loans, provide technical expertise, and aid the management of socially responsive projects. To take just one example, in 1981 Prudential Insurance loaned $1.5 million to purchase farmland where minority group members will be trained to produce and market livestock and vegetable crops through cooperative farming. The project is located in east central Alabama, an area with high unemployment.

The auto insurers supply my favorite example of enlightened self-interest. Without their vigilance and deep pockets, the Reagan Administration would have done far more toward ending the campaign for automobile safety than it did. Among other initiatives, they took the Administration to the Supreme Court to get the airbag regulation reinstated.

The industry sponsors the Center for Corporate Public Involvement. It publishes a bimonthly newsletter, *Response,* which details the social investments various insurance companies and some other corporations are making. For a negative view of the industry's business practices, consult the National Insurance Consumer Organization.

Three Interesting Insurance Companies. Three companies stand out as examples of good insurers. The *Consumers United Group* (CUG) offers a unique opportunity to be involved with a socially committed organization. It provides a wide range of insurance products and services to members of nonprofit associations and cooperatives. These services include term life insurance and health insurance, as well as naturopathic care and acupuncture. CUG's stated goal is "to create a world of peace and justice made up of self-actualized human beings." This minority-owned cooperative is strongly committed to social change at the grass-roots level. Its owners run their company responsibly — group decisions on firings, cooperative participation in management, and no layoffs. The company reinvests proceeds in community development projects aimed at ending racism and poverty. CUG has also invested in programs to retrain convicts and to promote minority housing and small business projects. The company is 80% female and 75% black.

Aetna Life & Casualty Company is one of the best of the large insurers. Its Corporate Responsibility Investment Committee defines the company's investment policy and reviews proposed projects and investments. This committee has served as a model for other companies. Aetna reserves some funds for social investments which do not meet normal financial justification standards. About $30 million per year goes into social investments. Most of this money has gone into housing projects, but some has financed hospitals, colleges, and minority-owned businesses.

The Equitable Life Assurance Society has a strong commitment to social change. *Savvy* has listed it as one of the best places for women to work, and *Black Enterprise* lists it as one of the best places for blacks to work. At the board of directors level, Equitable's Social Performance Committee monitors the company's total business conduct. Its Office of Corporate Social Responsibility assists management in reviewing progress toward corporate social performance goals. The Equitable emphasizes minority business financing. Its minority enterprise small business investment company is the largest privately owned business of its type. The company purchases everything from paper clips to computers from firms run by minority group members, women, or the handicapped. The Equitable also banks with minority-owned institutions and allocates not less than 10% of its advertising budget to minority-owned media.

Not everyone is happy with the Equitable. The Service Employees International Union, representing claims processors at Equitable's Syracuse Group Benefits Office, successfully sought an NLRB order compelling Equitable to begin negotiating with them for a contract. According to the *AFL-CIO News*, the union head instituted a boycott of the company's insurance policies because of the Equitable's illegal delaying tactics in bargaining with its employees.[5]

Bank deposits, money market fund shares, and some life insurance policies are investments very similar to debt securities. Because of their access to vast sums of liquid assets, institutions offering these vehicles can profoundly influence the direction society takes. But with the notable exception of the institutions mentioned in this chapter, they are remarkably resistant to change. In the next chapter, we'll see how activist investors are beginning to move reluctant institutions and corporations.

13 SHAREHOLDER ACTIVISM

I N 1983 proxy wars filled the financial pages like *E.T.* filled the theaters. Superior Oil shareholders successfully sought to change its bylaws to facilitate its sale. Mesa Petroleum tried to swallow Gulf Oil. Dissident Trans World Corp. shareholders lost a proxy battle to force the sale of its money-losing airline, but then won the war when the company proposed to spin it off as a separate corporation. Meanwhile, dissidents at Condec Corp. (heavy equipment and valves) succeeded in electing five members to its board, replacing among others the company's chairman and CEO.

In these battles the stakes were obvious: the fates of companies worth billions of dollars. But few understand the mechanism — the proxy — for conducting the war. Still fewer realize that shareholder activists use this same mechanism to force corporations, their shareholders, and their management to consider their social responsibilities.

Shareholder activists identify companies that don't meet their standards. But instead of avoiding them, activists attempt to reform them through education and example. Their principal means is the shareholder resolution, which appears on the corporation's proxy statement. These resolutions are the means by which the shareholder-owners control policy. In the early 1970s Ralph Nader and other social reformers, and churches such as the Church of Christ began using shareholder resolutions as instruments of social change, and today remain its most consistent exponents.

What does shareholder activism have to do with ethical investing?

Everything. When you invest positively, you make a statement about what you consider vital. Your actions speak to others. The cumulative effects of positive investing are noticed, as the recent torrent of articles on the subject proves. But that is not enough.

If the drive for corporate responsibility is to have real force, two things must happen. First, more shareholders must become aware of their duty to influence corporate action. The proxy mechanism offers the means for creating that awareness. Second, corporations which have not responded to shareholder concerns must be compelled to face these issues. That is not to say that shareholder activists, for example, should force American Electric Power (AEP) to stop strip mining coal. There are at least two sides to that question. What it does mean is that AEP should at least acknowledge the social, economic, and environmental impact of their operations.

THE PROXY MECHANISM

Apart from civil or criminal litigation, the only institutionalized mechanism for affecting corporate awareness is the proxy. *Proxy* means the authority or power to act for another. In this specific case it refers to the power of attorney to vote corporate stock. In order to understand the proxy's central function in governing corporations, a brief look at how corporations are organized is in order.

By law, every corporation must hold an annual meeting of its owners — its shareholders. There they exercise their ownership rights by voting on corporate policy and for directors who manage the corporation on their behalf. Each share — not each shareholder — is entitled to one vote. For shareholders in a small company, a proxy is a convenience. A shareholder simply signs a letter authorizing someone to vote her shares either in a particular manner or at the agent's discretion, and she can skip the annual meeting. But if the corporation is as large as General Electric, proxies are a necessity. With tens of thousands of shareholders holding half a billion shares of stock, the corporation has to have an effective means of tallying votes. The proxy mechanism serves that purpose.

The law requires the corporation to notify shareholders in advance of the annual meeting of its date, time, and place, as well as the matters which will be put to a vote. This notification takes the form of a *proxy statement* — a pamphlet which describes the candidates for the corporation's board and contains the text of the resolutions on which the shareholders will vote. Accompanying the proxy statement is a card — the actual proxy instrument — which instructs the corporation as to how the shareholder wishes to vote. In order to vote, shareholders must either submit their proxies to the corporation before the meeting or attend and submit the card there.

The use of proxies is not new. But in order to see how they are used to further social causes, a brief look at the proxy movement's origin is in order.

ETHICAL PROXY RESOLUTIONS

In 1934, when it created the Securities Exchange Commission (SEC), Congress stated that "fair corporate suffrage is an important right that should be attached to every equity security bought on a public exchange."[1] In 1942 the SEC held that shareholder suffrage requires companies to publish shareholder resolutions in their proxy statements. In 1972 Ralph Nader's efforts showed that these resolutions could include social issues.

Philosophical Debate

The social proxy movement arose in the late 1960s and early 1970s. Civil rights, Vietnam, environmental issues, and more prompted people to look at the corporation's role in society. But it is an outright misrepresentation to claim, as many do, that it is a relic of an aberrational era. The truth is that since early corporations first appeared at the dawn of the modern era, political theorists have debated their role in society. In 1725 the British House of Commons, appalled by their corrupting influence, effectively banned them.

What about modern corporations? Do they have any social responsibilities as I have used the term in this book? You and I may think the answer to this question is obvious. But for Milton Friedman, the answer to that question is entirely different.

> I have called [the doctrine of corporate social responsibility] a "fundamentally subversive doctrine" in a free society and have said that in such a society, "there is one and only one social responsibility of business — to use its resources and engage in activities designed to increase its profits so long as

FIGURE 13-1   Top 25 Corporate Pension Funds

Rank	Fund	Assets ($ millions)
1	American Telephone & Telegraph Co.	45,600
2	General Motors Corp.	15,800
3	General Electric Co.	9,368
4	International Business Machines	6,986
5	Ford Motor Co.	6,611
6	E. I. du Pont de Nemours and Co.	6,143
7	U.S. Steel & Carnegie Pension Fund	5,566
8	Exxon Corp.	5,510
9	GTE Corp.	3,900
10	Eastman Kodak Co.	3,665
11	Mobil Oil Corp.	3,500
12	Rockwell International	3,500
13	United Technologies Corp.	3,325
14	Boeing Co.	3,200
15	Shell Oil Co.	3,172
16	Sears, Roebuck & Co.	3,056
17	Westinghouse Electric	2,815
18	McDonnell Douglas Corp.	2,778
19	Lockheed Corp.	2,729
20	Standard Oil Co. of California	2,645
21	United Air Lines, Inc.	2,510
22	Standard Oil Co. (Indiana)	2,320
23	Atlantic Richfield Co.	2,100
24	Union Carbide Corp.	2,051
25	Caterpillar Tractor	2,020

Source: Reprinted with permission from *Pensions & Investment Age,* January 24, 1983, pp. 1–27. © Crain Communications, Inc., 1983.

it stays within the rules of the game, which is to say, engages in open and free competition without deception or fraud."[2]

"Fundamentally subversive doctrine" — those are strong words, indeed. But is a movement demanding that business acknowledge its leadership in society really subversive? Is the corporation, as Milton Friedman would have us believe, some sort of neutral economic force? A Delaware court has ruled that "shareholders have the inherent right to assert their individual interests within their company, however bizarre, unpopular, or unusual they may be."[3] The contradiction between the law's view that shareholders own the corporation and Friedman's that "'business' as a whole cannot be said to have responsibilities"[4] brings into focus the challenges activists face.

The Movement's Origins

Many arguments against shareholder involvement in corporate policy making only forwarded the movement. For instance, without adequate information, corporate executives claimed, shareholders could not understand the basis of corporate policies. So shareholders began to demand information. At first these inquiries received rebuffs. Robert S. Potter, then Chancellor of the Episcopal Diocese of New York and a partner in a major New York law firm, telephoned the chairman of a company in which the church held 6000 shares. Potter wanted to set up a meeting to discuss the company's Puerto Rican mining operation and its plans for relocating families, environmental protection, and land reclamation. The chairman's response was curt. "I won't see either you or your bishop. The Episcopal Church has no business getting into the matter whether as a stockholder or otherwise. You can send me a memorandum if you wish."[5]

The social proxy movement actually began with Campaign GM. The Project on Corporate Responsibility, a Ralph Nader organization, targeted General Motors because it was then the largest industrial corporation in America. It offered nine resolutions to GM for submission to its share-

FIGURE 13-2   Federal Government Receipts, 1950–1982, by Major Category, as Percent of Total Receipts*

Fiscal year	Personal tax and nontax receipts	Corporate profits tax accruals	Indirect business tax and nontax accruals	Contributions for social insurance
1952	44.2	29.6	14.9	11.2
1956	44.4	27.9	14.3	13.5
1960	44.9	23.5	13.9	17.6
1964	43.9	22.2	13.5	20.4
1968	44.7	20.7	10.7	24.0
1972	47.1	16.0	9.3	27.6
1976	43.6	16.7	7.7	32.1
1980	47.6	13.3	6.6	32.4
1982	49.0	8.1	8.2	34.7

* Components may not total 100 percent due to rounding.

Note: In 1982, if contributions for social insurance are excluded, receipts from personal taxes are 75 percent, corporate taxes 12.4 percent, and indirect taxes 12.6 percent of the total.

Source: Adapted from Joint Committee on Taxation, "Study of 1982 Effective Tax Rates of Selected Large U.S. Corporations," 98th Cong., 1st Sess. (1983), pp. 10, 16, based on the Economic Report of the President, 1970 and 1983.

holders at its 1970 annual meeting. These resolutions dealt with the needs of minorities, workers, and consumers.

General Motors challenged its shareholders' right to raise these questions in proxy resolutions. After a lengthy debate, the SEC ruled that two of the nine had to be submitted to the shareholders. One of the resolutions asked that the GM board be expanded to make it more broadly representative of the public at large. The other sought to establish a committee for corporate responsibility. Neither resolution received even the 3% of the votes then needed under SEC regulations for resubmission at the next annual meeting. But the movement had been born.[6]

As shareholders began to exercise their right to put resolutions before annual meetings, many corporations opposed resolutions or refused to put them in the proxy statement. Often shareholders were thereby forced to bring a costly lawsuit in order to enforce their rights. Because they lost these cases routinely, the corporations tried another tack. In 1983 they persuaded the SEC to impose restrictions on the resolution mechanism. The SEC increased the percentage of affirmative votes required to reintroduce a resolution. Since social issue shareholder resolutions rarely receive more than 5% of the vote, these requirements may have a devastating effect on the activists' educative efforts. Timothy Smith, director of the Interfaith Center, says, "These new regulations represent a tilt toward those businesses which may attempt to exclude legitimate stockholder concerns. But the basic process itself appears to be intact: concern about the ethical conduct of corporations is too widespread among churches and other socially responsive investors to be shut down or sidetracked at this point."[7]

New Procedural Hurdles

What are the effects of the SEC's new rules on shareholder resolutions? Carl Olson, one of the leading conservative activists, counted 15.

1. At the time of submitting his proposal, a stockholder must own 1% or $1000 in market value of the company's stock. In effect this means owning considerably more than $1000 to guard against a stock market downturn.
2. A stockholder must own the same stock for at least a year before submitting a proposal. Thus a stockholder must actually own a stock at least 18 months before an annual meeting, since a proposal must be submitted about six months before the meeting.

3. A proposal may not be on the same subject matter as any other which during the previous five years failed to receive a prescribed vote percentage at any meeting.
4. A proposal must involve 5% or more of the total corporate assets.
5. A proposal must involve 5% or more of the total corporate net earnings.
6. A proposal must involve 5% or more of the total corporate gross sales.
7. Proposals dealing with the last part of a fiscal year are discriminated against, because a proposal has to pass all three 5% tests for the entire most recent fiscal year.
8. Proposals dealing with the past years of corporate activity are discriminated against, especially in a quickly growing company, for the same reason.
9. A stockholder may not make a mailing to stockholders who own 25% or more of the voting stock in the corporation.
10. A stockholder must report the dates when he acquired the stock he owns in the corporation, regardless of how many separate acquisitions — including stock splits, stock dividends, dividend reinvestments, payroll deduction — are involved and when those transactions took place.
11. A proposal must be submitted at least 120 days before the corporation proxy statement is to be sent out. The previous rule was 90 days.
12. A stockholder may sponsor only one proposal. Previously, the number was two.
13. The proxy statement may state the number of shares held by a resolution's proposer and her name and address. If not printed, this information must be made available to anyone on request.
14. Proposals must receive a 5% affirmative vote in order to be brought up at the next year's meeting. The previous rule was 3%.
15. Proposals must receive an 8% affirmative vote in order to be brought up at a third annual meeting. The previous rule required 6%.[8]

Although these regulations set up some new barriers to stockholder activism, they don't mark the end of the road for the social proxy movement. Its history over the last decade argues for its continued health.

THE CURRENT SCENE

Since the early 1970s, when company managements reacted with outrage to social proxy resolutions, great advances have been made. Now a spirit of cooperation exists in many — but not all — companies. Allen R. Nelson, secretary of Connecticut General Life Insurance (now part of CIGNA) has said, "I believe the effectiveness of the shareholder movement has been demonstrated in several different ways — through the higher levels of management involvement, the significant number of companies dialoguing with shareholders, the increased sophistication of the resolutions themselves, and most important, the impact the resolutions are having on companies."[9]

Each year more American companies make an effort to demonstrate their concerns on social issues. As Derald H. Ruttenberg of Studebaker-Worthington put it some years ago, "The 'ethical' investor movement gives managers a chance, I think, to share the limitations on their ability to change things and other problems with activists, large institutional investors, and the general public."[10] Today companies are more willing to meet with shareholders and to implement their suggestions without going through a proxy vote. Now more companies understand the point made by James E. Heard, director of the Investor Responsibility Research Center, who said, "Shareholder resolutions have a beneficial effect simply because to answer questions at the annual meeting, company executives have to be briefed on the issues raised."[11]

The 1983 Resolutions

In 1983 more than two hundred social responsibility resolutions were proposed for proxy statements, compared with two in 1973. Here is just a sampling of the issues.

Trade with Communist Countries. Exxon, IBM, Pepsico, Control Data, and Occidental Petroleum received resolutions asking that they not buy goods or services produced by slave or forced labor in Communist countries.[12]

Weaponry. William Whistler submitted a resolution to General Electric asking the company "to support efforts to ban weapons in space; to direct research and development funds to peaceful uses of space; to cease involvement in the use of space for nuclear warfare-related systems; and to stop nuclear weapons manufacture."[13]

Antiunion Activities. On behalf of members of the International Typographical Union (ITU), the League for Industrial Democracy submitted a resolution to Capital Cities Communications requesting reports on its labor

FIGURE 13-3   Soviet Siberian Pipeline

The U.S. State Department has accused the Soviet Union of using forced labor on the Siberian Pipeline. The following corporations were asked to make public a statement that they did
not benefit from such a practice.

Caterpillar Tractor
Dresser Industries
General Electric
Ruhrgas — buyer of the gas
        major stockholders are
            Exxon
            Mobil
            Shell
            Texaco

Source: Stockholders for World Freedom, Carl Olson, Chairman, P.O. Box 7273, Alexandria, VA
22307, (703) 780-0180. Reprinted with permission.

policies. The company had a history of poor relations with the ITU and
the Newspaper Guild. The ITU solicited support from Capital Cities'
shareholders, including Morgan Guaranty Trust Company, State Street
Research & Management, and Citibank, and from more than one hundred
union funds. The resolution received 11.5% of the votes cast. No labor
resolution had ever reached that level without management support. The
union will keep pushing for the report in 1984. Observing the success of
the J. P. Stevens campaign, it intends to enlist other unions to put pressure
on Capital Cities' lenders.

South Africa. Church groups attempted to commend First Boston Corp.,
Chemical Bank, Sears, Roebuck & Company, and Shearson/American
Express for policies restricting loans to South Africa. The proponents chose
proxy resolutions on the theory that shareholders read the proxy materials
more carefully than other materials sent to them.[14] Some activists question
the wisdom of using the proxy for commendations. It seems to trivialize
the process and to give credence to objections based on cost and irrelev-
ance. Letters to the board and senior management would seem a better
route.

Some state legislatures have acted on the South Africa issue. In 1982
Connecticut became the first state to establish social performance criteria
for state investments. Connecticut now requires all companies in which it
owns stock which do business in South Africa to sign the Sullivan Principles (see Appendix D for more details). In 1983 Massachusetts followed

with a measure prohibiting the investment of state funds in companies or banks doing business in South Africa.

Contributions to Political Candidates

The nascent movement received its strongest impetus from the financial support — both legal and illegal — corporations generated for President Nixon's reelection campaign.

Watergate showed all too clearly that not all corporate contributions are directed toward charities. In 1973 and 1974 a total of 21 corporations or their executives or both were indicted for illegally contributing corporate funds to political campaigns.[15]

Since Watergate, corporate political action committees have become legal vehicles for political contributions. In 1981–82, corporate PACs took in $47.1 million, while labor organization PACs took in $37.4 million.

FIGURE 13-4   1981–82 Top Ten Corporate PAC Contributors to Federal
                Candidates

Tenneco Employees Good Government Fund (Tenneco Inc.)	$454,150
Sunbelt Good Government Cmte. of Winn-Dixie Stores (Winn-Dixie Stores, Inc.)	281,375
Harris Corporation Federal Political Action Committee (Harris Corporation)	249,250
American Family Political Action Committee (American Family Corporation)	232,775
Fluor Corp. Public Affairs Committee (Fluor Corporation)	233,200
Litton Industries Inc. Employees Pol. Assistance Cmte. (Litton Industries, Inc.)	218,550
United Technologies Corporation PAC (United Technologies Corporation)	204,275
Amoco Political Action Committee (Standard Oil Company — Indiana)	193,327
Grumman Political Action Committee (Grumman Corporation)	189,978
Philip Morris Political Action Committee (Philip Morris Inc.)	188,327

Source: Federal Election Commission.

Others, like the Realtors PAC, the American Medical Association PAC, and the League of Conservative Voters — received $43.2 million. PACs of all types — including the National Rifle Association's and the National Conservative Political Action Committee — spent $190.3 million during 1981–82.[16] Perhaps the most disturbing corporate contributions are those gifts meant to influence the outcome of various ballot referenda. For instance, Ralston Purina, the food company, gave $15,000 in 1980 to defeat a Missouri nuclear power referendum. Not surprisingly, Union Electric contributed $1,150,000 and Westinghouse $100,000, for they had stakes in power plants in Missouri. But why Ralston Purina? Other corporations have made large contributions on both sides of tax limitation efforts, antinuclear referenda, and gun control initiatives. These donations and others like them have led to shareholder concern.

FIGURE 13-5   25 Companies Paying No Federal Income Taxes on Earnings in 1981

Company Name	Pre-Tax Earnings (in $ millions)
1. Xerox Corp.	1,179,900
2. Tenneco, Inc.	1,089,000
3. Dow Chemical Co.	733,000
4. BankAmerica Corp.	647,950
5. Union Pacific Corp.	594,416
6. Chase Manhattan Corp.	564,041
7. Amerada Hess Corp.	545,593
8. CSX Corp.	523,400
9. Burlington Northern, Inc.	418,975
10. TRW, Inc.	385,989
11. Signal Companies, Inc.	355,800
12. Santa Fe Industries, Inc.	331,400
13. Security Pacific Corp.	331,159
14. Southern Railway Co.	330,876
15. Anheuser-Busch Companies, Inc.	325,200
16. Weyerhaeuser Co.	310,644
17. Chemical Bank	288,312
18. Deere & Co.	280,363
19. IMC Corp.	254,400
20. Banker's Trust Co.	253,799
21. IC Industries, Inc.	233,800
22. Georgia-Pacific Corp.	230,000
23. Southern Pacific Co.	223,300
24. McDonnell Douglas Corp.	218,400
25. Air Products & Chemicals, Inc.	202,483

Source: Adapted with permission from "Effective Corporate Tax Rates in 1981; A Special Supplement Prepared by the Editors of Tax Notes," Arlington, VA, Tax Analysts, 1982.

GROUPS IN THE SOCIAL PROXY ARENA

The groups proposing shareholder resolutions are both small and large. Action on Smoking and Health (ASH) held one share in 16 of the 21 airlines to which it proposed a number of smoke-free flights or nonsmoking areas in airport terminals — a situation that the new SEC rules will keep from happening again. At the other end of the spectrum, a proposal to Xerox on its operations in South Africa was cosponsored by holders with 1,324,589 shares. Here are some of the more prominent activists.

Religious Groups

Churches at the national level have about $25 billion to invest in the market. (This figure is not so astronomical when you consider that the value of the stock of the top five hundred publicly traded firms tops $1.8 trillion.) Some churches and religious orders, like the Sisters of Loretto, have used their stock effectively.

United Church of Christ. Dr. Audrey Smock oversees investments for the United Church of Christ, which has roughly $500 million to invest. The church's pension fund owns stocks in about 130 of the Fortune 500. Dr. Smock reports that when Sears bought the investment firm of Dean Witter Reynolds, many church groups protested its new subsidiary's sale of bonds for South Africa. "At first, Sears would not respond," she says, "so we filed shareholder resolutions. The company then agreed to undertake a policy review and, after the study, not only changed the policy but went further and asked the churches to help write the policy."[17]

Interfaith Center of Corporate Responsibility. One of the most active groups is the Interfaith Center of Corporate Responsibility (ICCR). Its members include one hundred seventy Roman Catholic orders and dioceses and seventeen Protestant denominations.[18]

The center has sponsored resolutions on issues including employment practices, nuclear weapons, investments in South Africa, and mining in Brazil. In 1983 ICCR asked Atlantic Richfield and Exxon to "describe and evaluate the projects in which they are involved in Chile." They also proposed that Upjohn "report to shareholders on its manufacture of Depo-Provera, a drug that has not been approved for use in the United States

FIGURE 13-6   Results of Annual Meeting Votes Spring 1983

Following are votes on resolutions sponsored by church groups that appeared on the ballots at corporate annual meetings the spring of 1983. These votes have been confirmed by the companies unless marked with an asterisk (*):

Corporation	Issue	% of total
Abbott	WHO Code compliance	4.1
Alcan	Report on investment in South Africa	7.2
Allied	Extraordinary session on involvement in nuclear weapons production	2.8
Allis-Chalmers	Plant closings	3.9
American Home Products	Report on drug lobbying in Bangladesh	3.1
AT&T	Termination of Department of Energy nuclear weapons contract	4.0
Bristol-Myers	WHO Code compliance	4.4
	Secret ballot	6.7
Caterpillar Tractor	Plant closings	4.7
Chase Manhattan	Weatherization loans in low income neighborhoods	5.7
	Report on loans to Chile	4.7
Chemical Bank	Commendation of policy on South Africa	78.3
	Report on loans to Chile	2.5
Cincinnati Gas & Electric	Nuclear power	5.9
Citicorp	No loans to South African government	4.6
Consolidated Edison	Disclosure on Indian Point	6.2
	Lifeline rates	4.1
Continental Illinois	Disclosure on international loans	5.3
Control Data	Review of contracts with South African government	6.8
Crocker National	Disclosure on loans to South Africa	2.5
Detroit Edison	Nuclear power	10.5
Dresser Industries	Report on Sullivan Principles	8.1
Dun & Bradstreet	Sullivan Principles	9.9
Eaton	Sullivan Principles	11.7
	No expansion in South Africa	9.3
Exxon	Mining on Indian lands	2.5
First Chicago	Krugerrand sales	3.2
Fluor	Report on operations in Chile	4.1
General Dynamics	Withdraw bid on cruise; no bids on weapons affected by freeze	1.0*
General Electric	No expansion in South Africa	2.7
	Plant closing in California; expansion in Brazil	2.1
	Position on nuclear freeze; criteria for Department of Defense contracts	1.6

Source: Interfaith Center for Corporate Responsibility, *The Corporate Examiner,* June 1983, N.Y., NY, pp. 1, 4, 5.

FIGURE 13-6   *(continued)*

GTE	MX contingency planning committee	3.8
Houston Industries	Nuclear power	7.3
Ingersoll-Rand	No expansion in South Africa; sign Sullivan Principles	11.2
IBM	Criteria for Department of Defense contracts	2.1
ITT	Minority employment	3.4
Internorth	Weatherization	3.0
McDonnell Douglas	Secret ballot	6.6
	Withdraw bid on Cruise; no bids on weapons affected by freeze	1.8
Mobil	Relationship to Montgomery Ward	4.8
Monsanto	Termination of Department of Energy nuclear weapons contract	1.8
Morgan (J. P.)	No loans to South African government	4.8
	Report on loans to Chile	6.0
Motorola	No loans to South African government	10.3
	Operations in South Korea	8.6
N. Carolina Nat'l Bank	No loans to South African government	4.9
Occidental Petroleum	Right to speak at shareholders' meeting	7.4*
	Toxic waste	6.4*
Pacific Gas & Electric	Nuclear power	5.8
Phibro-Salomon	No loans to South African government	3.8
Philadelphia Electric	Nuclear power	10.3
Republic New York	Disclosure on international loans	1.0*
	Disclosure on loans to Chile	10.9*
Reynolds (R. J.)	Tobacco sales in the Third World	3.5
Rockwell International	Consider ethical and legal objections to nuclear weapons involvement	3.7
Singer	Criteria for Department of Defense contracts	4.7
Tenneco	Criteria for Department of Defense contracts	2.9
Texaco	No sales to South African police and military	7.3
Texas Instruments	Criteria for Department of Defense contracts	1.9
TRW	Reevaluate and terminate MX contract	2.6
Union Carbide	Commend for withdrawal from Oak Ridge	1.8
Union Electric	Nuclear plant construction	5.6
	Report on nuclear plant accident costs	8.0
U.S. Steel	Report of plans to reinvest in steel; plant closing	11.6
Wells Fargo	No loans to South African government	8.2
	Report on loans to Chile	6.3
Westinghouse	Employment practices	6.4
	Discontinue operations in South Africa	2.1
Xerox	No expansion in South Africa	5.2
	No sales to South African police and military	6.9

as a contraceptive but is marketed for that use in a number of other countries."[19]

Tim Smith, ICCR's director, notes, "Most companies now give us grudging respect. Most corporations now agree that they should act — although they may not — in a responsible manner. Of course, there is room for disagreement on what is responsible."

Disagreement there is, and not just on what is responsible. D. J. Kirchoff, chief executive officer of Castle & Cooke (processed and fresh foods), has dubbed church activists "anti-business radicals in clerical garb." Kirchoff quotes Reginald Jones, GE's former CEO, as saying of them, "like revolutionists everywhere, their end justifies their means, and we are sometimes shocked by their hypocritical distortion of facts to fit ideological preconceptions and prejudices."[20]

Political Groups

Accuracy in Media. AIM submitted proposals to CBS asking the network to settle a libel suit filed against it by General William C. Westmoreland. AIM wanted CBS to "offer compensation to Westmoreland and air a program to inform the public of the errors in the original broadcast."[21]

The American Jewish Congress. In 1983 the AJC proposed resolutions to the 23 companies requesting reports on their lobbying efforts to sell Airborne Warning and Control Systems (AWACS) to Saudi Arabia. (See Figure 13-7.)[22] In 1976 and 1977, the AJC sponsored resolutions at over 30 companies asking for disclosure of their roles in the Arab boycott of Israel.[23]

The Foundation for the Study of Philanthropy. This foundation has sponsored resolutions asking corporations to stop making charitable contributions to universities which forbid their professors and researchers to work with the Central Intelligence Agency or which allow any Communist, Marxist, Leninist, or Maoist to work at the school.

Shareholders for World Freedom. Shareholders for World Freedom regularly proposes resolutions against doing business with Communist countries. Carl Olson, its chairman, also heads Stockholders Against the Government Burden and the Stockholder Sovereignty Society, which deal respectively with taxpayer and corporate suffrage issues.

FIGURE 13-7   American Jewish Congress Resolution on Sale of AWACs
to Saudi Arabia, 1982

In 1982 the American Jewish Congress (AJC) submitted proxy resolutions to the 23 companies listed below requesting that the companies report on: steps taken to influence congres-
sional and public opinion; company funds spent on AWACs lobbying in 1981 and lobbying on
general Middle East issues in 1982; what part of those expenses would be claimed as tax-
deductible; whether management planned further lobbying on Mideast issues; and how lobbying on Mideast issues has advanced the interests of the corporation.

Alcoa	GTE
American Airlines	Halliburton
Blount, Inc.	H. J. Heinz
Boeing	Kellogg
John Deere	Mobil Oil Corp.
Dravo	NL Industries
Dresser Industries	Owens-Illinois
Eastern Airlines	Republic Steel
Fluor Corp.	SmithKline-Beckman
FMC	United Technologies
Ford	Westinghouse
Greyhound	

Source: IRRC News for Investors, February 1983, pp. 23, 24. Reprinted with permission.

The Emergence of Institutions

Currently over $400 billion in assets rests in pension funds. (See Figures
13-8 through 13-10.) Observers estimate that figure will reach $3 trillion
by 1995.[24] Add the hundreds of billions in charitable foundations, college
and university endowments, church funds, and mutual funds, and you have
a powerful force for social change over the years ahead.

Pension Funds. Pension funds, for instance, hold close to half of the equity
in U.S. corporations. In 1976 just three bank trust departments — Morgan
Guaranty Trust, Bankers Trust, and Citibank — held over $47 billion in
equities within their pension trust portfolios. At that time the Morgan
Guaranty Trust was the largest single holder of stock in IBM, Exxon,
Eastman Kodak, General Electric, Ford, Mobil, Philip Morris, DuPont,
Union Carbide, and ITT.[25]
    Most trust officers hold the voting rights of the stock they administer.
The Superior Oil proxy fight in 1983 highlighted the dilemma this can
create both for the trust officers and for those on whose behalf they are
administering the funds. Dissident shareholders sought a change in the
company's bylaws to facilitate selling the company. Citibank's trust de-

FIGURE 13-8   Top 25 Public Pension Funds

Rank	Fund	Assets (in $ millions)
I	New York State Common Retirement Fund	16,968
2	New York City Retirement System	15,953
3	California Public Employees Retirement System	13,507
4	New York State Teachers' Retirement System	9,975
5	Teacher Retirement System of Texas	7,313
6	California State Teachers Retirement System	7,298
7	Michigan State Employees Retirement System	6,339
8	Ohio Public Employees Retirement System	6,291
9	Wisconsin Investment Board	6,184
10	Ohio Teachers Retirement System	6,176
I I	New Jersey Division of Investment	6,150
12	North Carolina Retirement System	6,073
13	Florida State Board of Administration	4,659
14	Pennsylvania School Employees Retirement System	4,230
15	Minnesota State Board of Investment	4,088
16	Washington State Investment Board	3,557
17	Los Angeles County Employees' Retirement Association	3,402
18	Oregon Public Employees Retirement System	3,400
19	Georgia State Retirement System	3,208
20	Alabama Retirement System	3,017
21	Pennsylvania State Employees Retirement System	3,008
22	Illinois Teachers' Retirement System	2,890
23	Maryland Teachers' Retirement System	2,890
24	Colorado Public Employees Retirement Association	2,760
25	Virginia Supplemental Retirement System	2,600

Source: Reprinted with permission from Pensions & Investment Age, January 24, 1983, pp. 1–27, © Crain Communications, Inc., 1983.

partment held one million shares of Superior for its clients. Superior Oil was also a Citibank client. Nonetheless, Citibank voted against Superior's management because the trust officers felt the resolution was in the best interest of their accounts. Donald C. Carter, who led the organization handling proxy solicitations for the dissidents, said that the institutions voted four to one in favor of their resolution.[26] Ten years ago that would have been unimaginable.

Institutional Activists. Many of the social proxy battles are now being led by institutional investors, such as pension funds and unions. They can threaten to reinvest their huge sums, thereby substantially affecting a stock's market value or a bank's cash flow. In 1981 the California teachers' pension plan, with a sizable investment in Standard Oil of Indiana

FIGURE 13-9   Top Ten Union Pension Funds

Fund	Assets (in $ millions)
Teamsters, Western Conference	3,789
Teamsters, Central States	3,721
United Mine Workers of America, Natl. H.Q.	1,912
International Brotherhood of Electrical Workers	1,282
Boilermakers, Blacksmiths National Pension Trust	1,075
Bakery and Confectionery Union & Industry	845
International Union of Operating Engineers	752
Marine Engineers Beneficial Association	643
Machinists and Aerospace Workers	600
Garment Workers International Headquarters	545

Source: Reprinted with permission from Pensions & Investment Age, January 24, 1983, pp. 1–27, © Crain Communications, Inc., 1983.

(Amoco), asked the company to reveal its hiring policies. Indiana Standard refused. This $7.5 billion fund bought more shares until its total investment reached 828,000 shares. Indiana Standard finally surrendered the information. "When you're talking about 828,000 shares, that's a little different than picketing from a church group," noted Stuart Baldwin, of the Council on Economic Priorities, a nonprofit research organization which monitors corporate activities.[27]

The willingness of big institutions to vote against management leads me to believe that more institutions can be persuaded to support social issue proxy efforts and similar campaigns. This is where the individual ethical investor can play an important role. The institutions will not move of their own accord. They respond to pressure. So it is critically important for ethical investors to know who controls their pension fund, for example. They should study the organizations in which they are involved — from colleges to charities — and see who runs their money. The right questions about their votes may yield interesting results. Remember: money managers work for their clients, not vice versa.

One of the best illustrations of successful lobbying of this type involves college and university portfolios. Harvard University now has an Advisory Committee on Shareholder Responsibility that suggests how the university should vote on public issue proxies. The Harvard Corporation Committee on Shareholder Responsibility reports the actual votes and the reasoning behind them. One area in which Harvard has not led is in divesting itself of securities issued by companies doing business in South Africa. By con-

FIGURE 13-10   Eight Largest Miscellaneous Funds

Fund	Assets (in $ millions)
United Nations Joint Staff Pension Fund	2,600
United Methodist Church	1,107
Tennessee Valley Authority	1,020
Southern Baptist Convention	947
World Bank Staff Retirement Plan	700
National Rural Electric Cooperative Association	690
United Presbyterian Church Pension Board	678
Episcopal Ministers' Church Pension Fund	600

Source: Reprinted with permission from *Pensions & Investment Age,* January 24, 1983, pp. 1–27, © Crain Communications, Inc., 1983.

trast, Michigan State has divested. Members of Harvard's class of 1983 have set up a separate alumni fund to be held in escrow until the university divests. If Harvard has not done so in 20 years, the money will go to charity. Meanwhile, income from the fund will finance annual lectures on conditions in South Africa.

Charitable Foundations. Charitable foundations have a great and largely unexplored potential in this field. Mary Camper-Titsingh, social responsibility analyst at the Ford Foundation, told me, "The Ford Foundation does not restrict its investment policy, but it uses proposals extensively to carry out policies trustees have set. Not too many foundations vote proxies. Since 1972 the Ford Foundation has, as has the Rockefeller Foundation. In the 1970s it was very eccentric if you voted proxies. Now that attitude has changed completely. More responsible organizations recognize the value of a forum for public concerns."

A FINAL THOUGHT

What drew me to ethical investing was my desire not to invest in certain types of companies. I soon discovered that ethical investing offered a means to invest my own and my clients' money positively, allowing us to make a personal statement about what we regard as the critical issues affecting our society. Only much later did I recognize the enormous potential for exercising collective power.

The key to the power of ethical investing is the recognition that corporations and institutions are owned and managed by people. Ethical investing insists on their humanity. It denies them the luxury of pretending to be impersonal economic forces. It requires a recognition of responsibility for one's actions, and it demands that others assume responsibility for theirs. As an instrument for change, both personal and social, ethical investing is unequaled.

Appendix A

SELF-ASSESSMENT OF FINANCIAL RESOURCES

Before starting an investment program, and every year after you start, you should assess your financial position to determine how much money you actually have to put into investments. I suggest that you make your lists using the charts that follow. These charts are designed to help you make calculations, as opposed to an inventory of assets and liabilities. Anyone you turn to for financial advice will want this information. You can save a good deal of time and trouble if you do the inventory in Chapter 1 and fill out these worksheets first.

Net Worth Analysis			
Assets (at fair market value)	Self	Spouse	Category Totals
Cash and bank accounts	$	$	$
Accounts receivable			
Residence(s)			
Home furnishings			
Personal effects (e.g., heirloom watch)			
Securities			
Cash value of insurance[a]			
Business interests			
Employee benefits[b]			
Miscellaneous			
Total	$	$	$

a. Face amount: self $
                 spouse $

   Additional amounts payable on death, not included above: self $
                                                     spouse $

b. Exclude benefits payable only on death, or those which are forfeitable. Verify data with employer.

Liabilities	Self	Spouse	Category Totals
Mortgages	$	$	$
Bank loans			
Accounts payable			
Insurance policy loans			
Other debts			
Pledges to charity			
Taxes			
Total	$	$	$
Net worth (assets less liabilities)	$	$	$

Income (by month)	Jan.	Feb.	Mar.	April	May	June	July
Salary/fees	$	$	$	$	$	$	$
Dividends							
Interest							
Capital gains							
Royalties							
Total income per month	$						

Income	Aug.	Sept.	Oct.	Nov.	Dec.	Total
Salary/fees	$	$	$	$	$	$
Dividends						$
Interest						$
Capital gains						$
Royalties						$
Total income per month	$					
Annual income	$					
Average income per month (annual income divided by 12)						$

Expenses (by month)	Jan.	Feb.	Mar.	April	May	June	July	Aug.	Sept.	Oct.	Nov.	Dec.	Total
Food	$	$	$	$	$	$	$	$	$	$	$	$	$
Mortgage													$
Property taxes													$
Maintenance													$
Utilities													$
Transportation													$
Clothing													$
Toiletries													$
Entertainment													$
Medical													$
Dental													$
Education													$
Insurance premiums													$
Investments													$
State taxes													$
Federal taxes													$
Local taxes													$
Total expenses per month	$												
Annual expenses	$												
Average expenses per month (annual expenses divided by 12)													$

Appendix B

DIRECTORY OF ORGANIZATIONS

Hundreds of organizations monitor corporate activities in dozens of fields. The organizations I've included here are some whose work I've seen over the last several years. My apologies to those I've omitted.

ANTICOMMUNIST ISSUES

Stockholders for World Freedom
Carl Olson, Chairman
P.O. Box 7273
Alexandria, VA 22307
(703) 780-0180

BACKGROUND INFORMATION

Bureau of Economic Analysis
Department of Commerce
1401 K Street, N.W.
Washington, D.C. 20230
(202) 523-0777
(statistics on economic subjects)

Bureau of Industrial Economics
Department of Commerce
1401 K Street, N.W.
Washington, D.C. 20230
(202) 523-0777
(information about a company or industry)

Bureau of Labor Statistics
Division of Information Services
441 G Street, N.W.
Washington, D.C. 20212
(202) 523-1208
(statistics about labor prices, growth, and productivity)

Commission for the Advancement of Public Interest Organizations
1875 Connecticut Avenue, N.W.
Suite 1013
Washington, D.C. 20036
(202) 462-0505
(*Citizen's Guide to Periodicals of Public Interest*)

Corporate Data Exchange
198 Broadway
New York, NY 10038
(212) 962-2980

Data Center
464 19th Street
Oakland, CA 94612
(clipping service and corporate observers)

Data Users Services Division
Bureau of the Census
Suitland & Silver Hill Roads
Washington, D.C.   20233
(301) 763-1386
(census information)

Federal Information Center
General Services Administration
18th & F Streets, N.W.
Washington, D.C.   20405
(202) 566-1937
(where and how to get information)

Government Printing Office
Superintendent of Documents
Washington, D.C.   20402
(202) 783-3238
(federal publications, but try to get
   them through your congressman
   — they're free that way)

League of Women Voters of the U.S.
1730 M Street, N.W.
Washington, D.C.   20036
(202) 429-1965

National Resource Center for
   Consumers of Legal Services
1302 18th Street, N.W.
Suite 303
Washington, D.C.   20036
(202) 338-0714
(prepaid legal services and clinics)

Washington Center for Study of
   Services
1518 K Street, N.W.
Washington, D.C.   20005
(202) 347-9612
(bibliography, guide to national
   businesses)

Worldwatch Institute
1776 Massachusetts Avenue, N.W.
Suite 701
Washington, D.C.   20036
(202) 452-1999

CORPORATE RESPONSIBILITY

Center for Corporate Public
   Involvement
1850 K Street, N.W.
Washington, D.C.   20006
(202) 862-4047

Corporate Accountability Research
   Group
1346 Connecticut Avenue, N.W.,
   #415
Washington, D.C.   20036
(202) 833-3931

Council on Economic Priorities
84 Fifth Avenue
New York, NY   10011
(212) 691-8550

INFORM
381 Park Avenue
New York, NY   10016
(212) 689-4040

Interfaith Center for Corporate
   Responsibility
475 Riverside Drive
Suite 566
New York, NY   10115
(212) 870-2293

Investor Responsibility Research
   Center, Inc.
1319 F Street, N.W.
Washington, D.C.   20004
(202) 833-3727

DEFENSE ISSUES

American Friends Service Committee/
    Narmic
1501 Cherry Street
Philadelphia, PA   19102
(215) 241-7175
(defense industry information)

Nuclear Free America
2521 Guilford Avenue
Baltimore, MD   21218
(301) 633-8478

SANE
514 C Street, N.E.
Washington, D.C.   20002
(202) 546-7100

Union of Concerned Scientists
1346 Connecticut Avenue, N.W.
Suite 1101
Washington, D.C.   20036
(202) 296-5600

ENERGY

Citizen/Labor Energy Coalition
    (C/LEC)
1300 Connecticut Avenue, N.W.
Suite 401
Washington, D.C.   20036
(202) 857-5153

Energy Conservation Coalition
1001 Connecticut Avenue, N.W.
Suite 535
Washington, D.C.   20036
(202) 466-5045

National Consumer Law Center
236 Massachusetts Avenue, N.E.
Washington, D.C.   20002
(202) 543-6060

Residential Utility Consumer's Action
    Group (RUCAG)
P.O. Box 19312
Washington, D.C.   20036

Solar Lobby
1001 Connecticut Avenue, N.W.
Suite 510
Washington, D.C.   20036
(202) 466-6350

ENVIRONMENT

Citizens for a Better Environment
59 E. Van Buren
Suite 1600
Chicago, IL   60605
(312) 939-1530

Clean Water Action Project
1341 G Street, N.W., #205
Washington, D.C.   20005
(202) 638-1196

Clean Water Fund
1341 G Street, N.W., #205
Washington, D.C.   20005
(202) 638-3013

Environmental Action Coalition
417 Lafayette Street
New York, NY   10003
(212) 667-1601

Environmental Action Foundation
Dupont Circle Building
Suite 724
Washington, D.C.   20036
(202) 659-9682

Environmental Action, Inc.
1346 Connecticut Avenue, N.W.
Suite 731
Washington, D.C.   20036
(202) 833-1845

Environmental Policy Center
317 Pennsylvania Avenue, S.E.
Washington, D.C.   20003
(202) 547-5330

League of Conservation Voters
317 Pennsylvania Avenue, S.E.
Washington, D.C.   20003
(202) 546-5246

National Audubon Society
950 Third Avenue
New York, NY   10022
(212) 546-9100

National Clean Air Coalition
530 7th Street, S.E.
Washington, D.C.   20003
(202) 543-8200

Sierra Club
530 Bush Street
San Francisco, CA   94108
(415) 981-8634
           or
330 Pennsylvania Ave., S.E.
Washington, D.C.   20003
(202) 547-1144

The Environmental Fund
1302 18th Street, N.W.
Washington, D.C.   20036
(202) 293-2548

EQUAL EMPLOYMENT

MS Foundation for Women
370 Lexington Avenue
New York, NY   10017
(212) 689-3475

NAACP (National Association for the
    Advancement of Colored People)
1790 Broadway
New York, NY   10019
(212) 245-2100

Operation PUSH, Inc.
930 East 50th Street
Chicago, IL   60615
(312) 373-3366

Women's Legal Defense Fund
2000 P Street
Suite 400
Washington, D.C.   20036
(202) 887-0364

PUBLICATIONS

Business & Society Review
870 Seventh Avenue
New York, NY   10019
(212) 977-7936
(corporate social responsibility
    quarterly)

California Management Review
350 Barrows Hall
University of California
Berkeley, CA   94720
(415) 642-7159
(quarterly journal on corporate
    accountability issues)

CEP Newsletter
Council on Economic Priorities
84 Fifth Avenue
New York, NY   10011
(212) 691-8550
(monthly newsletter on corporate
    activities)

Concerned Investors Guide
Resource Publishing Group
P.O. Box 390
Arlington, VA   22201

The Corporate Examiner
Interfaith Center for Corporate
    Responsibility
National Council of Churches
475 Riverside Drive, Room 566
New York, NY   10115
(212) 870-2936
              or
3410 19th Street
San Francisco, CA   94110
(415) 863-8060
(monthly newsletter corporate
    activities)

Environmental Action
Suite 731
1346 Connecticut Avenue, N.W.
Washington, D.C.   20036
(202) 833-1845
(monthly magazine with broad focus)

Good Money
The Center for Economic
    Revitalization, Inc.
Box 363
Calais Stage Road
Worcester, VT   05682
(802) 223-3911
(newsletters, networking for ethical
    investors)

INFORM
381 Park Avenue South
New York, NY   10016
(212) 689-4040
(corporate activities bimonthly
    newsletter)

*Insight: The Advisory Letter for
    Concerned Investors*
Franklin Research and Development
    Corporation
222 Lewis Wharf
Boston, MA   02110
(617) 723-1670
(investment advisory newsletter for
    concerned investors)

IRRC News for Investors
Investor Responsibility Research
    Center, Inc.
1319 F Street, N.W.
Washington, D.C.   20004
(202) 833-3727
(newsletter emphasizing proxy issues)

Label Letter
Union Label and Service Trades
    Department, AFL-CIO
815 16th Street, N.W.
Washington, D.C.   20006
(labor issues, subscriptions to members
    only)

Labor & Investments
Industrial Union Department, AFL-
    CIO
815 16th Street, N.W.
Washington, D.C.   20006

Multinational Monitor
Corporate Accountability Research
    Group
1346 Connecticut Avenue, N.W.
Room 411
Washington, D.C.   20036
(202) 833-3932
(newsletter)

Renewable Resource and Conservation
    Report
P.O. Box 1177
Syracuse, NY   13201

Response
Center for Corporate Public
    Involvement
1850 K Street, N.W.
Washington, D.C.   20006
(202) 862-4047
(corporate social responsibility
    monthly newsletter)

HEALTH AND NUTRITION

Center for Science in the Public
    Interest
1755 S Street, N.W.
Washington, D.C.   20009
(202) 332-9110
(health, food, and nutrition issues)

Disability Rights Center
1346 Connecticut Avenue, N.W.,
    #1124
Washington, D.C.   20036

National Women's Health Network
224 7th Street, S.E.
Washington, D.C.   20003
(202) 543-9222

Public Citizen Health Research
P.O. Box 19404
Washington, D.C.   20036
(202) 872-0320

INSURANCE

Center for Corporate Public
    Involvement
1850 K Street, N.W.
Washington, D.C.   20006
(202) 862-4047
(industry group)

National Insurance Consumer
    Organization
344 Commerce Street
Alexandria, VA   22314
(consumer group)

LABOR

AFL-CIO
Industrial Union Department
815 16th Street, N.W.
Washington, D.C.   20006
(202) 842-7800

Disability Rights Center
1346 Connecticut Avenue, N.W.,
    #1124
Washington, D.C.   20036

INFORM
381 Park Avenue
New York, NY   10016
(212) 689-4040

New Ways to Work
149 9th Street
San Francisco, CA   94103
(415) 552-1000

9 to 5, National Association of
    Working Women
1224 Huron Avenue
Cleveland, OH   44115
(216) 566-9308

MISCELLANEOUS PUBLIC INTEREST GROUPS

Aviation Consumer Action Project
P.O. Box 19029
Washington, D.C.   20036
(202) 223-4498

Center for Auto Safety
1346 Connecticut Avenue, N.W.,
    #1223
Washington, D.C.   20036
(202) 659-1126
(auto recalls and complaints)

Center for Development Policy
418 10th Street, S.E.
Washington, D.C.   20003
(202) 547-6406

Center for Law & Social Policy
1751 N Street, N.W.
Washington, D.C.
(202) 872-0670

Center for Law in the Public Interest
1575 I Street, N.W.
Washington, D.C.
(202) 371-0199

Center for Responsive Governance
1100 17th Street, N.W.
Washington, D.C.
(202) 223-2400

Center for Responsive Politics Inc.
6 E Street, S.E.
Washington, D.C.
(202) 544-7966

Center for Study of Responsive Law
P.O. Box 19367
Washington, D.C.   20036

Citizen Action
1501 Euclid Avenue
Suite 500
Cleveland, OH   44115
(216) 861-5200

People and Taxes
P.O. Box 14198
Washington, D.C.   20044
(property and income tax reform)

Public Interest Research Group
1346 Connecticut Avenue, N.W.,
   #415
Washington, D.C.   20036
(202) 833-3934

Tax Reform Research Group
215 Pennsylvania Avenue, S.E.
Washington, D.C.   20003
(202) 544-1710

Telecommunications Research and
   Action Center
P.O. Box 12038
Washington, D.C.   20005
(202) 462-2520

MUTUAL FUNDS

Calvert Social Investment Fund
1700 Pennsylvania Avenue, N.W.
Washington, D.C.   20006
(800) 368-2748 and (301) 951-4820

The Dreyfus Third Century Fund, Inc.
600 Madison Avenue
New York, NY   10022
(800) 645-6561 and (212) 895-1206

New Alternatives Fund, Inc.
295 Northern Boulevard
Great Neck, NY   11021
(516) 466-0808

Pax World Fund, Inc.
224 State Street
Portsmouth, NH   03801
(603) 431-8022

The Pioneer Group, Inc.
60 State Street
Boston, MA   02109
(617) 742-7825

Renaissance Asset Management
1427 Shrader Street
San Francisco, CA   94117
(415) 664-6812

MONEY MARKET FUNDS

Working Assets Money Fund
230 California Street
San Francisco, CA   94111
(800) 223-7010; in Pennsylvania call
    collect (215) 786-6760

Calvert Social Investment Fund
1700 Pennsylvania Avenue, N.W.
Washington, D.C.   20006
(800) 368-2748

NUCLEAR POWER

Abalone Alliance
2940 Sixteenth Street
Room 310
San Francisco, CA   94103
(415) 861-0592

Alliance for Survival
1473 Echo Park Avenue
Los Angeles, CA   90026
(213) 617-2118

Council on Economic Priorities
84 Fifth Avenue
New York, NY   10011
(212) 691-8550

Critical Mass
215 Pennsylvania Avenue, S.E.
Washington, D.C.   20003
(202) 546-4790

Nuclear Information and Resource
    Service
1346 Connecticut Avenue, N.W.
4th Floor
Washington, D.C.   20036
(202) 296-7552

Union of Concerned Scientists
1346 Connecticut Avenue, N.W.
Suite 1101
Washington, D.C.   20036
(202) 296-5600

PENSIONS

Pension Rights Center
1346 Connecticut Avenue, N.W.,
    #1019
Washington, D.C.   20036

POLITICAL INVOLVEMENT

Common Cause
2030 M Street, N.W.
Washington, D.C.   20036
(202) 833-1200

Congress Watch
215 Pennsylvania Avenue, S.E.
Washington, D.C.   20003
(202) 546-4996

Council on Economic Priorities
84 Fifth Avenue
New York, NY   10011
(212) 691-8550

League of Women Voters of the U.S.
1730 M Street, N.W.
Washington, D.C.   20036
(202) 429-1965

Public Citizen, Inc.
2000 P Street, N.W.
Washington, D.C.   20036
(202) 293-9142

Public Citizen Litigation Group
2000 P Street, N.W., #700
Washington, D.C.   20036
(202) 785-3704

SOUTH AFRICA

International Council for Equality of
    Opportunity Principles, Inc.
1501 North Broad Street
Philadelphia, PA   19122
(215) 236-6757 or 6758
(for Sullivan Principle rankings)

WOMEN'S ISSUES

Catalyst
14 East 60th Street
New York, NY   10022
(212) 759-9700

MS Foundation for Women
370 Lexington Avenue
New York, NY   10017
(212) 689-3475

9 to 5, National Association of
    Working Women
1224 Huron Avenue
Cleveland, OH   44115
(216) 566-9308

Women's Legal Defense Fund
2000 P Street
Suite 400
Washington, D.C.   20036
(202) 887-0364

TAX SHELTER INFORMATION

Brennan Reports
Office Colony, Suite 245
P.O. Box 882
Valley Forge, PA 19482

Investor's Tax Shelter Reports
Investment Search, Inc.
223 Duke of Gloucester Street
Annapolis, MD   21041

Limited Partners Letter
P.O. Box 1146
Menlo Park, CA   94025

The Stanger Report
623 River Road
Fairhaven, NJ   07701

INVESTMENT HELP

Joan Bavaria
Franklin Research and Development
222 Lewis Wharf
Boston, MA   02110
(617) 723-1670
(money managers)

Amy Domini
Moseley, Hallgarten, Estabrook &
    Weeden
44 Brattle Street
Cambridge, MA   02138
(800) 225-5372
(617) 876-5700
(stock brokers)

George D. Kinder and Associates
16 Wendell Street
Cambridge, MA   02138
(617) 492-6223
(investment adviser/financial planner)

Jim Lowell
Lowell and Blake Assoc.
5 Doane Street
Boston, MA   02109
(617) 227-0454
(investment adviser/financial planner)

Marcy Murningham
Mitchell Investment Management Co.
    Inc.
1000 Massachusetts Avenue
Cambridge, MA   02138
(617) 661-6354
(money manager – consultant)

Bob Schwartz, David Sand, Michael
   Moffitt
Shearson/American Express Inc.
666 Fifth Avenue
New York, NY   10103
(800) 223-6024
(212) 974-3241
(money managers/stock brokers)

Tamsin Taylor
Strategic Investment Advisors
142 Lincoln, Suite 781
Santa Fe, NM   87501
(505) 983-9370
(investment adviser/financial planner)

Robert Zevin, Steve Moody, Larry
   Litvak
U. S. Trust Company
40 Court Street
Boston, MA   02108
(617) 726-7250
(money managers)

Affirmative Investments, Inc.
Harvard Square, Box 801
Cambridge, MA 02238
(617) 491-4578
(tax shelter advisers)

Appendix C

ETHICAL MUTUAL FUND HOLDINGS*

CALVERT SOCIAL INVESTMENT FUND — MANAGED GROWTH PORTFOLIO, SEPTEMBER 30, 1983

U.S. Government Agencies and Instrumentalities
  Federal Farm Credit Banks, 9.00%, due 10/14/83
  Federal Home Loan Bank Board, 10.85%, due 10/26/92
  Federal National Mortgage Association, 10.90%, due 1/11/93
  Federal Home Loan Bank Board, 11.70%, due 7/26/93
  Federal Home Loan Bank Board, 11.95%, due 8/25/93
  Federal Farm Credit Banks, 11.90%, due 10/20/97

Bank Money Market Deposits
  Riggs National Bank

Repurchase Agreements, for Delivery at Cost, Collateralized by Securities
  Issued or Guaranteed by the U.S. Government
  Drexel Burnham Lambert, Inc., 10.00%, due 10/3/83 (collateralized by
  $255,000 FNMA, 10.30%, due 5/10/90)

Equity Securities
  Business Machines and Services
    Commodore International, Ltd.
    R. R. Donnelley & Sons Company
    SEI Corporation

* Lists are supplied by the funds.

225

Equity Securities, *continued*
  Communications
    MGM Home Entertainment
      Group, Inc.
    The Washington Post Co.
  Financial Services
    Core States Financial
      Corporation
  First Virginia Banks, Inc.
    Federal National Mortgage
      Association
  Hospital
    Humana, Inc.

Industrials
  Fort Howard Paper Company
  Hannaford Brothers Co.
  Mercantile Store Company, Inc.
  Phillips-Van Heusen Corp.
  Stride Rite Corporation
Petroleum
  Sonat, Inc.
Utilities
  Citizens Utilities Co. Class B
  Magma Power Company
  Southwestern Public Service
    Company

THE DREYFUS THIRD CENTURY FUND, INC., MAY 31, 1983

Common Stocks

Aerospace
  General Dynamics
Aluminum
  Kaiser Aluminum & Chemical
Building and Industrial Supplies
  Norton
  U.S. Gypsum
Coal
  AMAX
  Cleveland-Cliffs Iron
Copper
  Ranchers Exploration &
    Development
Drugs
  SmithKline Beckman
  Warner-Lambert
Engineering and Construction
  Dravo
  Fluor
  Morrison-Knudsen

Environment
  Dome Petroleum
  Dorchester Gas
  Ionics
  KMS Industries
  Magma Energy
  Magma Power
  Rockcor
  Woodside Petroleum, A.D.R.
Fast Foods
  Jerrico
Finance and Financial Services
  Ahmanson (H.F.)
  Alexander & Alexander Services
  Crocker National
  Golden West Financial
Gas Pipelines
  Transco Companies
Health
  ADAC Laboratories
  Century Laboratories
  Coherent

Source: Reprinted with permission of the Dreyfus Third Century Fund, Inc., May 31, 1983.

DEKALB AgResearch, Cl.B.
Genetic Systems
Gist-Brocades
Life Imaging
LymphoMed
Ribi ImmunoChem Research
Ribi ImmunoChem Research
    (Units)
Leasing
    U.S. Leasing International
Machinery
    Caterpillar Tractor
    Raymond Corp.
Multi-Markets
    RCA
Oil Drilling and Services
    Cameron Iron Works
    Crutcher Resources
    Rowan Companies
Paper and Forest Products
    Georgia-Pacific
    International Paper
Petroleum Producers and Marketers
    Atlantic Richfield
    Pogo Producing
    Sun Co.
    Unocal
Publishing/Books
    Addison-Wesley Publishing,
        Cl.B.

Railroads
    Rio Grande Industries
    Santa Fe Industries
    Southern Pacific
Supermarkets
    Jewel Companies
Telecommunication
    International Telephone and
        Telegraph
Transportation
    Sundance Oil

Convertible Preferred Stocks

Hansford Data Systems
Industrial Vision Systems
W. J. Schafer Associates, Cl. A.

Convertible Notes and Bonds

Mapco, Adjustable Rate Sub. Notes
Rockcor, Sub. Deb.

Short-Term Investments

Chemical Bank (London)
Crocker National Bank (London)

NEW ALTERNATIVES FUND, INC., NOVEMBER 30, 1983

Name of Stock	Relationship to Fund Concept
Acro Energy	Solar Heating
AFG Industries	Solar Glass and Photovoltaic Cells
Alagasco	Natural Gas and Methane Vehicles
American Water	None
American Solar King	Solar Heating
Ametek	Photovoltaic Cells
Astrosystem	Photovoltaic Cells
Bairnco	Efficient Lighting
Baldor	Efficient Electric Motors
Bethlehem Corp. (ASE)	Fuel Cells; Burners for Alternative Fuels
Browning Ferris	Waste Burning for Energy
Central and Southwest	Gas Utility
Certain-teed	Insulation
Chronar	Photovoltaic Cells
DWG	Natural Gas
Deltak	Cogeneration
Energy Conversion Devices	Photovoltaic Cells
Fischer & Porter	Energy Management Systems
Foster Wheeler	Fluidized Bed Burners
General Signal	Energy Management Systems
Geothermal Resources	Geothermal Energy
Hawaiian Electric	Geothermal, Biomass & Wind Energy
Helionetics	Lasers for Solar Cell Manufacture
Idaho Power	Hydroelectric
Johnson Controls	Energy Management Systems
Laclede Gas	Natural Gas
Magma Power	Geothermal Energy
Montana Dakota Util	Environmentally Sound Utility
Mor Flo	Solar Heating
Mountain Fuel Supply	Natural Gas
National Fuel Gas	Natural Gas
Nortek	Photovoltaic Cells
Novan	Solar Heating
PPG	Temperature Control Glass
Peabody	Cogeneration, Waste Burning
Piedmont Natural Gas	Natural Gas
Pulte Home	Insulated Homes
Robert Shaw Controls	Energy Management Systems
St. Joseph Light & Power	Clean Utility
Signal Co.	Cogeneration
Vermont American Corp.	None
Jim Walter Corp.	Insulation
Zurn Industries	Environmental Control Systems

PAX WORLD FUND, INC., JUNE 30, 1983

Common Stocks

Hazelton Labs
Servamatic Solar Systems, Inc.
Western Union Co.
Dart & Kraft, Inc.
Maytag Co.
Nike, Inc.
Merck & Company
Central Hudson Gas & Electric
Walt Disney
H. J. Heinz Co.
Lifemark Corporation
U.S. Home Corp.

Bard (C. R.), Incorporated
American Sterilizer Co.
American Natural Resources Co.
Consolidated Natural Gas Co.
Enserch Corporation
Northwest Energy Co.
Pennzoil Company
Texas Oil & Gas Corp.
Sealed Air Corp.
Burlington Northern, Incorporated
CSX Corp.

Bonds

Corporate

Becton, Dickinson & Company, 5%, Convertible Subordinated Debentures, due December 1, 1989

Jim Walter Corporation, 5¾%, Convertible Subordinated Debentures, due January 15, 1991

National Medical Enterprises, 12⅝%, Convertible Subordinated Debentures, due November 13, 2001

Government

Federal Farm Credit Bank, 13.85%, due March 1, 1984

Federal Home Loan Bank System, 10.80%, due March 25, 1985

Federal National Mortgage Association, 14.25%, due May 10, 1984

International Bank for Reconstruction and Development, Washington, D.C., 14.625%, due December 15, 1986

Twelve Federal Land Banks, 8.65%, due July 20, 1983

Source: Reprinted with permission from Pax World Fund, Inc., June 30, 1983.

Appendix D

1983 SULLIVAN PRINCIPLES RATINGS FOR FIRMS DOING BUSINESS IN SOUTH AFRICA

STATEMENT OF PRINCIPLES

Principle 1: Nonsegregation of the races in all eating, comfort, locker room, and work facilities.

Principle 2: Equal and fair employment practices for all employees.

Principle 3: Equal pay for all employees doing equal or comparable work for the same period of time.

Principle 4: Initiation and development of training programs that will prepare Blacks, Coloreds, and Asians in substantial numbers for supervisory, administrative, clerical, and technical jobs.

Principle 5: Increasing the number of Blacks, Coloreds, and Asians in management and supervisory positions.

Principle 6: Improving the quality of employees' lives outside the work environment in such areas as housing, transportation, schooling, recreation, and health facilities.

EXPLANATION OF RATING CATEGORIES

I.   Making good progress.
II. Making progress.

Source: International Council for Equality of Opportunity Principles, Inc.; 1501 North Broad St., Philadelphia, PA 19122. (Copies of full report are available for $15.)

III.   Needs to become more active.
    A. Received low point score.
    B. Did not pass basic requirements.
IV.   Endorsers.
    A. With no employees.
    B. With ten or fewer employees.
    C. Holding less than 19% equity.
V.   New signatories.
VI.   Signatories which did not report.
VII. Signatory with headquarters outside the U.S.
VIII. Nonsignatories.

A complete alphabetical list of the Signatory Companies indicates the rating category of each Signatory. More than one rating category is listed for some Signatories whose South African subsidiaries were rated separately and received different ratings.

ALPHABETICAL LIST OF SIGNATORIES

AFIA Worldwide		Butterick Company, Inc.	IIIA
Insurance	IIIA		
Abbott Laboratories	II	CBS Inc.	IIIA
American Cyanamid		CIGNA Corporation	II
Company	I, VI	CPC International, Inc.	II, IVA
American Express		Caltex Petroleum	
Company	IVB	Corporation	I
American Home		Carnation Company	IIIB
Products		Carrier Corp.	V
Corporation	V	J. I. Case Corporation	IIIA, IVA
American Hospital		Caterpillar Tractor Co.	II
Supply Corporation	II	Celanese Corporation	IIIA
American International		The Chase Manhattan	
Group, Inc.	IIIB	Corporation	II
Armco Inc.	II, IVB	Chicago Bridge & Iron	
Ashland Oil, Inc.	IIIA, IVA,	Company	V
	VI	Citicorp	I, IVC
		The Coca-Cola	
Borden, Inc.	I	Company	I, II
Borg-Warner Corp.	II	Colgate-Palmolive	
Bristol-Myers Company	II	Company	I
Burroughs Corporation	I		

Marsh & McLennan		See Del Monte	
Companies	VI	Corporation	
Masonite Corporation	IIIB	See Heublein, Inc.	
McGraw-Hill, Inc.	I	Richardson-Vicks Inc.	IIIA
Measurex Corporation	VI	Rohm and Haas	
Merck & Co., Inc.	I,II	Company	IIIA,IVB
Mine Safety Appliances			
Co.	IIIB	Schering-Plough Corp.	II
Minnesota Mining &		Sentry Insurance	
Manufacturing		A Mutual Company	IIIA
Company	I	SmithKline Beckman	
Mobil Oil Corporation	I	Corporation	II,V
Monsanto Co.	I	Sperry Corporation	I
Motorola, Inc.	IIIA	Squibb Corporation	IIIA
		[Standard Oil Company	
NCNB Corporation	IVB	of California]	
NCR Corp.	IIIA	See Caltex Petroleum	
Nabisco Brands Inc.	II	Corporation	
Nalco Chemical		The Standard Oil Co.	
Company	IIIB	(Ohio)	II,IIIA
Norton Company	II,IIIA,IVB	The Stanley Works	II
Norton Simon, Inc.		Sterling Drug Inc.	IIIA
(Avis, Inc.)	IVA		
		Tampax Incorporated	I
Olin Corporation	IIIA,IIIB,	[Tenneco, Inc.]	
	VI	See J. I. Case	
Oshkosh Truck		Corporation	
Corporation	IVA	[Texaco Incorporated]	
Otis Elevator Co.	II	See Caltex Petroleum	
		Corporation	
The Parker Pen Co.	II	J. Walter Thompson Co.	VI
Pfizer, Inc.	I,II	Time Incorporated	IVB
Phelps Dodge		The Trane Company	IIIB
Corporation	IIIA,VI		
Phillips Petroleum		Union Carbide	
Company	II	Corporation	I,II,IVB
		[United Technologies	
Reader's Digest		Corporation]	
Association, Inc.	IIIA,IVA	See Carrier Corp.	
Rexnord Inc.	IIIA	See Otis Elevator Co.	
[R. J. Reynolds		The Upjohn Company	II,IIIA
Industries, Inc.]			

Appendix E

COMPANIES WITH WOMEN ON THEIR BOARDS OF DIRECTORS (1984)*

Abbott Industries
ACF Industries, Inc.
Aetna Life & Casualty
Affiliated Publications
Alberto-Culver Co.
Albertson's, Inc.
Alexander & Baldwin, Inc.
Allegheny Power System, Inc.
Allied Corp.
Allied Stores Corp.
American Airlines, Inc.
American Brands, Inc.
American Broadcasting Co.
American Can Co.
American Electric Power Co., Inc.
American Express
American Family Corp.
American Home Products Corp.
American Hospital Supply Corp.
American Motors Corp.
American National Life Insurance Co.

American Security Corp.
American Stores Company
American Telephone & Telegraph Co.
American United Life Insurance Co.
AmeriTrust Corp.
AMF, Inc.
AMFAC
AM International
Amstar Corporation
Anchor Hocking Corp.
Anheuser-Busch, Inc.
Archer Daniels Midland
ARA Services, Inc.
Arizona Public Service Co.
Armstrong World Industries
Ashland Oil, Inc.
Associated Dry Goods Corp.
Atlantic Richfield
Avon Products, Inc.

* List compiled from the top 1000 industrial corporations and top 300 diversified financial service and retail firms through January 31, 1984.

Source: Catalyst, New York City, NY.

Baldwin-United Corp.
Ball Corp.
Baltimore Gas & Electric Co.
BanCal Tri-State Corp.
Bandag, Inc.
Bank of New York Co.
Bank of Tokyo Trust Co.
BankAmerica Corp.
Bankers Trust New York Corp.
George Banta Co.
Baxter Travenol Labs., Inc.
Beatrice Foods Co.
Beneficial Corp.
Bird & Son, Inc.
Block Drug Co.
Blue Bell, Inc.
Bohemia, Inc.
Boise Cascade Corp.
Borden, Inc.
Bristol-Myers Co.
Burlington Industries, Inc.
Burlington Northern, Inc.
Burroughs Corp.
Butler Manufacturing Co.

Cameron Iron Works, Inc.
Campbell Soup Co.
Carlisle Corp.
Carolina Power & Light Co.
Carter Hawley Hale Stores, Inc.
Castle & Cook, Inc.
Caterpillar Tractor Co.
CBS, Inc.
Ceco Corp.
Celanese Corp.
Certain-teed Corp.
Champion International Corp.
C.H.B. Foods Inc.
Checker Motors Corp.
Chemical New York Corp.
Chesebrough-Ponds, Inc.
Chrysler Corp.
Chubb Corp.

CIGNA Corp.
Church & Dwight Co., Inc.
Citicorp
City Federal Savings & Loan
    Association
Clorox Co.
Cluett, Peabody & Co., Inc.
Coachmen Industries, Inc.
Coca-Cola Co.
Coleco
Coleman Co.
Colgate-Palmolive
Columbia Gas System, Inc.
Commonwealth Edison Co.
Cone Mills Corp.
Consolidated Edison Co.
Consolidated Foods Corp.
Consolidated Papers, Inc.
Continental Corp.
Continental Group
Continental Illinois Corp.
Continental Telephone Corp.
Control Data Corp.
Corning Glass Works
CPC International, Inc.
Crown Zellerbach Corp.
CSX Corp.
Cummins Engine Co., Inc.
Helene Curtis Industries, Inc.

Datapoint Corp.
Dart & Kraft, Inc.
Dean Foods Company
Delta Airlines
Dentsply International, Inc.
Detroit Edison Co.
Digital Equipment Corp.
Walt Disney Productions
Dover Corp.
Dow Chemical Co.
Dow Jones & Co., Inc.
Duke Power Co.
E. I. du Pont de Nemours & Co.
Dyneer Corp.

E-Systems, Inc.
Eastern Air Lines, Inc.
Eastman Kodak Co.
Emhart Corp.
Equitable Life Assurance Society
Esmark, Inc.
Esterline Corp.
Everest & Jennings International
Exxon Corp.

Facet Enterprises, Inc.
Farmer Brothers Co.
Federal National Mortgage Assoc.
Federated Department Stores, Inc.
Financial Corp. of Santa Barbara
Firestone Tire & Rubber Co.
First Bank System, Inc.
First Charter Financial Corp.
First Chicago Corp.
First City Bancorp of Texas
First Maryland Corp.
First National Boston Corp.
First Union Corp.
First Western Financial
First Wisconsin Corp.
Fischer & Porter Co.
Florida Power & Light Co.
Ford Motor Co.
Foremost-McKesson, Inc.
Forest Oil Corp.
Fort Howard Paper Company
Franklin Electric Co.
H. B. Fuller Co.

GAF Corp.
Gannett Co.
General Electric Co.
General Foods Corp.
General Mills, Inc.
General Motors Corp.
General Telephone & Electronics
    Corp.
Gerber Products Co.

Giant Foods, Inc.
Gibraltar Financial Corp. of California
Gillette Co.
Golden West Financial Corp.
Goodyear Tire & Rubber Co.
Grand Union Co.
Great Atlantic & Pacific Tea Co.,
    Inc.
Great Western Financial Corp.
Greyhound Corp.
Grumman Corp.
Guilford Mills, Inc.
Gulf States Utilities Co.
Gulf Oil Corp.
Gulf & Western Industries, Inc.

Halliburton Corp.
John Hancock Mutual Life Insurance
    Co.
Harcourt Brace Jovanovich, Inc.
Harper & Row Publishers, Inc.
Harris Bancorp
Harte-Hanks Communications
Hershey Foods Corp.
Heublein, Inc.
Hewlett-Packard Co.
Hexcel Corp.
H. F. Ahmanson Bank & Trust Co.
H. J. Heinz Corp.
Home Life Insurance Co. of America
Honeywell, Inc.
Hon Industries
Hospital Corporation of America
Houghton Mifflin Co.
Household Finance Corp.
Huffy Corp.
E. F. Hutton Group, Inc.

IBM Corp.
IC Industries Inc.
Illinois Power Co.
Imperial Sugar Co.
International Flavors & Fragrances,
    Inc.

International Harvester Co.
International Minerals & Chemical
    Corp.
International Multifoods Corp.
International Paper Co.
International Telephone & Telegraph
    Corp.
Interpace Corp.
Interpublic Group
Irving Bank Corp.

Jewel Companies, Inc.
Johnson & Johnson

Kaiser Aluminum & Chemical Corp.
Kaiser Cement Corp.
Kellogg Co.
Kemper Corp.
Kimball International Corp.
Kimberly-Clark Corp.
K-Mart Corp.
Knight-Ridder Newspapers, Inc.
Koppers Co., Inc.
Kroger Co.
Kuhlman Corp.

Lear Siegler, Inc.
Lee Enterprises, Inc.
Leslie Fay, Inc.
Levi Strauss & Co. Inc.
Lincoln Corp.
Litton Industries, Inc.
Long Island Lighting Co.
Lucky Stores, Inc.
Lukens Steel Co.

Malone & Hyde Inc.
Manhattan Industries, Inc.
Manufacturers Hanover Corp.
Marine Midland Bank
Marriott Corp.
Mary Kay Cosmetics, Inc.
Massachusetts Mutual Life Insurance
    Co.

Mattel, Inc.
May Department Stores Inc.
MCA Inc.
Mercantile Bancorporation, Inc.
Mead Corp.
Merck & Co., Inc.
Mercury Savings & Loan Assoc.
Meredith Corp.
Metromedia, Inc.
Metropolitan Life Insurance Co.
Michigan General Corp.
Michigan National Corp.
Midland Glass Co.
Midlantic Banks Inc.
Milton Bradley Co.
Minnesota Mining & Manufacturing
    Co.
Minnesota Mutual Life Insurance Co.
Mobil Corp.
Mohasco Corp.
Monogram Industries
Monsanto Corp.
Moog, Inc.
J. P. Morgan & Co., Inc.
Morrison-Knudson Co., Inc.
Motorola, Inc.

Nabisco Brands, Inc.
National Bank of North America
National City Corp.
Natomas Co.
NBD Bancorp, Inc.
NCR Corp.
New England Mutual Life Insurance
    Co.
New York Life Insurance Co.
New York Times Co.
Niagara Mohawk Power Corp.
NIBCO, Inc.
Norlin Industries
Norstar Bancorp., Inc.
Northeast Utilities Service Co.
Northern States Power Co.

Northwest Bancorp.
Northwestern National Life Insurance
    Co.
Norton Co.
Noxell Corp.

Occidental Petroleum Corp.
Ogden Corp.
Ohio Edison Co.
Overhead Door Corp.
Owens-Illinois, Inc.

Pacific Gas & Electric Co.
Pacific Lighting Corp.
Pacific Lumber Co.
Pacific Mutual Life Insurance Co.
Pacific Power & Light Co.
Papercraft Corp.
Penn Mutual Life Insurance Co.
J. C. Penney Co., Inc.
Pennsylvania Power & Light Co.
Pennwalt Corp.
Petrolite Corp.
Pfizer, Inc.
Philadelphia Electric Co.
Philips-Van Heusen, Inc.
Philip Morris Inc.
Phillips Petroleum Co.
Pillsbury Co.
Pitney-Bowes, Inc.
Phoenix Mutual Life Insurance Co.
Polaroid Corp.
Potlach Corp.
Procter & Gamble Co.
Provident Mutual Life Insurance Co.
Prudential Insurance Company of
    America
Public Service Co. of Indiana
Public Service Electric & Gas Co.

Quaker Oats Co.

Ralston Purina Co.
Ranier Bancorporation

Rapid-American Corp.
Rath Packing Co.
Raytheon Co.
RCA Corp.
Republic Bank Corp.
Revlon, Inc.
Reynolds Industries, Inc.
R. H. Macy & Co., Inc.
Roadway Express, Inc.
Rockwell International
Rohm & Haas Co.
Rorer Group, Inc.
Rubbermaid, Inc.

Safeco Corp.
Safeway Stores
Santa Fe Industries
Scholastic, Inc.
Scott Paper Co.
Seafirst Corp.
Sealaska Corp.
Sears, Roebuck & Co.
Security Pacific Corp.
SFN Companies, Inc.
Shaklee Corp.
Shawmut Corp.
Signal Companies
Singer Co.
SmithKline Beckman Corp.
Southern California Edison
Sperry Corp.
Springs Industries
Squibb Co.
Standard Motor Products, Inc.
Stanhome, Inc.
Standard Oil of California
Stanley Works
State Mutual Life Assurance Co.
State Street Boston Corp.
Sterling Drug, Inc.
Stop & Shop Companies, Inc.
St. Paul Companies, Inc.
Sun Company, Inc.

Supermarkets General Corp.
Super Value Stores, Inc.

Tampax, Inc.
Texaco, Inc.
Texas Commerce Bancshare, Inc.
Textron Inc.
Thomas & Betts Corp.
TIAA/CREF
Time Inc.
The Times Mirror Co.
The Travelers Corp.
Transamerica Corp.
Trans World Corp.

UAL, Inc.
Union Bank, Inc.
Union Mutual Life Insurance Co.
United Banks of Colorado, Inc.
United Brands Co.
United Technologies Corp.
United Telecommunications, Inc.
Upjohn
U.S. Bancorp
U.S. Fidelity & Guaranty Co.

Valley National Bank of Arizona
Varco International, Inc.

Vermont American Corp.
V.F. Corp.
Virginia Electric & Power Co.
Vulcan Materials Co.

Wachovia Corp.
Waldbaum's Inc.
Warner Communications, Inc.
Warner Lambert Co.
Washington Post Co.
Watkins Johnson
Wells Fargo Co.
West Point-Pepperell
Westinghouse Electric Corp.
Westvaco Corp.
Wickes Companies, Inc.
Winnebago Industries, Inc.
Wolverine World Wide, Inc.
F. W. Woolworth Co.
Work Wear Corp.
William Wrigley, Jr. Co.

Xerox Corp.

Zayre Corp.
Zurn Industries, Inc.

Appendix F

QUESTIONS
FOR SHAREHOLDERS*

There are many kinds of questions that shareholders, and potential shareholders, ought to ask about the companies in which they invest. Here are some suggestions.

COMPENSATION

- Does the company have any compensation agreements that guarantee executives' salaries in case of a takeover or merger ("golden parachute contracts")?
- What are the terms, and under what conditions can they be exercised? What is the total amount for which the company could be obligated?
- What was the highest bonus paid to a company officer this year? What did the individual receiving the largest bonus do to warrant such a payment?
- How can management and the board of directors justify the recent large increases in executive salaries in light of the operating results for the current year?
- Was the executive compensation increased when the company did not increase dividends (or did not pay dividends)?
- Are executive incentive plans structured to emphasize the company's long-term objectives rather than short-term ones?
- Has the company loaned money to employees to enable them to exercise stock options? If so, what interest rate are they being charged? Is the rate lower than the company's borrowing rate? If so, why? Has the company guaranteed any bank loans to employees to enable them to exercise stock options?

* *Source:* "For Shareholders Who Wonder about Firms, Here Are Some Questions," by Martin Baron, © *Los Angeles Times*, 1983. Adapted by permission.

MANAGEMENT

- Did the outside directors have any major disagreements with management representatives on the board of directors?
- Did the board reject any major proposals that were recommended by management?
- Why are there so many "insiders" (persons who are also employed by the company) on the board?
- Why did a certain officer resign? Did the company grant any severance benefits?
- How long does the board of directors plan to keep the founder of the company employed?
- In view of the company's recent expansion into a particular new business, has consideration been given to appointing some new directors with experience in that field?

PERFORMANCE AND OPERATIONS

Lou Levy, Peat Marwick's partner in charge of Securities and Exchange Commission matters, says this area "ought to be the most important" for shareholders. "How are they doing vis-à-vis the competition? How are they doing in the recession? If a major company goes bankrupt, how will that impact this company?" Has the level of product complaints, product returns, warranty costs risen? What action has management taken to reduce or prevent these problems?

Other questions shareholders can ask about a company's performance include:

- Are any suits pending on the company's products?
- How do the return-on-investment percentage, earnings-to-sales ratio, and so on compare with industry averages?
- How much business is dependent on government spending? Will federal budget cuts or changes in defense spending have an impact on the company?
- How will the reductions in the level of expenditures for capital projects and research and development affect the company's long-term prospects?
- What is the impact of reduced inflation and recession on the company? How does this impact compare with that on the company's competitors?
- Will the company's new financing be based on short-term debt? Will any new financing dilute current shareholders' interests?
- How does the company ensure that its technology is not stolen by other companies?

MERGERS AND ACQUISITIONS

"There has to be a financial reason for going ahead with a merger or acquisition," says Joseph V. O'Donnell, managing partner of Cooper, Lybrand's Los Angeles office. "Shareholders interested in the financial viability of a company and the direction of growth have a right to know what the reason for an acquisition was." O'Donnell notes that with mergers there is "usually a lot of money involved, money that might be used for another purpose."

Additional merger and acquisition questions which could be asked include:

- What is management's expertise in the industry in which the acquired company operates? Did the purchase price significantly exceed book value?
- What would management's reaction be to a tender offer above the company's current market price? How do we know management would not fight such an effort to protect its own interests even though the offer would be attractive to the shareholders? What steps have been taken to make a takeover more difficult?

SHAREHOLDER ISSUES

- Has the company purchased any shares from individual or corporate investors at higher-than-market prices?
- Are there proposals submitted by shareholders but not included in the proxy statement? If so, why were they excluded?

SOCIAL AND POLITICAL ISSUES

David Landsittel of Arthur Andersen notes that many investors believe "their relationship to a company as an investor is influenced by how the company runs its business in the social responsibility area." Joseph O'Donnell adds that issues such as charitable contributions are becoming increasingly important as the federal government cuts back on social spending. Some social issue questions include:

- How many minority or women employees are in policy-making positions? What are the highest levels of management they occupy?
- Have the company's employees experienced any job-related diseases during the past year? Is the rate of such disease increasing? What is being done to correct the situation?
- How much were charitable contributions this year? How were recipients of the company's contributions selected? How did the company benefit from its contributions? Do company officers or directors serve on the bords of those charitable organizations?

- What is the nature of the company's lobbying activities? How much did those activities cost the company in 1982?
- How much did the company's employees contribute to its political action committee (PAC)? Which political candidate or issues did the PAC support? Why?
- Does the company have equal opportunity policies with regard to individuals over 40 years of age or individuals who are handicapped?

LITIGATION

- How does the company compare to other similar companies in terms of the magnitude and number of lawsuits against it? What litigation was settled and why? What was the cost to the company?
- What about "hidden" litigation? Is the company vulnerable to future product or worker liability claims? What are the potential costs?

AUDITORS

- Were there any disagreements with the company's independent auditors? If so, what was the disagreement, and how was it resolved?
- Were new independent auditors engaged this year? Did the new auditors' report differ from that of the previous auditors? If so, why?
- Were any problems discussed in the independent auditors' internal control report for which remedial action has not been taken?

Then there are some specific questions that apply to particular industries. For example:

BANKS

- What is the bank's exposure on loans to Argentina, Brazil, Mexico, Poland? Does the refinancing of loans for countries experiencing financial difficulties just postpone the recognition of defaults and losses?
- To what extent has the bank purchased or participated in loans originated by others? Do you perform credit reviews on loans purchased from other banks?
- Does the bank enter into repurchase agreements? If so, how does it protect itself from losses such as those caused by the recent failures of certain securities dealers?

OIL AND GAS CONCERNS

- Is the company discovering new reserves as fast as it is depleting its old reserves?
- How would the company's financial stability be affected if oil prices were to decline to $25 per barrel?
- Has the recent domestic natural gas surplus significantly affected the company's earnings and cash flow? Will it in the future?

PUBLIC UTILITIES

- What can be done about the disposal of spent nuclear fuel if there is no away-from-reactor storage? What is the cost of expanding existing spent-fuel pools?
- Does the company have the ability to finance the construction programs currently under way or expected to be necessary in the near future? What are the company's financing plans for this year?

TRANSPORTATION

- Does the company have the lowest operating costs among its competitors on routes served?
- How will the company be affected by recently enacted tax increases on fuel, excise taxes on new trucks and parts, and highway use taxes on trucks?

Appendix G

PUBLICLY TRADED FIRMS THAT DEAL WITH COMMUNIST COUNTRIES (1976)

Abbott Laboratories
Air Products & Chemicals
Alaska Airlines
Allis Chalmers
Aluminum Company of America
American Broadcasting Company
American Can Company
American Cyanamid
American Express Company
American Home Products
American Standard
Applied Magnetics
Armco Steel Corporation
Atlantic Richfield Company
Avco
Avon Products, Inc.

Baxter Labs
Bendix Corporation
Berkey Photo, Inc.
Boeing Company

Borden, Inc.
Borg-Warner Corporation
Bristol Meyers
Brown and Sharpe
Brunswick Corporation
Burr-Brown Corp. .
Burroughs Corporation

CMI Corporation
Cabot Corporation
Cameron Iron Works
Carpenter Technology Corporation
Caterpillar Tractor Corporation
Celanese Plastics Company
Chrysler Corporation
Cincinnati Milacron, Inc.
Cities Service International
Clark Equipment Company
Coca-Cola Company
Colgate-Palmolive Company
Combustion Engineering, Inc.

Source: Adapted from "Complete Listing of Firms That Do Business with Reds," 1976, Stockholders for World Freedom, Carl Olson, Chairman, P.O. Box 7273, Alexandria, VA 22307, (703) 780-0180. Reprinted with permission.

Continental Can Company
Control Data Corporation
Cooper Industries
Corning Glass Works
Crompton and Knowles
Crutcher Resources

Daniel Industries
Detroit Edison Company
Diamond Shamrock
Dow Chemical Company
Dresser Industries
E. I. du Pont de Nemours Company
Dynatech Corporation

E.G. & G., Inc.
Eagle-Picher Industries, Inc.
Eastern Airlines
Eaton Corporation
Edo Corporation
El Paso Natural Gas Company
Engelhard Minerals & Chemical
    Corporation
Exxon Corporation

FMC International
Firestone Tire & Rubber
Fleetwood Enterprises
Fluor Corp.
Ford Motor Company
Foster Wheeler Corporation
Foxboro Company

GAF Corporation
Gearhart Industries
Gelman Sciences
General Binding
General Dynamics Corporation
General Electric Company
General Instrument Corporation
General Magnaplate
General Mills
General Motors Corporation
General Tire

Gerber Products
Giddings and Lewis
Gleason Works
B. F. Goodrich
Gould, Inc.
GTE-Sylvania
Gulf + Western Industries, Inc.
Gulf Oil Corporation

Halliburton Company
Hanna Mining
Harnischfeger Corporation
Hayes-Albion
Hewlett-Packard Company
Holiday Inns, Inc.
Honeywell, Inc.

Illinois Industries
Ingersoll-Rand Company
Instrument Systems Corporation
Intel
International Business Machines Corp.
International Harvester Company
International Paper Company
IU International Corporation

John Deere Company
Johnson & Johnson
Joy Manufacturing Company

Kaiser Aluminum and Chemical
Kaiser Steel Corporation
Kearney National
Kennemetal, Inc.
Kevex Corporation

Lear Seigler
Litton Industries, Inc.
Lockheed

MTS Systems Corporation
MacMillan Inc.
Mark Controls Corporation
Martin Marietta Corporation

Maxwell Laboratories
McDonnell-Douglas
McGraw-Edison
McNeil Corporation
Mead Corporation
Measurex
Mine Safety Appliances Company
Minnesota Mining and Manufacturing
Monsanto Company
Moog, Inc.
Morrison-Knudsen Company

Nashua Corporation
NCR
New Brunswick Scientific Company
Norton Simon, Inc.

Occidental Petroleum Corporation
Olin Corporation
Oregon Metallurgical Corporation
Orion Research

PPG Industries
Pan American World Airways
Pepsico, Inc.
Perkin-Elmer Corporation
Pfizer, Inc.
Philip Morris, Inc.
Phillips Petroleum Company
Pitney-Bowes, Inc.
Polaroid Corporation

RCA Corporation
R. J. Reynolds Industries, Inc.
Ramada Inns, Inc.
Raytheon Company
Reichhold Chemicals, Inc.
Revlon, Inc.
Reynolds Metals Company
Rockwell International
Rohm and Haas
Rohr Industries

Sears, Roebuck

Singer Corporation
Spectra-Physics
Sperry
Standard Oil of Indiana
Stauffer Chemical Company
Sterling Drug
Storage Technology
Syntex Corporation

TRW, Inc.
Tektronix
Teledyne Inc.
Telex Corporation
Tenneco, Inc.
Texas Eastern Transmission
    Corporation
Texas Instruments
Texas Utilities Services, Inc.
Textron, Inc.
Thermo Electron Corporation
Time Inc.
Timken Company
Tinsley Laboratories
Trans World Airlines

U.S. Industries, Inc.
Union Carbide Corporation
Uniroyal
United Aircraft Prod.
United Brands
United States Steel Corporation
Upjohn Company

Varian Associates

Wavetek
Webb Corporation
Westinghouse Electric Corporation
Whittaker Corporation
Wickes Corporation

Xerox Corporation

Zurn Industries, Inc.

Appendix H

COMPANIES WITH BLACKS
IN THEIR BOARDROOMS

Compare this list with the list that follows. In 1982 blacks sat on the boards of 136 American corporations. In 1971 that number was 16.

COMPANIES WITH BLACK CORPORATE DIRECTORS, 1982

Alcoa
Allied Corporation
AMAX
American Airlines
American Broadcasting Companies
American Can
American Express
American Security Bank
American Telephone & Telegraph
AmeriTrust
Arkansas Power & Light
Avon Products

Bank of America
Bankers Trust

Bendix
Borden
Burroughs

Campbell Soup
CBS
Celanese
Chase Manhattan
Chemical Bank
Chrysler
CIGNA
Citicorp
Coast Federal Savings & Loan
Coca-Cola
Commonwealth Edison

Source: M. Moskowitz, "The 1982 Black Corporate Directors Lineup." Reprinted by permission from *The Business & Society Review,* Fall 1982, #43, pp. 51–54; copyright 1982. Warren, Gorham & Lamont Inc., 210 South Street, Boston, MA. All rights reserved.

Consolidated Edison
Continental Illinois
Cummins Engine

Dart & Kraft
Dayton Power & Light
Delta Airlines
Detroit Edison
Dow Jones
Du Pont

Eastern Air Lines
Eastman Kodak
Entex, Inc.
Equitable Life Assurance
Exxon

Federated Department Stores
Fireman's Fund
First Commercial Bank (New York)
First Pennsylvania Banking & Trust
Foote, Cone & Belding
Ford Motor
F. W. Woolworth

Gannett
General Foods
General Mills
General Motors
Gerber Products
Girard Trust
Golden West Financial
Goodyear Tire & Rubber
Great Western Financial
Greyhound
Grumman

Harte Hanks Communications
Heublein

IBM
Illinois Bell
International Harvester

J. C. Penney
Jewel Companies
John Hancock Mutual Life
Johnson & Johnson

K-Mart
Kaiser Aluminum & Chemical
Kellogg
Knight-Ridder

Lloyd's Bank of California
Lockheed Aircraft

Manufacturers Hanover
Merck
Metromedia
Metropolitan Life Insurance
Mid-South Utilities
Miller Brewing
Mississippi Power & Light
Mobil
Monsanto
Morse Shoe
Mutual of New York

National Bank of North America
Natomas
NBD
New Orleans Public Service
New York Life Insurance
Northwestern Bell Telephone
Norton Simon

Ohio Edison

Pacific Telephone
Pan American World Airways
Penn Mutual
Peoples Gas
PepsiCo
Pfizer
Philadelphia Electric
Philip Morris

Phillips Petroleum
Polaroid
Potomac Electric Power

RCA
R. J. Reynolds Industries
Rohm & Haas

Saxon Industries
Schlitz Brewing
Scott Paper
Sears, Roebuck
Seven-Up
Signal Companies
Singer
SmithKline
Sperry & Hutchinson
Supermarkets General
Systems Planning Corp.

Texas Commerce Bancshares

Time Inc.
Times-Mirror
Trans World Airlines
Travelers

Union Carbide
United Airlines
United California Bank

Virginia Electric & Power

Warner-Lambert
Washington Gas Light
Wells Fargo Bank
Westinghouse Electric
W. R. Grace

Xerox

Zenith Radio
Zurn Industries

COMPANIES WITH BLACK CORPORATE DIRECTORS, 1971

A&P
CBS
Chase Manhattan Basnk
Commonwealth Edison
Equitable Life
First National Bank of Washington,
    D.C.
First National City Bank of New York
    (now Citibank)

General Motors
Harcourt, Brace, Jovanovich
Metropolitan Life
Michigan Consolidated Gas
Pan American World Airways
Potomac Electric
Standard Oil of Ohio
Westinghouse Broadcasting
W. T. Grant (now defunct)

NOTES

Prologue

1. H. J. Mankiewicz and O. Welles, "Citizen Kane: The Shooting Script," in *The Citizen Kane Book* (Boston: Little, Brown & Co., 1971), p. 151. Copyright © 1971 by Bantam Books, Inc. By permission of Bantam Books, Inc. All Rights Reserved.

Chapter 1

1. D. Lindorff, "Making a Killing on Peace," *Mother Jones*, December 1982, p. 60.
2. "Corporations and Social Action," *The Christian Century*, November 24, 1982, p. 1191.
3. *NCC Guidelines for Mission Investments*, Corporate Information Center, Room 846, 475 Riverside Drive, New York, NY 10027.
4. *Market Conscience*, July 1, 1983, p. 1.
5. R. Lowry, *Is the Peaceful Atom a Good Investment?* (Worcester, VT: Catalyst Press and the Center for Economic Revitalization, Inc., 1983), pp. 16, 18–19.
6. M. Brauer, "Issues to Consider in Social Investing," *Pension World*, June 1983, p. 29.
7. R. Barber and J. Rifkin, *The North Will Rise Again* (Boston: Beacon Press, 1978), p. 122.

Chapter 3

1. L. Sloane, "The Role of Investment Counselors," *New York Times*, November 20, 1983, sec. 12, p. 70.

Chapter 4

1. "Zellerbach, Other Firm to Pay Total $750,000 to U.S. in Civil Fines," *Wall Street Journal*, May 19, 1983; "C. Z. Gets Award," *San Francisco Chronicle*, June 2, 1983.
2. J. Train, "Lessons of the Masters," *Harvard Magazine*, Vol. 84, no. 5, May–June 1982, pp. 8, 10–12.

3. Johnson Products Company, Inc., 1982 annual report, p. 20.

4. A. Abelson, "Up and Down Wall Street," *Barron's*, June 13, 1983, pp. 1, 41.

Chapter 5

1. B. W. Ketchum, Jr., "How Growing Companies Grow New Jobs," *Inc.*, July 1979.

2. M. E. Enowitz, "Solar Stocks Soar," *Sun Times*, January–February 1983, p. 14.

3. "Adopt-A-Drug," *Vogue*, March 1983, p. 270.

Chapter 6

1. S. Sanomeet, "Disney Has Big Hopes for Pay TV," *Wall Street Journal*, April 7, 1983, p. 31.

2. W. A. Haas, Jr., "Corporate Social Responsibility: A New Term for an Old Concept with New Significance," Bradshaw and Vogel, eds., *Corporations and Their Critics* (New York: McGraw-Hill, 1982), p. 135.

3. "McDonald's Pledges 30,000 Summer Jobs," *San Francisco Chronicle*, April 22, 1983.

Chapter 7

1. "Companies are Roaring Back into Convertible Bonds," *Business Week*, May 30, 1983, p. 78.

2. R. P. Lowry, *Is the Peaceful Atom a Good Investment?* (Worcester, VT: Catalyst Press and the Center for Economic Revitalization, Inc., 1983).

3. G. C. Hill, "Lender Beware," *Wall Street Journal*, March 19, 1984, pp. 1, 27.

Chapter 8

1. Quoted in "Firms Launch Alternative Investment Mutual Funds," *Labor and Investments*, December 1982–January 1983, p. 1.

2. "Barron's/Lipper Gauge," *Barron's*, November 14, 1983, p. 69.

3. *Ibid.*, p. 70.

4. "'Socially Responsible' Funds Pique Interest, but Results Often Have Been Unimpressive," *Wall Street Journal*, November 18, 1982, p. 33.

5. "Barron's/Lipper Gauge," p. 73.

Chapter 10

1. I borrowed this term from Perkins and Rhoades, *The Women's Investment Handbook* (New York: Plume, 1983).

Chapter 11

1. "Planning For Retirement? It's Never Too Soon," *U.S. News & World Report*, January 24, 1983, pp. 51, 54.

Chapter 12

1. N. Gall, "Games Bankers Play," *Forbes*, December 5, 1983, pp. 172, 184.

2. *IRRC News for Investors*, January 1983, pp. 8–9.

3. "Is the Mellon Bank Really a Good Neighbor?" *Business Week*, June 20, 1983, p. 27; "USW Asks Members to Withdraw Funds from Mellon Bank," *Wall Street Journal*, June 2, 1983. By November 1983 the Steelworkers and the denominations had withdrawn

their support from the Mellon confrontation. Local churches and individuals were carrying on the fight.

4. Prospectus, Working Assets Money Fund, San Francisco, CA, 1983.

5. *AFL-CIO News*, May 21, 1983, p. 2.

Chapter 13

1. Quoted in S. D. Lydenberg, "A Setback for Corporate Democracy," *New York Times*, September 4, 1983, p. F2.

2. M. Friedman, "A Friedman Doctrine — The Social Responsibility of Business is to Increase its Profits," *New York Times Magazine*, September 13, 1970, p. 126.

3. *Loretto Literary & Benevolent Institution v. Blue Diamond Coal Co.*, 444 A.2d 256, 261 (Del. Ch. 1982).

4. Friedman, "A Friedman Doctrine," p. 123.

5. R. S. Potter, "The Investment Responsibilities of Boards Concerned About Human Welfare: A Response to the Threshold Objections to the Notion of Social Investment," in C. W. Powers, ed., *People/Profits: The Ethics of Investment* (New York: Council on Religion and International Affairs, 1972), p. 3.

6. D. Vogel, "Trends in Shareholder Activism: 1970–1982," *California Management Review*, spring 1983, pp. 68–69.

7. Lydenberg, "A Setback for Corporate Democracy."

8. Information provided by Carl Olson, Chairman, Stockholder Sovereignty Society, P.O. Box 7273, Alexandria, VA 22307.

9. T. V. Purcell, "Thinking Ahead," *Harvard Business Review*, September–October 1979, pp. 40, 44.

10. Ibid., p. 44.

11. P. Cowen, "The Freeze Heats Things Up," *Boston Globe*, April 5, 1983, pp. 35, 49.

12. "Checklist of 1983 Shareholder Resolutions," *IRRC News for Investors*, February 1983, pp. 48–52.

13. "Special Report: 1983 Proxy Season Gets Under Way," *IRRC News for Investors*, February 1983, p. 33.

14. "Commendation Resolutions Receive Cool Reception," *IRRC News for Investors*, February 1983, p. 27.

15. H. E. Alexander, "Corporate Political Behavior," in Bradshaw and Vogel, eds., *Corporations and Their Critics* (New York: McGraw-Hill, 1982), p. 35.

16. Information provided by Sharon Snyder, Federal Election Commission. See also *FEC Reports on Financial Activity, 1981–1982, Interim Report No. 4: Party and Non-Party Political Committees.*

17. A. Taft, "Churches Use Investment Power," *Miami Herald*, July 16, 1983, p. 20A.

18. T. Smith, "Manager's Journal," *Wall Street Journal*, September 22, 1980.

19. "1983 Proxy Season Gets Under Way," pp. 28, 31.

20. D. J. Kirchoff, "Antibusiness Radicals in Clerical Garb," *Business and Society Review*, winter 1979–80, p. 164.

21. "1983 Proxy Season Gets Under Way," p. 46.

22. Ibid.

23. Vogel, "Trends in Shareholder Activism," p. 72.

24. Ibid.

25. J. Allen, "The Exercise of Voting Rights by Large Institutional Investors," 1977, reprinted in Subcommittee on Reports, Accounting, and Management of the Senate Committee on Governmental Affairs, Voting Rights in Major Corporations, S. Doc. No. 95-99, 95th Cong., 2d Sess. 602 (1978).

26. A. C. Wallace, "The New Activists: Big Investors," *New York Times*, June 12, 1983, p. 4F.

27. S. Trausch, "Ethical Investing: Putting Your Money Where Your Social Sense Is," *Boston Globe*, April 14, 1981, p. 40.

BIBLIOGRAPHY

In addition to the books, magazines, and newsletters discussed in the text, here are some other publications worth your attention.

ACCOUNTING AND FINANCIAL STATEMENTS

S. Davidson et al. *Accounting: The Language of Business,* 2nd ed. Glen Ridge, NJ: Thomas Horton & Daughters, 1975.
J. Tracy. *How to Read a Financial Report.* New York: John Wiley & Sons, 1980.

BONDS

D. Darst. *The Complete Bond Book.* New York: McGraw-Hill, 1976.
————. *The Handbook of the Bond and Money Markets.* New York: McGraw-Hill, 1981.
Homer & Leibowitz. *Inside the Yield Book: Tools for Bond Market Strategy.* Englewood Cliffs, NJ: Prentice-Hall, 1973.

CORPORATE SOCIAL RESPONSIBILITY

Bradshaw & Vogel, eds. *Corporations and Their Critics.* New York: McGraw-Hill, 1982.

ETHICAL INVESTING

R. Barber and J. Rifkin. *The North Will Rise Again.* Boston: Beacon Press, 1978.

S. D. Lyndenberg. *Minding the Corporate Conscience: Public Interest Groups and Corporate Social Accountability.* New York: Council on Economic Priorities, 1978.

————. *Minding the Corporate Conscience: Annual Meetings Round-Up.* New York: Council on Economic Priorities, 1980.

————. *Bankrolling Ballots Update 1980.* New York: Council on Economic Priorities, 1981.

R. L. Nelson. *The Investment Policies of Foundations.* New York: Russell Sage Foundation, 1967.

C. W. Powers. *Social Responsibility and Investments.* Nashville: Abingdon Press, 1971.

C. W. Powers, ed. *People/Profits: The Ethics of Investment.* New York: Council on Religion and International Affairs, 1972.

J. G. Simon, C. W. Powers, and J. P. Gunnemann. *The Ethical Investor: Universities and Corporate Responsibility.* New Haven, CT: Yale University Press, 1972.

State of California. *Governor's Public Investment Task Force, Final Report.* North Highlands: General Services, Publications Section, 1981.

FINANCIAL PLANNING

F. Amling & W. Droms. *Personal Financial Management.* Homewood, IL: Richard D. Irwin, Inc., 1982.

S. H. Archer, G. M. Choate, and G. Racette. *Financial Management: An Introduction.* New York: John Wiley & Sons, 1979.

J. Barry. *Financial Freedom: A Positive Strategy for Putting Your Money to Work.* Reston, VA: Reston Publishing Co. Inc., 1982.

D. Brownstone & J. Sartisky. *Personal Financial Survival: A Guide for the 1980s and Beyond.* New York: John Wiley & Sons, 1981.

S. Lee & K. Hassay. *Women's Handbook of Independent Financial Management.* New York: Van Nostrand Reinhold Co., 1979.

S. Porter. *Sylvia Porter's New Money Book for the 80s.* Garden City, NY: Doubleday & Co., 1979.

J. Quinn. *Everyone's Money Book.* New York: Delacorte Press, 1979.

INSURANCE

Consumer's Union. *The Consumer's Union Report on Life Insurance,* 4th ed. New York: Holt, Rinehart & Winston, 1980.

INVESTING, GENERAL

L. Engel, in collaboration with P. Wyckoff. *How to Buy Stocks*, 6th rev. ed. Boston: Little, Brown & Co., 1976.

B. Graham. *The Intelligent Investor: A Book of Practical Counsel*, 4th rev. ed. New York: Harper & Row, 1973.

C. Hardy. *Dunn & Bradstreet's Guide to Your Investments*. New York: Lippincott, 1981.

G. Loeb. *The Battle for Investment Survival*. New York: Simon & Schuster, 1972.

C. Rosenberg, Jr. *Stock Market Primer*, rev. ed. New York: Warner Books, 1976.

L. Silk. *Economics in Plain English*. New York: Simon & Schuster, 1978.

K. Sokoloff. *The Thinking Investor's Guide to the Stock Market*. New York: McGraw-Hill, 1978.

————. *The Paine Webber Handbook of Stock and Bond Analysis*. New York: McGraw-Hill, 1979.

A. Tobias. *The Only Investment Guide You'll Ever Need*. New York: Harcourt Brace Jovanovich, 1978.

J. Train. *The Money Masters*. New York: Harper & Row, 1980.

J. Tuccille. *Everything the Beginner Needs to Know to Invest Shrewdly*. New York: Arlington House, 1978.

INVESTMENT AND FINANCIAL BIBLIOGRAPHIES

"Financial Planning Bibliography"
College for Financial Planning
9725 E. Hampden
Denver, CO 80321
(enclose self-addressed, stamped envelope)

S. Mechanic, "Investment Bibliography"
Sylvia Mechanic
Business Librarian
Brooklyn Public Library
280 Cadman Plaza West
Brooklyn, NY 11201
(enclose self-addressed, stamped envelope)

POLITICAL ACTION COMMITTEES

Fraser Associates. *The PAC Handbook: Political Action for Business*. Cambridge, MA: Ballinger, 1981.

RETIREMENT PLANNING

C. Hemphill. *Wills and Trusts: A Legal and Financial Handbook for Everyone.* Englewood Cliffs, NJ: Prentice-Hall Inc., 1980.

TAX SHELTERS, BOOKS

R. Haft et al. *1982 Tax Sheltered Investments Handbook.* New York: Clark Boardman Co. Ltd., 1981.

R. Stanger. *Tax Shelters in the 80s.* Rumson, NJ: Robert A. Stanger & Co., 1980.

R. Swanson & B. Swanson. *Tax Shelters: A Guide for Investors and Their Advisers.* Homewood, IL: Dow Jones-Irwin, 1982.

NAME INDEX

Dow Chemical Co., xv, 4, 102, 135,
151, 170, 202, 232, 236, 247
Dow Jones & Co., Inc., 236, 250
Dravo Corp., 207
Dresser Industries Inc., 33, 200, 204,
207, 247
Dreyfus Corporation, 99
Dreyfus Third Century Fund, 29–30,
128, 131, 133–134, 221, 226–227
Duke Power Co., xiv, 236
Dun & Bradstreet International Limited,
33, 204
du Pont (E. I.) de Nemours & Co., 62,
102, 151, 170, 195, 207, 232, 236,
247, 250
Dyco, 154, 160
Dynascan, 47

Eagle-Picher Industries, Inc., 247
Early California Industries, Inc., 29
The East Asiatic Co. (S.A.) (Pty) Ltd.,
232
Eastern Airlines, 102, 207, 237, 247,
250
Eastman Kodak Co., 62, 102, 104, 151,
195, 207, 232, 237, 250
Eaton Corp., 33, 102, 136, 204, 247
Echerd (Jack), 67
Echlin Manufacturing Co., 33, 63
Econo-Therm Energy Systems, 78
Edo Corp., 247
E. G. & G., Inc., 247
Electro-Biology, 93
Elizabethtown Water Company,
122
El Paso Co., 144, 247
El Pueblo State Bank, 181
Elsinor Corp., 91
Emerson Electric Co., 136
Emhart Corp., 237
Emons Industries, 28
Empire State Fund, 141
Energy Conversion Devices, 80, 93
Engelhard Corp., 102, 232
Engelhard Minerals & Chemical Corp.,
247
Enterprise Savings & Loan Association
(Long Beach), 186
Entex, Inc., 250
Entropy Limited, 81
Envirodyne Industries, 78
Environmental Testing and Control, 67

Episcopal Ministers' Church Pension
Fund, 210
Equinox Solar, Inc., 81
The Equitable Life Assurance Society of
the United States, 23, 46, 100,
190–191, 237, 250, 251
Equitec, 154
Ernst & Whinney, 88
Esmark, Inc., 27, 237
Estee Lauder, 10
Esterline Corp., 237
E-Systems, Inc., 136, 237
Everest & Jennings International, 237
Excel Insurance Co., 54
Export-Import Bank (EX-IM), 116
Exxon Corp., 21, 23, 44, 62, 70, 79, 96,
102, 125, 147, 151, 195, 199, 203,
204, 207, 232, 237, 247, 250

Facet Enterprises, Inc., 237
Fafco, Inc., 80, 81, 98
Falstaff Brewing Corporation, 29
Family Savings & Loan Association (Los
Angeles), 186
Farmer Brothers Co., 237
Farm House Foods Corp., 115
Fedco Foods Corp., 48
Federal-Mogul Corp., 232
Federal National Mortgage Association,
237
Federated Department Stores, 162, 237,
250
Ferro Corp., 232
Ferrofluidics, 95
Fidelity Union Bancorporation, 44
Financial Corp. (Santa Barbara), 237
Fireman's Fund, 250
Firestone Tire & Rubber Co., 102, 232,
237, 247
First Atlanta Corp., 44
First Bank National Association (Cleve-
land), 183
First Bank System, 237
First Boston Corp., 200
First Charter Financial Corp., 237
First Chicago Corp., 237
First Chicago Investment Corp., 84, 102,
204
First City Bancorp of Texas, 237
First City Properties, 10
First Commercial Bank (New York), 250
First Enterprise Bank, 183

SUBJECT INDEX